Praise for `sendmail` Performance Tuning

"Other `sendmail`-related books are available, but none of them cover performance tuning in any great depth—if at all. This book is specifically aimed at tuning and covers much more than any others I have seen."
—Gregory Neil Shapiro, Developer, Sendmail Consortium

"*sendmail Performance Tuning* is an excellent book aimed at the more sophisticated `sendmail` user. A definite need exists for this book, and Nick Christenson offers focused, practical information that I can readily deploy."
—Alan M. Strassberg, Global Network Engineer, Seagate, LLC

"This book fills an important niche that simply hasn't been addressed until now, and I believe it will be an excellent addition to the reference shelf for any mail systems administrator. If you want to learn how to build a large-scale mail system or optimize your own for best price and performance, there simply aren't any other choices available. You can either repeat all the work Nick has done or take advantage of his extensive knowledge on the subject. Nick is one of the few people in the business I'd trust to write my bible for me."
—Brad Knowles, Senior Consultant, Snow, BV

"This has the makings of an excellent book, and I know of no other that covers this material. Certain aspects of the book may well be covered elsewhere, but this is the first book I have encountered that attempts to collect all this information under one cover."
—Tim Bosserman, R&D Engineer, Earthlink

"Nick shows junior sysadmins how a senior sysadmin analyzes a complex system: `sendmail` itself, the operating system, its hardware, and the Internet at large. `sendmail` graybeards will find themselves saying 'I hadn't thought of that.' Repeatedly."
—Scott Lystig Fritchie, Caspian Networks

sendmail Performance Tuning

`sendmail` Performance Tuning

Nick Christenson

✦✦ Addison-Wesley

Boston · San Francisco · New York · Toronto · Montreal
London · Munich · Paris · Madrid
Capetown · Sydney · Tokyo · Singapore · Mexico City

The publisher offers discounts on this book when ordered in quantity for special sales. For more information, please contact:

U.S. Corporate and Government Sales
(800) 382-3419
corpsales@pearsontechgroup.com

Visit Addison-Wesley on the Web: www.awprofessional.com

For sales outside of the U.S., please contact:
International Sales
(317) 581-3793
international@pearsontechgroup.com

Library of Congress Cataloging-in-Publication Data

Christenson, Nick
    Sendmail performance tuning/Nick Christenson.
        p. cm.
    Includes bibliographical references and index.
    ISBN 0-321-11570-8
    1. Electronic mail systems.   I. Title.
    TK5105.73 .C49 2003
    004.692—dc21   2002074382

ISBN 0-321-11570-8

Text printed on recycled paper.
1 2 3 4 5 6 7 8 9 10—MA—0605040302
First printing, September 2002

Contents

Preface

Most people consider email to be the "killer application" of the Internet. An astounding amount of email crosses the globe every day. These messages flow from server to server in ever-increasing quantities. Some email servers originate email, some relay it from one network to another, some store email for later retrieval, and some perform all of these tasks. This book explores the intricacies of email communication, focusing on `sendmail`-based solutions, and suggests how one can build, design, and tune email servers that will accomplish each of these tasks more efficiently. Applying the suggestions in this book will help email servers perform better under increasing load, expedite the delivery of their messages, and make them more resistant to accidental and malicious load-related incidents. These pages contain detailed descriptions of precisely what actions go on behind the scenes on an email server, information about email software features and ways that options for deploying this software might affect performance, suggestions on methods and pitfalls to effectively test email server configurations, and actual test data to support the claims made in this book.

This book is intended to be read primarily by system administrators of UNIX-based email servers. Other system administrators and email application developers, however, may find many of the topics discussed here to be useful. While the thrust of this book targets the use of the Open Source `sendmail` software package, much of the information presented here should prove useful in non-`sendmail` environments as well. However, this is not a book on basic system administration, `sendmail` administration, or general UNIX performance tuning. I assume that the reader of the book either understands these issues, if only at a basic level, or knows where to look if clarification or more information about some point is necessary. While some duplication of material between this book and others is both necessary and beneficial, I've tried to repeat information that can be found in other books as little as possible. My recommendations on excellent books that provide this information are available in the concluding chapter, and I strongly recommend them to readers of this text.

This book is intended to be read sequentially. Chapters build on information found in previous chapters, so skipping around may prove confusing. One exception involves the `sendmail` introduction chapter (Chapter 2), which may be safely skipped by readers who are familiar with `sendmail` and especially comfortable with building version 8.12 `sendmail.cf` files using M4.

At the end of each chapter, a "Summary" section lists the key points discussed in the chapter. While these summaries are not substitutes for reading the chapter, the reader should find them useful in reinforcing some of the more important points that have been discussed.

In this book, literal information as it might be expressed on a computer system is rendered in a fixed-width `Courier` font. This includes actual file names, commands as they are typed into a computer, source code of any form, and variable names as they appear in configuration files. A variable is indicated by the use of *`Courier italic`*. For example, `/var/mail/`*`username`* would indicate a variable file name that should be replaced with a real username, and this file resides in the `/var/mail` directory.

Many people have helped make this a better book. I'd like to thank William von Hagen for his assistance on the topic of Linux filesystems. I couldn't have asked for a better team of reviewers, and this book was much improved by their contributions. These people were Claus Aßmann, Tim Bosserman, Scott Lystig Fritchie, Brad Knowles, Jim Larson, and Alan Strassberg. I'd also like to thank the editing team at Addison-Wesley, Karen Gettman and especially Jessica Goldstein, for making the process of writing this book much easier for me than I had feared. Also deserving of thanks are Tyrrell Albaugh for holding everything together, and Jill Hobbs for improving my sloppy writing. Finally, I'd like to single out the contribution of Gregory Neil Shapiro, who gets a "gold star" for the effort he put in to improve this book. If the reader happens across an especially interesting bit of `sendmail` information in these pages, there's a good chance it has been included because Greg suggested it to me. Of course, I take full responsibility for any errors or omissions that might have occurred.

I hope you enjoy this book.

Nick Christenson
El Cerrito, California

Chapter 1

Introduction

There is a considerable amount of information available in print and on the Internet on the topic of configuring electronic mail systems running `sendmail`, but comparatively little information on how to tune these systems to handle anything except the most nominal amount of email traffic. Of course, as the most straight-forward installation of `sendmail` and a Post Office Protocol (POP) daemon under UNIX on a commodity desktop box can easily accommodate more than 1,000 individual users and handle more than 100,000 modestly sized email messages per day, at many sites performance tuning of these systems isn't critical. Nonetheless, as email rapidly becomes the preferred method for much of the communication that occurs in the world today, more and more systems are feeling the strain. For tuning tips, one can glean some well-known tricks by scouring old Usenet news postings and mailing list archives, but these methods have not been widely disseminated, much less gathered together in a single document. Even so, this book contains many suggestions that, I believe, have been documented for the first time.

This book focuses on solutions based on `sendmail`, but also references other UNIX-based Open Source email software packages. Much of the information in this document is applicable to email systems not based on `sendmail` or, for that matter, non–Open Source or non–UNIX-based systems.

This book does not try to answer all possible questions about running elec-tronic mail systems. For example, aside from a brief introduction to the Open Source `sendmail` package in Chapter 2, it does not discuss changing the logical behavior of one's `sendmail`-based email system. Instead the focus is entirely on making a single email server perform its duties more efficiently. If the reader is interested in reducing spam, filtering email, or making any number of other con-figuration changes, many good sources for this sort of information [SEN] [SG98] exist; however, this book is not one of them. Further, the topic of increasing capacity by running email as a distributed system is not considered here in depth. Instead,

1

this book focuses on tuning individual machines to perform their email-related tasks better. For information on building a distributed email system, the reader may want to consider other sources [CBB97] [SHB+98].

1.1 Performance Tuning Examples

Several places in this book cite real performance numbers that I measured on a test network. It is appropriate that some information be provided up front about the system and test methodology used in arriving at the data presented in this book.

The systems used to generate the data found in this book are not configurations that I would recommend using in actual practice. This discrepancy is intentional. I selected these particular configurations as test platforms for the following reasons:

1. It is important to understand how performance can be affected in both CPU-bound and I/O-bound server situations. Therefore, I use server configurations that have been artificially manipulated to be CPU bound and I/O bound. In fact, these two configurations will be referred to as "CPU-bound" and "I/O-bound" servers in this book.

2. The extent to which the tuning advice provided in this book affects different servers at different sites will vary widely. For example, changing the delivery mode employed by `sendmail` will affect a two-processor Sun Enterprise 220R with a Sun Netra st A1000 disk storage array differently than it affects a 2.0GHz Linux server using software RAID to stripe four disks together. It would be improper to make assumptions about the effects on a site's performance based on data gathered under a different configuration. Hopefully, the temptation to do so will be reduced if data are presented regarding server configurations that no one would use.

3. It is easier to be confident in results obtained using a small number of machines as part of a test network. The fewer and simpler the machines involved, the less likely that someone would forget to go through all the tasks necessary to ensure that the conditions have been repeated exactly from one test run to the next. To make the testing easier by making the load generation facilities simpler, the bottlenecks in the test systems cited in this book have been exaggerated. Of course, in "real life," we don't always have a lot of choice in how complex an environment we want to test. Because this book will be read by many people, however, it is especially important to get the test results correct here.

4. With whatever environment is being tested, it is important to ensure that sufficient load generation capacity and network bandwidth, not to mention adequate power and cooling, are available to perform accurate tests. At the time of this writing, I don't have unlimited access to a high-performance test lab. Nevertheless, interesting results can be obtained from just about any available hardware.

For the purposes of this book, we're primarily interested in whether a given change will affect system performance positively or negatively. We're also interested in how large an effect we might expect each change to have on our system, although we need to be skeptical that precise numbers generated in one environment will apply in another environment.

Now that the disclaimers have been made, let's look at the two test servers. The CPU-bound server has the following configuration:

- The server is a Sun Sparc 5 (not Ultra 5, Sparc 5) clone, vintage circa 1996.
- It has a single 85MHz MicroSPARC II processor.
- It has 32MB of RAM.
- It's running Solaris 2.6 with some of the jumbo patches installed. No attempt has been made to tune the kernel.
- It contains two 2GB Seagate Hawk (5400 RPM) disks on a SCSI-2 bus.
- It has a single 10 Mbps Ethernet card to connect it to the test network.

The I/O-bound server has the following configuration:

- The server is a contemporary PC-based server.
- It has a single 1.6GHz Intel Pentium 4 processor.
- It has 256MB of RAM.
- It's running the Linux 2.4 kernel—specifically, Red Hat 7.2. The operating system is unpatched.
- It has a 4GB Seagate Hawk (5400 RPM) disk for the operating system and home directories. A second 2GB Seagate Hawk (also 5400 RPM) is used for testing. It has been split into two 1GB partitions. The inner (slower) partition is used for all testing. These are SCSI-2 disks.
- Its mainboard provides a single 100 Mbps Ethernet connector to connect it to the test network.

1.2 `sendmail` Versions Covered

This book discusses issues involved in performance tuning several different versions of sendmail, not just the most recent release. This choice was made for several reasons. First, not every organization feels that it can use the most up-to-date version of sendmail at its site. These organizations will still find valuable information in this book. Second, some organizations have elected not to use sendmail because of historical problems that may not affect more recent versions. If someone has had a bad experience in the past with sendmail performance, it's entirely possible that the reasons for the problem no longer exist in the code. In such a case, I want to give the reader the full opportunity to understand what might have happened and why it might no longer present a problem. Third, by the standards of most Internet applications, sendmail is a very old program. That is, sendmail in some form has been in operation for more than 20 years. The program itself is now older than some people charged with installing and maintaining it. The sendmail Mail Transfer Agent (MTA) has a lengthy history, and despite most of the code having been rewritten, often several times since then, good programmers don't like to break compatibility with older behavior. As a consequence, the way sendmail works now owes a great deal to evolutionary changes in the code over a long period of time. Some of the ways in which sendmail chooses to implement certain features might seem strange, and understanding its history can help lead to understanding about why things are as they are.

Historically, sendmail adds new features or changes its behavior only when the middle number in its version changes. That is, its behavior should be expected to change between versions 8.9.3 and 8.10.0, but should remain relatively stable between versions 8.11.5 and 8.11.6. Revisions that alter the rightmost number typically represent bug fixes or possibly refinements or minor tunings in the operation of sendmail. Recently, each of the changes associated with the advancement of the middle release number has largely been associated with a single theme. The changes between versions 8.8 and 8.9 centered on spam control. The Open Source release of version 8.10 added a large number of smaller features to the MTA; a partial list of these features has been documented [SA99]. Version 8.11 added cryptographic support to the Open Source release of sendmail. The focus of sendmail version 8.12 is most relevant to this book, as its advances occurred primarily in the realm of performance. Although by no means was every new feature in successive sendmail versions associated with that release's theme, many were. In any case, email administrators running sendmail who are concerned with performance would be well advised to try to install the latest version of sendmail, especially if they are currently working with some revision of 8.11 or earlier.

Just for reference, we can test the CPU-bound server described earlier in this chapter to measure the benefit of upgrading to `sendmail` 8.12 from version 8.11. Using the most generic `sendmail.cf` file appropriate for each version of `sendmail`, queueing and then delivering one approximately 1KB message to the mailbox of one of 50 randomly selected users on that machine, we get a throughput of 221 messages/second using `sendmail` 8.11.6, and 242 messages/second using `sendmail` 8.12.2. This difference represents a performance gain of about 11%. The server was CPU bound during this test, so it just measures improvements in the efficiency of the code. This improvement is quite modest, but it can be obtained "for free." As we will see, we can make additional changes to a `sendmail` 8.12 configuration file that will improve these numbers further.

1.3 Definitions

Before going any further, let's define some terms used when discussing email services. The Mail Transfer Agent (MTA) is responsible for moving email between different email servers using the Simple Mail Transfer Protocol (SMTP), defined by RFC 2821 [KLE01]. Examples of UNIX MTAs include `sendmail`, `postfix` [POS], Exim [EXI], and `qmail` [QMA]. MTAs temporarily store email that they have accepted but not yet delivered in the message queue (or mail queue, or just queue). The Local Delivery Agent (LDA) is the program that receives email from an MTA and places it in the message store or mail spool. The message store is a data repository where email messages reside, typically sorted by user. A user queries this repository using a Mail User Agent (MUA) such as Eudora or Netscape. The query is performed via one of several mechanisms, such as the Post Office Protocol (POP), which is the service provided by most ISPs, or Internet Message Access Protocol (IMAP), which is commonly used by many businesses. A program such as `mailx` or `elm` may also be referred to as an MUA, but these applications access the message store via the filesystem on the same server on which the email is stored. Common Open Source POP daemons used on email servers include Qpopper [QPO] and CUCIpop [CUC], and version 3 of POP itself is defined in RFC 1939 [MR96]. The three most common Open Source IMAP servers are Cyrus [CYR], UW-IMAP [UWI], and the Courier IMAP [COU] packages. Version 4r1 of IMAP is defined in RFC 2060 [CRI96]. Some organizations allow email access via a World Wide Web (WWW) interface. Often called Web Mail solutions, these systems won't be covered in depth in this book. A good overview on obtaining, building, installing, and running Open Source IMAP and Web mail services is available in *Managing IMAP*, by Dianna and Kevin Mullet [MM00]. A good overview of the email protocols mentioned here is found in David Wood's book, *Programming Internet Email* [WOO99].

1.4 Email Server Tasks

The tasks performed by an email server running `sendmail` can be roughly broken down into the following categories:

1. Receive and queue email for delivery to other servers
2. Receive email and store it in the appropriate mailbox
3. Send locally generated email to other servers

The server may also run other tasks, such as allowing access to messages via POP or IMAP, but these tasks are unrelated to `sendmail`.

Most email servers perform each of the three aforementioned tasks, although some servers may perform one or two of these tasks far more frequently than others. The first task is representative of the workload handled by an email gateway. Large organizations often use gateways to provide a limited point of access for email to flow into and out of a network. The second task usually dominates the performance experienced by an email hub where mailboxes are stored and accessed via MUAs. The third task dominates the load experienced by an email server that handles large mailing lists or sends internally generated email out to the Internet. While many of the individual operations that constitute each of these actions remain the same from task to task, enough differences exist that this division of action becomes a convenient way to consider various aspects of email system tuning. Each of these aspects will be discussed in its own chapter in this book.

1.5 Tuning Isn't Always Necessary

While this book focuses on email tuning, a large percentage of email systems on the Internet today simply don't deal with enough traffic to justify buying expensive hardware and spending a great deal of time tuning applications to handle their load. This statement doesn't mean that email performance tuning won't offer any benefit for these systems, but merely that extreme measures aren't justified. This section aims to identify the thresholds at which the most naive email server implementation is likely—although not guaranteed—to work just fine. Typically, storage I/O speeds limit email server performance, as we shall see. In the scenarios that follow, however, we assume that each server in question has a sufficiently fast I/O system such that it can move data near the maximum capability of its CPU, memory, and networking subsystems.

The first scenario under which no email server tuning is likely to be necessary is if a site's Internet connection is limited to T1 (1.544 Mbps) or lower speeds.

Even obsolete computers, such as the Sparc Station 2 (circa 1991 for readers who may only have encountered these machines in history books) or any PC with an Intel 80486 or equivalent chip, can easily saturate a T1 line if it does not attempt to perform complex computations on all data that flow through it. If a site sends a majority of its email to and from the Internet (rather than within the organization), and the corporate Internet connection is a T1, then a single Sparc 2 would probably perform admirably as a corporate mail gateway server. If it doesn't and the email server slows down, the true source of the problem likely isn't the server. Rather, the network is probably the culprit.

A low-end Pentium box (with a capable networking card, a description fitting all the cards currently on the market) can easily saturate a 10 Mbps Ethernet segment with unfiltered traffic and, even if performing significant stateful modification of the packets, can saturate a T1 with very little difficulty. A Pentium II box, any UltraSparc, or any system based on an Alpha chip can easily saturate a 10 Mbps Ethernet while substantially modifying incoming data. Further, almost any server based on these processors can quite easily pass 100 Mbps of raw data through it if its networking is adequate. A four-processor Sun E420R, or equivalent server from another vendor, with a high-quality, well-tuned storage system acting as an email hub, can process in excess of 100 Mbps of email traffic (SMTP and POP). It makes no sense to purchase such a powerful server, tune it, and then have it serve email via a 10 Mbps network. As a corollary, if email traffic peaks at or around 10 Mbps, that site would waste its money by buying a multi-CPU machine, even if the vendor classifies it as a "workgroup server."

Before anyone can object to the veracity of the numbers cited here, let me state that these are rough rules of thumb. These figures are drawn from personal experience with real loads using commonly available software to handle Internet traffic. While research projects have driven 100 Mbps networks to capacity with low-end processors using specially written software, that case isn't of particular interest here. On another note, while this book discusses tuning email systems, it will only occasionally discuss tuning the source code of the email applications themselves.

Often, those intending to send large quantities of email during the course of a day greatly overestimate the resources needed to accomplish this task. Sending 1 million email messages in a 24-hour period sounds like a much more tractable problem if it is restated as sending a little less than 12 messages/second. If the message body remains the same in all cases and is short and stored in one place (so that it can be held in memory), such as might be the case on a mailing list server, generating messages at this rate is not at all difficult. Even the network bandwidth isn't difficult to handle. If each message is 10KB in size, and no optimization can be achieved by sending the same message to multiple recipients at the same site through a shared connection, at 12 messages/second this case involves only 1 Mbps of network traffic (just counting the message data itself). Of course, this scenario doesn't consider packet overhead, DNS requests, the potential for ICMP traffic, and traffic used in failed transmission attempts. Nevertheless, if this is the sum of the network traffic consumed and either the load is well spread out over the day or modest delays in email sent at peak times are acceptable, then a single T1 line would suffice to accommodate this load. As we have seen, it doesn't take a particularly beefy machine by today's standards to fill a T1 with email. In fact, the only likely performance problem in this scenario involves how to deal with messages that aren't deliverable in the first pass as they back up in the queue. If 1 out of every 100 of these 1 million messages are undeliverable for a day, the average number of messages in the queue will be 10,000 entries, a large enough number to significantly slow down filesystem access.

In any case, these sorts of numbers lie at the heart of building powerful email systems. The more information available on how the system will behave, the more accurately one can forecast the resources needed to get the job done.

1.6 Not So Fast...

After performing this sort of analysis, one might conclude that email performance tuning isn't necessary for a particular organization's system(s). However, before dismissing the rest of this book, some other factors might be worth considering. At most organizations, the number of people using email, the number of messages sent and received per person, and the average size of each email message are larger today than the corresponding numbers of a year ago. There's no reason to believe that these numbers won't be even bigger next year. At many sites where the email server(s) can easily handle the load, this situation might be only temporary. It's quite likely that more capacity will be necessary someday.

The rate at which email flows into and out of an organization might be quite modest and easily handled by an untuned system. If a site's connection with the Internet is large, the possibility always exists that demand may increase dramatically in short order. This increase may be due to malevolence, error, transient conditions, or an organization's marketing department suddenly cranking up an email campaign without informing the information technology folks. These things happen. While it's not out of the question that an organization's email loading might increase dramatically overnight, overwhelming whatever resources might currently be in play, a well-tuned system will provide overhead to reduce the chance of a catastrophic outage due to a sudden increase in load. Further, if the system does become overwhelmed, a well-tuned system will handle these situations more gracefully and recover from them more quickly than a naively configured system will.

While a low-bandwidth Internet connection may very well provide a choke restricting the amount of email flowing through a gateway, it doesn't mean that someone won't try to send out more email than can fit in the pipe. An organization with a T1 connection to the Internet may find that it needs to get critical patch information out to a million customers as soon as possible and decide that email is the most efficient way to accomplish this goal. For example, if the informational message is 2KB in size, there are 1 million recipients for the message at 500,000 different email domains, and one-third of the T1 is available for transporting email data, then it could not possibly take less than four hours to get all the email out. This estimate assumes that our email server is arbitrarily fast, no delays occur on the Internet, and everyone else's server is up and ready to go.

Unfortunately, real life is messier than this scenario. It's entirely possible that the folks responsible for sending these messages won't consider how badly their mailing will slam the email gateway, and they may not even be aware of how much (or how little) bandwidth exists between them and the Internet. The email server almost certainly will become overwhelmed with the sudden load. It will take a great deal of time to accept all those messages. This process will consume resources within the machine that will slow its ability to send those messages out to the Internet. If this scenario actually occurred, it's entirely possible that the email server would still be working on sending this email out days after it received the first message.

Even if the list of email addresses is of high quality, a fair percentage of the destination email addresses will not exist, potentially generating hundreds of megabytes of bounced email notifications. These notifications are extra messages that will return to the server, adding to its load. Some email addresses will be for hosts that should exist but don't respond for days. Even if this group represents a small percentage of the total number of recipients, it might entail several or many thousands of messages that can slow down the email server's queues for many days. While considering the sudden processing of 1 million email messages is an extreme example, any email system can experience significant problems handling sudden message volumes several orders of magnitude smaller than this case.

With today's Internet, it would be remiss to ignore the possibility of havoc caused to email servers by self-replicating viruses found in message attachments. Busy email gateways have been shut down because of these attacks [CER99]. In such cases, it is usually better if the shutdown occurs because someone made the decision to take this step, rather than because the gateway couldn't handle the load.

Finally, even a single careless message can cause a great deal of disruption to an email server. With today's drag-and-drop desktop operating systems, some simple-to-perform actions can have serious consequences. On most systems, the actions required to email a 100-word document are the same as those required to send a 100MB presentation or spreadsheet, and often a user is not aware of just how large the documents they're working on might be. On more than one occasion, the sending of a single ill-advised document has caused multihour email disruptions in large organizations.

A well-tuned email server provides not only additional capacity to handle high volumes of email, but also headroom against the occasional incident. Even if mishaps—whether accidental, caused by emergency, or due to maliciousness—are rare, email has become so important to most organizations that any outage can significantly disrupt business. Even if day-to-day email throughput doesn't require expensive hardware and hours of configuration, some relatively simple and inexpensive modifications to an existing system, if they can prevent even a single noticeable outage caused by transient events, can produce significant returns on investment.

1.7 Email System Profiling

More times than I care to remember, I've had a conversation with someone trying to specify an email system that went like the following:

Them: I need to build an email server using Sun equipment that will handle X number of users. What hardware should I buy?

Me: Well, that completely depends.

Them: On what?

Me: On their usage profiles. How many messages does each person send and receive each day? What is the average message size? How fast is your Internet connection? What percentage of your peak day's total traffic occurs during the peak hour?

Them: I don't know.

Me: Then I'm afraid I can't help you very much.

Them: Well, can you give me a rough estimate?

Me: Sure, you'll need a machine somewhere between a Sparc 2 with a 2GB disk and a 30-processor Sun E6500 with an EMC Symmetrix storage system.

When it comes to email servers, it seems that just about the only information anyone can obtain from a prospective client is the number of users. Unfortunately for performance purposes, this figure is just about the least useful metric for evaluating email service load. Getting the information that's really necessary to size a server often seems next to impossible, even from people who really ought to know better.

When all is said and done, the two most important pieces of information to consider regarding the load on a server almost always will be (1) the number of transactions (messages or connections) per second the server has to handle and (2) the average size (in bytes) of each transaction. Further, one really needs to know these data rates only for the busiest 15 minutes of the day. If the server can handle its busiest load, then except under the most unusual circumstances, it should provide acceptable service during the rest of the day.

Some secondary considerations shouldn't be ignored, however. The first relates to the overhead for each connection. For example, if an email server provides IMAP service, there will be a fixed overhead for each connected user. If there are a lot of users or if the overhead is considerable (e.g., the server has to spawn a process for each connection), then total overhead might be an issue, even if the vast majority of connections remain idle for extended periods of time and thus contribute very little to the total throughput load. Another secondary performance issue might be related to bottlenecks that are not easily solved. For example, if a site has a fixed-bandwidth network connection to the outside world that is not easily upgraded, and during much of the day that connection is at capacity, then that server may require a substantially larger message queue than is typical; that requirement might need to be reflected in the server's storage capacity. This case might also arise in those (rare, these days) situations where network connectivity is intermittent.

Unfortunately, these considerations are largely irrelevant. Rarely does someone who wants information on building an email service know and provide the key information necessary for sizing the system(s) that will run it. If an organization has this information, it probably doesn't need assistance. In most cases, what needs to be done is to accept the information that is available—the number of users—and find an appropriate profile for their usage patterns from which performance numbers can be drawn. This effort usually involves obtaining copies of the data the email applications log on the server, if possible. Chapter 7 covers obtaining information from these logs in more detail.

One problem is that typical Internet email usage patterns change constantly, which means that not only will the estimates provided here be immediately obsolete, but also the trends for estimating future growth will almost certainly become less valid as time passes. The best substitute for accurate information is a guess based on current information, so readers are strongly encouraged to treat what is presented here with a healthy dose of skepticism and, instead, perform their own research to the best of their ability. This point cannot be stated strongly enough. The numbers presented in the remainder of this chapter should be treated as guesses and over-generalizations, but are better than nothing (although in some cases, perhaps not much).

In the Internet Service Provider (ISP) market, the numbers of messages that a typical subscriber sends and receives per day vary widely. A reasonable estimate is that typical ISP users receive about twice as many messages per day as they send. This difference is largely due to mailing list traffic, opt-in advertising, Web action confirmation, and spam. As to absolute numbers of messages, some direct data are available. In the online newsletter *Messaging Online*, America Online (AOL) reported that it averaged receiving 3.5 messages per subscriber per day in 1998 and 5.6 messages per subscriber per day in 1999 [M-O00]. From this, we can project that by mid-2002, AOL subscribers may be receiving, on average, as many as 20 email messages per user per day.

America Online users have often been chastised as being "unsophisticated" compared to the customers of more traditional ISPs. While it does little good to debate this point, it certainly seems that traditionally they receive less email per capita. During 1999, most other ISPs received between 10 and 15 messages per subscriber per day, a number typically two to three times higher than their AOL counterparts. I would expect this gap to narrow over time, but not to vanish, at least for several years. I'd project that during 2002, the typical ISP subscriber will receive 20 to 30 email messages/day.

To date, the numbers for ISPs outside of the United States tend to be far lower than those for their U.S. counterparts. Data for European and Asian ISPs lead me to believe that per capita their subscribers average about one-third the number of messages received by U.S. subscribers. I also expect this gap to close over time. Some folks have used the model that European and Asian Internet loads tend to have the same sorts of numbers as the U.S. loads of two to three years ago. For now, this model seems reasonable except when it comes to wireless messaging, where Europe and especially Asia support much higher loads [UM].

Similar to ISPs are the email portals, such as Hotmail and Yahoo!. In my experience these sites have two types of users: those who use their email just as much as one would use ISP email, and those who hardly ever use it. A reasonable estimate seems to be that message loads average a little less than half of the per capita load of ISPs in the same region.

Of course, many more email servers do duty in a corporate environment than at an ISP. For these servers, profile information is much more variable and depends greatly on the sophistication of the users, the types of documents and storage formats typically in use at the site, other data transport mechanisms that are available, and the general corporate culture that has sprung up concerning email applications. Estimating corporate email usage is a daunting task, and without adequate information about the site in question it would seem to be nearly impossible to generate an accurate model. Despite this problem, site planners and administrators will be asked to make these predictions, so we do what we can.

At least one report, released early in the year 2000 [FON00], estimates that at that time the typical user received about 19 email messages per day and the average message was about 150KB in size. This report predicted that in 12 months, the typical corporate mailbox would receive 34 messages per day and the average size would jump to 286KB. In many environments, especially in the corporate world, it would not be atypical to find that 90% of email is entirely internal—that is, the sender and the recipient of the vast majority of messages use the same email server.

It is worth reemphasizing that these numbers are rough estimates, and that nothing here should serve as a satisfactory substitute for direct research concerning one's actual situation.

1.8 General Tuning Ideas

There are some general tuning tips that can improve the performance of email service applications in a broad way. Some are simple, common-sense ideas, but they bear mentioning nonetheless. Note that modern UNIX-like operating systems generally do a much better job of tuning themselves these days than they once did. That fact, coupled with the relatively large amount of RAM one can economically install in a system, has meant that the most common sorts of performance-tuning tricks that are described in many books on the subject are much less effective in bringing about an actual performance increase than they were, say, 15 years ago. These tricks might include removing kernel modules to free up memory or increasing kernel table sizes. This is not to say that one shouldn't take the time to remove unneeded kernel modules or check kernel table sizes, but these optimizations are less likely to produce noticeable performance increases than they once would. Other avenues of attack can probably yield much more substantial gains.

Performance gains via general operating system tuning can still be obtained, however. Documentation on general performance tuning is available for most operating systems from the vendor, on the Internet, or both. Some sources of general information can also prove quite useful, such as the second edition of *System Performance Tuning* [ML02]. Even if general tuning advice doesn't directly contribute to better email throughput, it often provides insights about what's happening "under the hood" on a server. Gaining a better understanding of how an important system functions is always a good thing.

This book cannot hope to be as thorough as these other sources when it comes to operating system specifics, nor can it cover every system. Instead, the book focuses primarily on the types of hardware that can be used and on ways to improve performance at the application level. The rest of this section examines other methods by which performance improvements may be obtained.

1.8.1 DNS

One area in which significant performance gains can be achieved is in the configuration of DNS services. Any server that handles a large number of connections to and from arbitrary sites on the Internet, such as a Web or email server, will typically perform reverse DNS lookups on the IP addresses from which connections are received to perform authorization checks, properly log the name of the connecting host, and so on. Depending on the software and the level of paranoia in the configuration, once this reverse lookup is done, a forward lookup may also be performed to confirm that the two results match. Many MTAs take this step to make certain that the remote machine to which an email server is talking is really who it says it is. Besides providing identity verification, such checks properly identify the correct machine to which a particular piece of email will be sent. Consequently, a server will likely perform a very large number of DNS lookups, the majority of which will apply to hosts outside the local domain. The processes that make these lookups will sit around waiting for responses to be returned before they proceed. Methods that cut down on the time required to complete these DNS requests will reduce the total duration of an email protocol session, which means that resources are freed up more quickly to handle other tasks.

The most obvious way to reduce the latency of DNS requests on an Internet server is to run a name service daemon on the server itself. For high-volume email servers, this is an excellent idea. One of the most commonly cited reasons why folks resist doing so is because DNS servers are perceived to increase the administrative effort required to maintain a server. It doesn't have to be this way. Busy servers should run their own name daemon and reference it as their first choice in the `/etc/resolv.conf` file.

To reduce the maintenance costs, the daemon should be of the caching-only variety, and no computer other than the server itself should query its name service daemon. This can be done by administrative fiat or packet filtering; alternatively, using BIND version 8, it can be enforced in the name server configuration. This step is worth taking. The caching-only nature of this name server means that the only zone files on the name server are (1) the cache zone file, which lists the root name servers, and (2) the loopback zone file, which contains host name-to-IP address translations for the loopback network interface, 127.0.0.1. The server does not hold zone files for the local domain. When an SMTP connection is made to a host in the local domain, the name server must query the root name servers to find authoritative sources of DNS information about these hosts. It will need to make this query only once to determine which name servers are authoritative, and then it will need to perform a query on each particular host only once before that information will become locally cached. Thus the fact that this DNS server maintains no explicit knowledge of its own domain information only marginally affects the performance of the first query for a local host, while keeping the number of requests that it must make over the network to a minimum.

A sample `named.conf` file that lists these two zones and administratively keeps remote hosts from querying it for BIND version 8 follows:

```
options {
        allow-query { 127.0.0.1; };
        allow-transfer { none; };
};

zone "0.0.127.in-addr.arpa" IN {
        type master;
        file "REV.127.0.0";
};

zone "." IN {
        type hint;
        file "named.root";
};
```

The appropriate contents for these zone files can be found on any properly running DNS server running BIND.

While it may not seem like a lot of traffic, the DNS load and the latency introduced by making these queries to another machine can be substantial. Consequently, with a caching-only name server that maintains almost no local state, very little increased maintenance overhead arises. Very little can go wrong in this situation.

Instead of running caching-only name servers, some DNS administrators like to run caching-forwarding name servers. They differ from caching-only name servers in two ways:

1. They do not contain a zone for the root name servers, nor do they ever query the root name servers directly.

2. When a server cannot answer a query directly (because the query asks for information that cannot be found in a locally maintained zone or because the information isn't in its cache), the request is forwarded to a predefined server or set of servers for resolution.

With this strategy, if the servers to which the caching server forwards its queries are authoritative for local domains, the extra round-trip request across the Internet for querying the root name servers when the caching server needs to look up DNS information about local hosts does not occur.

As has already been discussed, while it is more expensive to query the root name servers for local domain information, this happens very infrequently (unless the Time to Live [TTL] records on one's own domain are set unusually low—for example, less than 5 minutes), so it doesn't cost very much. On the other hand, every request that a caching-forwarder makes for information not in its cache, including the lookups for all remote servers with which it will communicate, must go through an extra hop: the forwarder. If the forwarder is sufficiently fast, is dedicated to this task, and is "near" the caching-forwarder ("near" in a network sense, meaning that sufficient bandwidth exists between the two servers to support their connection, and the latency between these two hosts is very low), then this effort may not cost the email server very much. Whenever possible, however, an email server should take the extra time to look up local zone information by querying the root name servers as caching-only servers than to have them forward every request through another host. Forwarding both slows down the query process and provides additional—perhaps even a single—points or point of failure.

The primary exception to this general rule arises when an organization's firewall configuration precludes an email server from making direct DNS queries to the root name servers. In this case, a caching-forwarding configuration must suffice, and is a much better option than directly querying the forwarder for all DNS information.

Servers based on `sendmail` are less susceptible to DNS-induced slowdowns than some other MTAs might be, because each `sendmail` process caches the DNS information it receives. Note: This cache is maintained on a process-by-process basis; it is not shared between separate instances of `sendmail`, even between parent and child processes. The results of this functionality are most pronounced when a `sendmail` process performs a queue run. For each host that has email bound for it in the queue, host canonicalization will be performed exactly once. Starting with `sendmail` 8.12, the MX record resolution of each host will also be performed exactly once (unless the resource record TTL is exceeded, at which point the request must be repeated). This point is also evident during the processing of `sendmail` rulesets. As recipient information is processed, `sendmail` must translate between host name and IP address, often parsing the same email address multiple times. Nonetheless, a DNS lookup on each unique host name or IP address is performed only once per `sendmail` instance.

In some environments, it would clearly be better for the name daemon running on an email server to be authoritative for its own domain. It's also certainly possible to envision a situation in which an email server should not run a name daemon at all. Even so, in the vast majority of situations, running a caching-only name daemon on busy email servers can improve performance considerably without creating a maintenance headache.

1.8.2 General Server Tuning

The arrangement of the server hardware acts as an important foundation for providing efficient email services. An email administrator will often decide that moving the message store and email queue to their own disks or, if necessary, disk controller, might be a good idea. It's important to understand that the reason for doing so is not only to improve the throughput of email I/O, but also to insulate the email system from things that might go wrong on the rest of the server. That is, if someone fills the / filesystem due to some administrative error, it would be a good thing if that mistake didn't directly affect the flow of email. Dedicating a disk (or at least a disk partition) for the storage of temporary files created by the email server software can be beneficial for the same reasons.

In general, regardless of the system's performance characteristics, I recommend one disk (or more if appropriate) for the general operating system, one disk (or disk system) for the message queue, and, if the server provides a message store for local mailboxes, one disk or disk system for the message store. Even if the message throughput or volume does not require multiple disks, it is worth taking this step on any dedicated server just to have the separation of the disks themselves available to act as a barrier against something going wrong on one part of the server affecting another.

With larger email servers, at some point it becomes prudent to provide a separate disk devoted to swap space, moving these data off the operating system disk, although in almost all cases these two disks will share the same disk controller. Swap areas should never be allocated on disks devoted to the email queue or message store, regardless of available space or apparent short-term need.

1.9 Summary

- This book presents some examples dealing with performance differences generated on nonoptimal equipment. While the actual numbers themselves aren't terribly interesting, it can be instructive to compare how configuration changes affect sample "before" and "after" data.

- Many new features have been added to `sendmail` in recent releases. The `sendmail` 8.12 release focused on performance improvements. Anyone running `sendmail` in a performance-sensitive environment would be well advised to upgrade to at least version 8.12.

- Determining appropriate hardware and software configurations to meet a set of email needs is difficult. Creating an appropriate load profile may prove more difficult than setting up the server.

- Running a caching-only DNS daemon on a busy email server can be a significant performance win.

`sendmail` Introduction

T his book uses examples focusing on the `sendmail` Mail Transfer Agent (MTA). It's generally assumed that the reader has some idea how to build and administer `sendmail`, although not necessarily at the expert level. If an email administrator is responsible for management of a `sendmail`-based system, then he or she should definitely read appropriate chapters from a general UNIX system administration handbook such as the *UNIX System Administration Handbook* [NSSH01] or, even better, a book specific to `sendmail` administration such as Craig Hunt's *Linux Sendmail Administration* [HUN01] or Bryan Costales' `sendmail` [CA97]. If none of these sources is immediately available, then the Sendmail Consortium Web site [SEN] and the *Sendmail Installation and Operation Guide* [ASA], which comes with the `sendmail` source distribution, are good places to start.

2.1 Obtaining `sendmail`

Most UNIX-like operating systems come equipped with a version of `sendmail` already installed and minimally configured to work with that system. For many environments, this setup is entirely sufficient for simple email sending and receiving. In most organizations, however, it makes sense to at least partially centralize email functions. Consequently, these configuration files are usually replaced with something more appropriate.

The version of `sendmail` that comes with an operating system release is typically not the latest version available from the Sendmail Consortium, scheduling and the cost of integrating a software package with an entire operating system being what they are. For most systems, the version that ships with the OS is entirely sufficient for moving email properly. For email servers, however, it usually makes sense to upgrade to the latest stable version available.

The sendmail source code distribution can be obtained via anonymous FTP from ftp.sendmail.org or via the www.sendmail.org Web site. The source code is distributed in a gzipped or compressed tar bundle that is unpacked in the usual ways. MD5 and PGP signatures of the files are available to help ensure the integrity of the tar bundles. Information on package signatures is available at the sendmail.org Web site.

2.2 Building **sendmail**

Unpacking the tar bundle will create a directory called sendmail-*version*/ (e.g., sendmail-8.12.2). Under this directory, several subdirectories will appear. This layout has changed somewhat over time, but here is an explanation of some of the more important pieces of the source bundle:

sendmail This directory contains the source for the sendmail MTA itself. This directory is not self-contained; rather, information and source code in other parts of the distribution are necessary to compile the MTA.

mail.local This directory contains the source for the mail.local Local Delivery Agent (LDA). It also depends on other parts of the source distribution.

cf This directory contains all information necessary to build sendmail configuration files. This directory tree is self-contained and can be copied to another location on the computer.

doc This directory contains one subdirectory, op, which houses an nroff and PostScript version of the *Sendmail Installation and Operation Guide*.

The source distribution includes a number of files that contain important information:

README This file contains general information about the sendmail package in question. Read it thoroughly before attempting to build any sendmail distribution.

INSTALL This file contains information on the installation of the sendmail package. Read it thoroughly before attempting to build the distribution. Don't assume that significant changes haven't occurred to the installation process. For example, in sendmail version 8.11, the default was to install the sendmail binary set-user-ID root. Starting in version 8.12, the default is to install it set-group-ID smmsp using two different queues and two different configuration files, depending on whether a message was submitted for delivery on the command line or via SMTP. Blindly upgrading between these two versions of `sendmail` without understanding the instructions in this file may break an email server.

`Build` This script is used to build the `sendmail` distribution. The binaries should be compiled with this mechanism. Anyone who finds that they've made modifications such that running the `Build` script no longer builds the distribution should reconsider what they've done. The build environment used by `sendmail` may be nontraditional and seem baroque at times, but it is all done for a reason. There is almost certainly a mechanism to effect any desired change within the build process. Circumventing it may have unintended consequences. `Build` is explained in the file `devtools/README`.

`RELEASE_NOTES` This file contains a list of changes to the `sendmail` distribution. All significant changes are logged dating back to `sendmail` version 8.1, so this file contains important information. When upgrading, the list of changes between the version that one is running and the version that one is installing should at least be browsed, although most people do not need to read it thoroughly.

`sendmail/README` This file contains information for modifying the `sendmail` compilation process. Anyone who wants to change the details of how `sendmail` is built would be well advised to read this file carefully.

Building `sendmail` is generally as easy as changing to the top of the distribution directory and running `sh ./Build`. The object and executable files will be created in a directory named `obj.`*`osname.architecture`* (e.g., `obj.FreeBSD.4.4-RELEASE.i386` or `obj.SunOS.5.6.sun4`). In this manner, if the package is built on a filesystem that is shared between multiple operating systems, builds for different operating systems can coexist in the same directory hierarchy.

It may become necessary to modify the standard build environment so as to support some nonstandard compile-time features. These modifications should be added to the file `site.config.m4` in the `devtools/Site` directory. For example, the following lines should be written to `site.config.m4` to compile in support for Wietse Venema's TCP Wrapper [VEN92]:

```
APPENDDEF(`conf_sendmail_ENVDEF', `-DTCPWRAPPERS')
APPENDDEF(`conf_sendmail_LIBS', `-lwrap')
```

After these changes have been made, then from the top of the distribution one should run `sh ./Build clean` and then run `sh ./Build` again. The `README` files in `devtools/Site` and `devtools` contain information on how to alter this file so as to make arbitrary compile-time modifications.

2.3 Creating a `.cf` file

When the `sendmail` program starts, it reads a configuration file called `send-mail.cf`, which is usually stored in the `/etc/mail` directory. The `sendmail.cf` file is a strange beast filled with arcane rules and bizarre variables. Following the flow of the `sendmail` rulesets can prove difficult even for someone who really understands them. For someone without deep `sendmail` experience, this file can seem daunting, to say the least.

In the "old days," before `sendmail` version 8, `sendmail.cf` files had to be written and maintained by hand. Typically, the sysadmin found one that worked for a given configuration or at another site and modified it to suit another purpose. Tweaking a `sendmail.cf` file was generally considered to require deep magic and was a task not to be undertaken lightly.

Fortunately, except for the most unusual of circumstances, this file no longer needs to be modified by hand. Doing so is almost invariably the wrong way to change `sendmail`'s behavior. Instead, it's better to create a file to act as a template for the creation of the `sendmail.cf` file in a simple macro language called M4. The m4 utility (it's a program as well as a language name) exists on almost all UNIX systems. On some very old operating systems, such as SunOS 4.x or earlier, the default m4 utility may not be capable of doing everything `sendmail` requires. In such a case, one can obtain and install the version of M4 provided by the Free Software Foundation and available via anonymous FTP at `ftp.gnu.org` (or from one of its many mirrors) in the `gnu/m4` directory. The fact that the GNU m4 source distribution hasn't been modified since 1994 indicates just how few contemporary systems will lack a sufficiently modern version of this utility.

In this book, all examples demonstrating how to implement and modify `sendmail` configurations are written using M4. Sometimes variables are mentioned that could be modified directly in the `sendmail.cf` file. Tempting as it might be, I urge the reader not to do this. Several sample M4 configuration template files are available to use as starting points or to learn from in the `cf/cf` directory of the `sendmail` distribution, where they are indicated by a `.mc` file extension. These files are referred to as `.mc` files. In creating a suitable `sendmail` configuration file, one typically chooses a template `.mc` file representative of the operating system in question and copies it to some appropriate name, such as `solaris-gateway.mc`. This file is edited and features appropriate to the given server are then added, deleted, or modified as necessary. Finally, the `.cf` file is created by running "`make solaris-gateway.cf`" in the same directory.

Several sample configuration files are available to copy from, although admittedly more examples would be useful. Generally, one should start with the "`generic-ostype.mc`" file appropriate to the operating system and modify it to taste. One file that's good to look through for ideas about good formats or what sorts of things to change is called `knecht.mc`. Eric Allman, the original author of `sendmail`, uses this configuration file on one of his own machines. Beyond these examples, all of the myriad options available for configuration within `sendmail` are documented in the `cf/README` file, with which every `sendmail` administrator should become intimately familiar.

This section isn't intended as a general tutorial on M4, but one trap into which people often fall is worth mentioning. Unlike many other scripting languages with which the reader might be familiar, M4 does not support the use of comments by beginning a line with the "#" character. Assume one puts entries like the following in an M4 file:

```
# Don't use the mailertable for now.
# FEATURE('mailertable', 'hash /etc/mail/mailertable')
```

The first line beginning with a comment will be added to the `sendmail.cf` file (as a comment), the second "#" will be added to the file on a line by itself, and M4 will interpret the `FEATURE()` directive as *adding* mailertable support. Don't comment out features using "#" in `.mc` files.

Comments can be added to `.mc` files by prefacing lines with `dnl`, which means "discard characters until the next newline." Thus the following accomplishes what the preceding example failed to do:

```
dnl Don't use the mailertable for now.
dnl FEATURE('mailertable', 'hash /etc/mail/mailertable')
```

2.4   Why Use M4?

Especially when someone is just starting to use M4, it can be irritating to pore through the `cf/README` file to find the option or macro one needs to modify `sendmail`'s behavior. What exactly is a macro—and what isn't? Why are some things set using `define()` and some using `FEATURE()`? Trying to understand this syntax can prove very frustrating, especially if one knows exactly which line or lines in the `sendmail.cf` file need to be changed, but can't figure out how to do it in M4. Nevertheless, consistently doing things via M4 will pay off through the long-term maintainability of the email servers.

Each new version of sendmail includes many new features. Additionally, because much more field test time has accumulated and Internet services have generally evolved, occasional small bugs or better ideas prompt revisions, usually minor, of the sendmail rules. Over time, a given sendmail.cf file will fall further out of date with respect to the feature set available within sendmail as well as what is considered best practice in terms of processing email. For this reason, it's desirable to update the sendmail.cf file with each installation of a new revision of sendmail.

If a configuration template is written in M4, then upgrading is as simple as copying the .mc file to the cf/cf directory of the new distribution tree and using make to generate an updated file. To see how different the resulting .cf files might be, try this technique with two significantly different versions of sendmail, such as 8.11.6 and 8.12.2. Generate two .cf files using these different source distributions but the same .mc file, and then run the UNIX diff utility to find out how much the output has changed. Porting these changes by directly editing the sendmail.cf file would involve much more work than figuring out how to express a configuration in M4, even for a true sendmail guru.

Directly modifying a sendmail.cf file is an almost certain way to create a legacy system, starting down the road to a long-term support nightmare. Someone will almost certainly regret this decision later. Even if the effort is fairly well documented, it's just so much easier to understand what has changed, what the intent was, and what the side effects might be in a 20- to 50-line M4 file than in a 1500- to 2000-line sendmail.cf file. Managing updates to the file with a version control system can help a great deal. Of course, even at the most disciplined sites, harried system administrators do not always check updates into the version control systems, and version control logs are occasionally neglected as configurations migrate from one machine to another. On occasion, I've been contracted to help upgrade an email server running off an ancient configuration file because someone hacked it to do something necessary, didn't document what was done and why clearly enough, and then left the company. Undoing this damage can prove far more expensive than doing things right the first time.

I have to admit, sometimes I might want to test a very minor configuration change and I really don't want to go to the effort of generating the new file using M4, or I might not know what the correct syntax will be so I want to test and iterate on the configuration before writing it out in M4. In those cases, even though I know it's the wrong thing to do, I will manually edit the sendmail.cf file, albeit with the intention of changing it back immediately after the test ends. Then, once I know exactly what I want, I'll make the change to the `.mc` file. Unfortunately, it's human nature to occasionally get distracted during these tests: The phone rings, someone enters the office, some disaster strikes, and undoing the change is forgotten. This possibility is a good reason to not make changes in this manner, but of course it's difficult to resist taking a "short cut." One can adopt some methods to make these sorts of quick changes less likely to cause a long-term problem. If I plan to make a temporary change, I always copy `/etc/mail/sendmail.cf` to `/etc/mail/sendmail.cf.REAL` before making the edit. Then, if I forget, I'll see the `.REAL` file the next time I attempt to manipulate it and remember to either undo the change or update the M4 file before I do any further damage. I find this technique represents a reasonable compromise between discipline and expediency.

Someone who is interested in more information about the M4 language itself would be well advised to read the paper written on this language available in the *4.4 BSD Programmer's Supplementary Documents* [KR94].

2.5 System Setup

In almost all cases, the `Build` system included in the `sendmail` distribution does an excellent job of ensuring that the `sendmail` installation and system setup coincide to allow email to work properly on the server. Mostly, this effort involves selecting the right Local Delivery Agent (LDA) and assigning proper permissions to the mail spool and queue(s). Under some scenarios, manual intervention might be warranted or required. This section covers some of these situations.

First, let's consider the way things are set up under a typical installation using either the stock `sendmail` that comes with the system or an Open Source installation using version 8.11 or earlier. Two distinct strategies for email delivery exist that are typically aligned with either the Berkeley or System V flavor of UNIX.

2.5.1 The Queue

In both cases, the message queue, `/var/spool/mqueue`, is owned by the `root` user and readable and writable only by `root`. In most cases, non-`root` users have no reason to access anything in the queue. Anyone who wants information about queued messages should use the `mailq` command. The `mailq` command is just a link to the `sendmail` binary. Invoking `mailq` works the same way as running `sendmail -bp`. A system administrator may prevent unprivileged users from seeing the contents of the queue by setting the restrictmailq variable in sendmail's privacy options in the .mc file:

```
define(`confPRIVACY_FLAGS', `restrictmailq')
```

Starting with sendmail 8.12, things work a bit differently. Namely, sendmail is no longer installed as set-user-ID root by default. Under this configuration, the sendmail daemon still runs as root at system start-up time. As a consequence, however, sendmail invoked by a non-root user on the command line will not have root permission. This result presents a dilemma. Should we then allow non-root access to the queue, or should we prevent the sending of email from the command line? The answer is "neither." The sendmail 8.12 default installation process creates two configuration files and two queues. The sendmail process started as a daemon by root at system start-up uses /var/spool/mqueue accessible by root only as its queue and /etc/mail/sendmail.cf as its configuration file. A sendmail process started by a non-root user for an interactive email session uses the directory /var/spool/clientmqueue as its queue directory and /etc/mail/submit.cf as its configuration file. Before the installation of sendmail 8.12, a new user and group—both named smmsp by default—must be created. The sendmail binary is installed as set-group-ID smmsp, and the /var/spool/clientmqueue directory is owned by the owner and group smmsp, with its permissions set to be owner and group writable; it is inaccessible to everyone else.

When upgrading a computer with sendmail 8.11 or earlier to 8.12, the smmsp user name and group are created first. Then an 8.12-compatible /etc/mail/sendmail.cf file is installed. The sh ./Build install process will do the other necessary tasks: install the binaries with the correct permission, install a submit.cf file, and create the clientmqueue directory with the proper permissions.

A non-set-user-ID sendmail installation is a very good thing. It strongly reduces the chances that a local security attack will involve the sendmail binary in the future. However, one should be aware of a couple of side effects. For example, non-root users can no longer use the mailq command to view the contents of /var/spool/mqueue. Sites should resist the temptation to "fix" this problem by allowing world read and execute permission on the queue directory itself. In addition, sendmail -bv, used to verify user names, may give misleading information as it may no longer be able to read .forward files in non-world readable directories.

Those sites that still wish to run sendmail set-user-ID root—that is, using version 8.11 and earlier behavior—may do so by running the Build script with the following argument: sh ./Build install-set-user-id.

2.5.2 The Message Store

Under Berkeley-derived UNIX systems, the default message store, /var/mail or
/var/spool/mail, is owned and writable by root and readable and executable
by everyone. Each person's mailbox will have the same name as its ownership; that
is, the mailbox named npc will be owned by the user npc. It will be readable and
writable by the owning user and unreadable and unwritable by everyone else.

On Berkeley-based systems, the LDA runs as root so it will always have
permission to put email in a user's mailbox. It is typically called either mail or
mail.local and is usually located in either /bin or /usr/libexec.

On some System V-based operating systems, the mail spool (typically /var/
mail) will be owned by the user root and the group mail. This directory will
be writable by both the owning user and the group, or the directory will be world
writable but with the "sticky" bit set (mode 01777). When the sticky bit is set on
a directory, anyone may create any file in that directory, but users may remove or
rename only files that they themselves own. Using the sticky bit is not a good way
to control file permissions in the message store, however. It means that when a
new account is created on that server, the account creation process should create
a stub mailbox in /var/mail for that user. If not, because the directory is world
writable, some malicious user could come along and create a file using someone
else's user name. If the LDA doesn't check the ownership of the file before delivering
messages, the wrong person could read someone else's email. If it does check the file
ownership, which it should, it will prevent that user from receiving any email. While
this antisocial behavior shouldn't be tolerated for very long, it would be better if
this possibility didn't exist.

In the spool, each mailbox is owned by its user, just as it is on a Berkeley-based
system, except that the group of the file will be mail and the mailbox will be
writable by both the owning user and the group. The LDA will run with its GID
as group mail, which will allow it to deliver messages to any mailbox. Today the
System V message store flavors seem to be falling out of favor, with Berkeley-style
message stores predominating in the UNIX world.

2.5.3 Modifying Permissions in the Spool

Other programs built for a particular operating system, including email readers such
as mutt or mush, automatically adapt themselves to the expected behavior of a
particular operating system during compilation. Obviously, other vendor-supplied
programs that access mailboxes, such as the Solaris mailtool or elm on HP-
UX, also expect the files and directories to have certain permissions associated

with them. If these sorts of programs will access users' mailbox files, permissions and ownership of files in the mail spool should not be modified in a manner inconsistent with these programs' expectations.

On many larger, centralized email servers, the only programs that access mailboxes might be the LDA, a POP daemon, and maybe an IMAP daemon. In such a case, the users with mailboxes on this machine need not log in to the mail server itself, so they won't have access to programs such as `elm` or `mailx`. In fact, they don't need valid login shells or home directories listed in the `/etc/passwd` files. In these cases it isn't as dangerous to modify permissions in the message store, as long as the LDA and POP and/or IMAP daemons remain compatible with the changes. The bottom line is that all programs that access the message store need to agree on its location, layout, permissions, ownerships, and locking mechanisms.

While most recent operating systems allow for billions of unique UIDs (user identifiers), some operating systems limit UIDs to a maximum value of 65,536; others limit this number range even more strictly. Many email servers exist that support a far greater number of users, but how? As long as the users don't have direct access to the server, it can suffice to use a single UID for all email-access-only accounts on the system. This strategy can simplify UID management considerably. Further, if every account that accesses email from the system does so using POP or IMAP, then all mailboxes could be owned by this single UID, which might be assigned to a suggestive-sounding account name such as `mailadm`. Then `/var/mail` could be owned and readable only by this account, the LDA would run as this account, and the POP daemon could change its EUID (effective UID, the UID under which it performs most of its operations) to that of the user in question. Note that on UNIX systems the POP server still needs to run as `root` when it binds to port 110. These changes are not required, but on a remote access-only email server with a very large number of active accounts, such a change may simplify operation.

More sweeping changes, such as bypassing the `/etc/passwd` file altogether, are also possible. Some of these ideas will be considered in Section 4.2.

2.6 Summary

- On servers whose main purpose is to handle email, it's usually advisable to obtain the most recent version of `sendmail` rather than to run what came with the machine.

- Use M4 to create and make changes to `sendmail.cf` files.

Chapter 3

Tuning Email Relaying

Often a server running `sendmail` acts as a gateway between the Internet and one or more internal email systems. If a site has a high-bandwidth connection to the Internet, and the network includes multiple internal email servers, then a gateway machine can easily become saturated with requests. Even if the network bandwidth available is small, a failure of some link in the local network, the Internet connection, a local mail server, or even a large remote email server can cause a tremendous amount of email to back up in the gateway's queue. These kinds of events can cause serious problems for a gateway email server. Luckily, some techniques are available to mitigate the damage.

3.1 What Happens During Relaying

Consider a high-level view of what happens on a `sendmail` system that acts as an email gateway. First, an external system opens an SMTP connection with the gateway. The message is sent to the gateway, which writes it to local storage and then acknowledges (and accepts responsibility for) the message. At that point, the sending machine closes the SMTP connection and can delete its own copy of the message. The gateway next opens an SMTP connection to the message's true destination (or perhaps the next hop). It transmits the message to this machine, waiting to hear that the remote machine has accepted the message. At that point, the gateway may close its connection and remove the message from its queue.

Of course, the details of this operation are far more complex and have significant ramifications on the performance of the gateway machine. The following list offers additional detail, assuming we're using `sendmail` version 8.9 or earlier and delivery is being attempted in "`background`" mode, the default mode in which `sendmail` is started at system start-up time. After reviewing the items in this list, we will examine which of these steps changed as the `sendmail` version changed.

1. The originator machine opens an SMTP connection with the gateway.

2. The gateway accepts the connection, and the master `sendmail` daemon spawns a new `sendmail` process to handle this connection.

3. The new `sendmail` process inspects the SMTP envelope (the envelope is distinct from the email message's header; see RFC 2821 [KLE01] or the *sendmail* book [CA97] for more details) to determine whether the message should be accepted by policy.

4. If the message is acceptable to the gateway, a `qf` file, which will eventually contain the message's header along with delivery information, is created in the queue, typically the `/var/spool/mqueue` directory. Next, the remote machine receives permission to send the message itself, and then the gateway creates the `df` file, which will hold the message's body, also in the queue.

5. The originator sends the message's header, which the gateway stores in memory temporarily, followed by the message body. As the body is received by the gateway, it is buffered and written out to the `df` file. This procedure ensures that the `sendmail` machine can handle a message larger than its virtual memory system, if desired.

6. Once the originator indicates that the message has been completely sent, the gateway adds its own "Received:" line to the header, modifies the message headers if necessary, and writes out the contents of the `qf` file. It then issues an `fsync()` command on the still-open `qf` and `df` file descriptors, closes the files, and acknowledges receipt of the message to the originator.

7. The `sendmail` process itself spawns a child whose process memory data segment inherits the memory image of the `qf` file from the parent process.

8. The originator of the now-queued message closes the SMTP connection if no more messages will be sent, and the `sendmail` process that queued the message exits.

9. By this time, the new child process has begun parsing the data that were written to the `qf` file to determine what to do with the message.

10. Once the destination machine has been determined, an SMTP connection is opened to the appropriate machine and an `xf` file is created in the queue, in which the MTA will log error messages associated with each delivery attempt.

11. The message envelope information is sent to the destination machine, which decides whether it will accept or reject the message.

12. Once the message envelope has been accepted by the destination machine, the message header is generated from the contents of the qf file held in memory and sent over the SMTP connection, followed by a blank line and then the body of the message, which is read out of the df file.

13. If the message cannot be sent to at least one intended recipient, the MTA creates a tf file. In this file it writes an updated version of the qf file, fsync()s the data, rename()s the file to atomically replace the old qf file.

14. Once the message is successfully delivered to all recipients, then sendmail can unlink the df files and then the qf files. If a tf file has been created, an exiting sendmail process will rename it to a qf file. The only time a tf or xf file might be left around in a mail queue is if the sendmail process that was working on the file crashes or if the entire machine stops functioning before cleanup can occur. Of course, in all circumstances, an intact qf file will remain present in the queue, so no email will be lost, although under certain rare circumstances a recipient might be sent the same message more than once.

Starting with sendmail 8.10, some minor differences occur to the sequence listed above. With this version of sendmail, the queue identifier for a given transaction will be guaranteed to be unique for more than 60 years. Needless to say, no item should stay in a mail queue for that long. Therefore, there is no need to create a qf file to reserve the queue ID, so creating and writing to this file are deferred until just before the MTA acknowledges the receipt of the message. When sendmail runs in background mode (the default case, signified by adding the -bd flag when starting sendmail), this activity does not typically result in the net saving of any I/O operations.

Besides the filesystem and network operations described previously, sendmail performs several DNS operations during this exchange. Typically, a reverse DNS lookup is performed on the IP address of the connecting host to check whether that host has permission to connect. Another DNS lookup is performed on the response to see whether a DNS A or IPv6 AAAA record exists that matches the PTR record returned in the previous request. A DNS lookup is then performed on the sender address. Next, a DNS lookup is performed on each recipient address to determine the machine for which the message is destined (it might be destined for the gateway itself) and to canonify the address (replace CNAME records with the host names to which they point). Once the sendmail process attempts to deliver the email message, the destination host is checked in DNS again. Each of these DNS checks of domain names are first checks for MX records, and then checks for CNAME and A records and possibly AAAA records if IPv6 support is enabled. Thus, if MX records for the destination server don't exist, two DNS lookups will be performed. For the typical relayed message bound for a single recipient, at least four DNS checks will occur, each of which may consist of two distinct queries.

Matters become simpler if the sendmail server's name server is located nearby. If a DNS server receives a request to answer a query about, say, an MX record, the name server will typically tack on a request to resolve any resource records to which the MX record points, on the theory that the additional information will be requested next. While this procedure doesn't reduce the number of requests between an application and its name server, it does reduce the number of requests sent between the application's name server and the authoritative repository for the DNS information. Communication between a site's DNS server and the rest of the Internet typically occurs much more slowly than communication between the application and its name server, especially if an email server is its own name server.

3.2 Synchronization

Any email system that cannot guarantee successful delivery of a message has a significant deficiency. Section 6.1 of RFC 2821 explicitly states:

> When the receiver-SMTP accepts a piece of email (by sending a "250 OK" message in response to DATA), it is accepting responsibility for delivering or relaying the message. It must take this responsibility seriously. It MUST NOT lose the message for frivolous reasons, such as because the host later crashes or because of a predictable resource shortage.

This is a significant statement, and it is an absolute requirement. Any email system that does not follow this guideline cannot claim to be compliant with the SMTP protocol. Essentially, this paragraph requires that once the message is accepted, it must be completely committed to stable storage before the acknowledgment can be returned to the sending server. Not only must the message be received, but to survive a machine crash, the filesystem buffer that contains the message must be flushed to stable storage. On UNIX-like systems, this requirement means that the fsync() or equivalent call must be made. This technique ensures that the message has actually been written to disk such that the data will still be available if the system crashes.

Since the early days of UNIX, significant advancements have been made regarding the speed at which data can be written to disk. The most significant involves buffering the data to memory rather than synchronously writing it to disk. When an application performs a write() call to a file, the data are just written to memory, which is much faster than writing it to a disk, before the system call returns indicating success. The kernel marks these data buffers as "dirty," and it knows that they need to be flushed to disk eventually. However, it waits until it can do so conveniently or until a timer has expired, so as to keep programs performing data write()s moving along and to more efficiently use system resources. The downside is that if the system crashes before the buffer is flushed to disk, the contents of the write() will be lost. Usually, this loss would involve only a few seconds of data—a small price to pay for vastly improved performance.

Conversely, this price is too large to pay for a machine that claims to support the SMTP standard. Therefore, an email server must perform much of its data updating synchronously, negating the most significant performance improvement in writing data to disk available to the system. Because few other applications must adhere to such strict requirements, the general I/O tuning literature pays little attention to synchronous disk operations. Few storage vendors test this scenario as it tends to make their products look as if they're not very fast, and few I/O benchmarks focus on this aspect of I/O performance. Even the PostMark [KAT00] filesystem benchmark, which is designed to mimic the behavior of an email system, falls short in this regard. While it does perform a large number of fairly random creates and deletes, it does not require that the target filesystem perform its updates synchronously.

These sorts of synchronous operations seem expensive from a performance standpoint, yet they are absolutely essential if people are to have any confidence that their messages will reach their intended destinations. Therefore, if it is necessary to support a large amount of email flowing through this system, one may have to be a bit clever in handling synchronous disk operations.

The necessity to synchronize writes to disk is true for both final email delivery and email queueing. Just because the machine queueing a message may not be its final destination does not mean that this server can have a cavalier attitude toward its integrity. Before a queued message is acknowledged—that is, before the machine performing the acknowledgment accepts responsibility for the message—we must be certain that the message has been committed to stable storage.

In sendmail configurations, a parameter called SuperSafe controls this behavior. By default, SuperSafe mode is turned on. In this case, after a series of disk write()s has occurred but before a close() is issued, an fsync() is performed on that file descriptor, ensuring the correct behavior as documented in RFC 2821. This feature can be turned off, although it should be done only under a very restricted set of circumstances. To turn off SuperSafe, add the following line to the .mc file:

```
define('confSAFE_QUEUE', 'False')
```

For example, if a large presorted batch of messages is being sent to nonlocal email addresses from an email server, sufficient accounting of what does and doesn't actually get accepted by another mail server might render the additional safety of SuperSafe unnecessary. However, it is strongly recommended that this feature not be turned off unless some other accounting system, as in this example, is present to determine whether all email messages have reached their intended destinations. In practice, meeting all of these criteria is unlikely in most situations, as this sort of record keeping is difficult to do.

Beginning with sendmail version 8.12, changes have been made to the way sendmail operates when run in "interactive" mode such that email from remote machines to local mailboxes (or remote servers) may be delivered via the delivery agent and committed to stable storage without creating intermediate entries in the mail queue. This goal can be accomplished using the following lines in the .mc file:

```
define('confDELIVERY_MODE','interactive')
define('confSAFE_QUEUE','interactive')
```

Setting confDELIVERY_MODE to "interactive" by itself can reduce the CPU overhead involved in handling mail transfer. With the addition of the confSAFE_QUEUE definition, a substantial reduction in I/O requirements in the queue will occur. With these changes, the sequence of events listed previously is modified as described next.

As is usual in any version of sendmail from 8.10 on, the qf file need not be created to reserve the queue identifier, and the qf file contents are held in memory. Also, the creation and buffering of the message body to the df file are deferred until the value defined by DataFileBufferSize is exceeded. By default, this value is 4,096 bytes. On most systems where the daemon will run predominantly in interactive mode, this value probably should be increased. A value of approximately 20KB seems a reasonable place to start for most machines, allowing most small messages to be held in RAM without exhausting the server of memory. If the system regularly needs to swap, then either add more RAM or lower this number. With interactive queueing, the xf file will also be buffered in memory rather than immediately written to disk as long as the value of the XScriptFile-BufferSize parameter isn't exceeded. The default value for this parameter is 4,096 bytes and will rarely be exceeded except on those servers where each message commonly has a very large number of recipients. In such a case, increasing this parameter seems reasonable. Adding the following lines to the .mc file will increase the xf file buffer to 16KB and increase the df file buffer to 100KB:

```
define('confXF_BUFFER_SIZE','16384')
define('confDF_BUFFER_SIZE','102400')
```

Unlike operations in `background` mode, in `interactive` mode, once the message has been received by a child `sendmail` process, another child process is not `fork()`ed to handle the subsequent delivery. Instead, the same process attempts delivery itself. When `confSAFE_QUEUE` is also set to `interactive`, it will attempt to do so without writing the message information out to disk unless it has to. This would be the case if none of the appropriate hosts to which the message could be sent is available or if the `DataFileBufferSize` buffer is exceeded. Then, and only then, are the `qf` and `df` files created in the queue and data written to them. After successful delivery of the message, the same `sendmail` process that performed this delivery will return an SMTP "250 OK" message to the originating machine signifying that the message has been transferred successfully to the next hop. The next hop may be a remote server, another delivery agent that takes responsibility for that message, or safe queuing of the message if initial delivery fails.

This algorithm will greatly reduce the amount of disk activity on the relaying machine, which would occur synchronously, at the cost of holding open the network connection from the server that originated the message for a small amount of additional time. In most cases, one would expect this method to considerably increase the number of messages per second a server that dealt predominantly in locally delivered email could handle. As a historical note, this change became available as an option in `sendmail` version 8.10 for systems, such as FreeBSD, that provided `stdio` function overrides.

Arguably, this network behavior is "less polite," as resources are consumed (the open connection) on the originating server when, strictly speaking, it isn't necessary. Nevertheless, I believe this behavior should be acceptable for a busy server because the resources consumed are very minor—just one outstanding process, a little bit of memory, and a socket. It does not impose any additional I/O or CPU load on the originating machine. At the same time, it does require the gateway machine to be expedient in its delivery. If the originating machine must wait for several minutes under any but the most extreme circumstances, that would cross the threshold between "acceptable" and "rude" behavior. One could also rationalize this behavior by noting that if, instead of running the master `sendmail` daemon in `interactive` mode, it were run in the default `background` mode, the same server might have significant problems keeping up with the load, inconveniencing the originating server to an even greater extent.

One other potential downside to running a gateway server in `interactive` mode is the greater chance that a message will be retransmitted unnecessarily and end up as a duplicate message in someone's mailbox. This problem can occur if a message is sent from the originator to the gateway machine, and the connection to the originator is terminated after the message is received by the gateway, but before the message has been accepted for delivery by the next hop or destination from the gateway. The originator won't know that the message is being successfully transmitted to its next destination and the message will be re-sent. The gateway won't know that the second message is a retransmission of the first one, so it will be relayed as well. This scenario can also occur if `sendmail` runs in `background` mode on the gateway, although the window within which this event might happen is much shorter. A message will be unnecessarily retransmitted in this case only if the SMTP connection from the originator becomes severed between the acceptance of the end of the message by the gateway and the receipt of the "250 OK" message by the originator. The duration of this window of vulnerability in `background` mode typically will be on the order of a one-way network trip between the gateway and originator plus the time it takes to make a single disk write. In total, this window typically would be on the order of 10 to 100 ms. If the gateway runs in `interactive` mode and the message is large, the window of vulnerability may last a little longer than the duration of an entire SMTP session between the gateway and the destination machine, perhaps in the range of several seconds, or even longer if the network connection is slow or the message is very large.

We can examine the effects of changing the delivery mode on the CPU-bound test server introduced in Chapter 1. In this experiment, we set up our test machine to relay email sent from one server to a second machine where the messages are delivered (the messages are actually discarded before final delivery, but our test gateway remains oblivious to this fact). The test gateway runs `sendmail` 8.12.2. In the first test, the gateway runs in `background` mode, and at saturation it can relay about 279 messages/minute before running out of CPU resources. During this time, disk that contains the mail queue runs at about 45% of its throughput capacity. If the delivery mode changes to `interactive`, throughput jumps to 450 messages/minute and the queue disk loading remains relatively constant, despite the increased I/O load, at about 47% of capacity. Finally, setting both the delivery mode and `SuperSafe` to be `interactive`, the test server can relay 512 messages/minute, while the queue disk loading drops to 0%.

From these results, we can see that considerably less CPU resources are consumed when running in `interactive` mode than when running in `background` mode. This difference primarily reflects the reduction in process forking and data copying. We obtain further CPU savings when we go to `interactive` queueing by eliminating the computational overhead involved in writing the data out to disk. If the gateway were disk bound rather than CPU bound, we would expect that not writing to the queue would result in an even more spectacular improvement in throughput. Even so, simply by changing the delivery mode and queue method in this test, we increased throughput by more than 80%, a tremendous improvement.

We can repeat these experiments on the I/O-bound test server also introduced in Chapter 1. We use the same configuration and testing methodology, using our target server as an email relay running `sendmail` 8.12.2 and using the Linux `ext2fs` filesystem in the queue. Queueing messages using `background` mode, we achieve a throughput of about 1,500 messages/minute. Changing the delivery mode to `interactive` reduces throughput slightly, to about 1,480 messages/minute. The switch to `interactive` mode changes the CPU workload of the server, but doesn't affect the I/O operations that must be performed, so it isn't surprising that the throughput essentially remains unchanged.

When we use `interactive` as the delivery mode and change `SuperSafe` to `interactive` as well, throughput jumps to 2,400 messages/minute. The restriction in this test, however, reflects CPU exhaustion on the machine sending the messages to our test server. At this point, the target machine we're testing handles the load easily. Memory consumption isn't a problem, no disks are used, and the CPU operates at about 21% of its maximum loading. While it is dangerous to extrapolate from these data, in this configuration our test server could potentially relay more than 10,000 messages per minute, an impressive amount of email.

3.3 Filesystems

For `sendmail`-based gateways, the single most common cause for a performance bottleneck is the rate at which files can be created and deleted in the mail queue directory, `/var/spool/mqueue` or its equivalent. The details of the implementation of the filesystem on which these messages are stored can contribute greatly to the overall performance of an email server. This section will discuss these issues.

3.3.1 FFS-Based Filesystems

Most of the more commonly used UNIX file systems are based on the venerable Fast File System (FFS) [MJLF84]. While this filesystem has been a workhorse for UNIX systems for more than 15 years, its characteristics can easily lead to performance problems under some types of loads. For instance, it does not perform terribly well when directories become too large—that is, when a single directory contains many files or subdirectories. It also performs relatively poorly when it must carry out quickly a large number of directory-modifying operations, such as creates and deletes, which are common on `sendmail` servers.

An example will illustrate this point. When it comes time to look up an entry in an FFS directory, the filesystem does a linear scan of that directory looking for any entity that matches the file name in question. On very large directories on extremely busy disks, the server might be so busy that a simple "`ls /var/spool/mqueue`" can take *minutes* to write the first line of output to the terminal. As this same delay will occur whenever a `sendmail` process looks up a particular queued message identifier, and will be exacerbated when a forked `sendmail` process begins a queue run, this delay can create a huge bottleneck. While a system will rarely get so bogged down that `ls` takes a minute to run, even adding a significant fraction of a second to each directory lookup can increase the amount of time it takes to process an email message by a considerable percentage.

Many higher-performance filesystems store their directory information in a hash table or balanced tree (often called a B-tree) structure, making the cost to perform such a lookup much less expensive when the directories get very large. Some that have this feature include VxFS [VER], XFS [SDH+96], and ReiserFS [REI]. On these filesystems, the directory hashing information is stored on disk. On FreeBSD version 4.4 or later, if the kernel is compiled with the "UFS_DIRHASH" feature, a hashed image of frequently accessed directories is stored in memory on the system. Do not underestimate this extremely strong potential performance improvement.

On FFS-based filesystems, when a file is deleted from a directory, updating of several on-disk data structures becomes necessary. First, the directory entry for this file is deleted, then the inode containing the file is placed on the free list. These operations must be performed in this order or else a directory entry could potentially point to invalid data. When a new file is created, an inode must be allocated for that file and then a directory entry created pointing to that inode. These operations must be performed in this order as the directory entry needs to know to which inode it ought to point. Consequently, some directory plus inode operations need to be performed in one order, whereas others need to be performed in the opposite order.

FFS solves this dilemma by performing its directory operations synchronously. When a file is to be created or deleted, first the directory is locked, then the inode and directory operations are performed synchronously on disk in the correct order, and finally the directory is unlocked. As a consequence, not only are directory operations performed synchronously, but a system where many file creations and deletions are trying to occur at the same time in a single directory will also have all these operations serialized and bracketed by locks. This strategy prevents taking advantage of the buffering designed to speed up disk I/O on modern systems, thereby making these operations perform poorly. Exactly this sort of activity takes place continuously in a `sendmail` mail queue and often causes mail machines to appear to run slowly. A more thorough discussion of the issues involving FFS filesystem consistency appears in [MBKQ96].

For this reason, many have been enticed by the prospect of running their filesystems in asynchronous mode. Asynchronous file system performance is so far superior to FFS's synchronous performance that it has proved a serious temptation even to people who ought to know better. As noted earlier, the email standards require that email that has been acknowledged as received must be able to survive a machine crash. If a filesystem runs in async mode, then not only will the data written to disk be buffered in memory, but the filesystem metadata operations (that is, operations that change file information rather than the file contents) will also be buffered. Thus data could be lost during a crash, and entire files or directories may be in jeopardy as well. In fact, the filesystem could reach such a state that a large percentage, or even all in extreme cases, might not be recoverable if the server crashes. Clearly, this approach is an unacceptable way to run an email system.

Soft Updates [GP94] is an extension to FFS that improves the performance of filesystem metadata operations. With Soft Updates, each modification of a directory entry is written in a particular way such that if the update is aborted, enough information is available to roll back or commit each individual operation. This approach has been implemented in practice in BSD 4.4-based operating systems [MG99] with metadata operation performance numbers that come very close to asynchronous performance without the potentially disastrous side effects. Researchers can debate whether journaling, which will be discussed later, or Soft Updates provides better performance (and they do—see [SGM+00], for example). For most practical purposes, however, which solution is adopted really doesn't matter. Both approaches have similar performance characteristics for most workloads, and both can offer dramatic improvements over slower synchronous metadata updates.

Even when an advanced filesystem is not available, queue performance in an FFS-based filesystem can be improved in several ways. One strategy is to turn off file access time updates for that filesystem.

On an FFS-based filesystem, each file is represented in a directory by an inode. The inode contains information such as the UID of the file's owner, the type of file, and the location on the disk of the data blocks that make up the file's contents. It also contains the times of three events: its creation time (when the inode was allocated), its modification time (when the file's metadata or data were last modified), and the access time (when the file was last read). Each time a file is read, the `atime` parameter in the inode is updated, which requires a disk write. Because `sendmail` never checks the access time of a file, we can safely turn this feature off and eliminate all of these inode updates.

This step typically is done by adding the `noatime` flag to the list of filesystem options given to the `mount` command during mounting of the filesystem. For example, on a gateway email server running FreeBSD, our `/etc/fstab` file might look like the following:

```
# Device              Mountpoint    FStype   Options        Dump   Pass#
/dev/da0s1b           none          swap     sw             0      0
/dev/da0s1a           /             ufs      rw             1      1
/dev/da0s1f           /usr          ufs      rw             1      2
/dev/da1s1h           /var/spool    ufs      rw,noatime     2      2
server:/export/home   /home         nfs      rw             0      0
/dev/cd0c             /cdrom        cd9600   ro,noauto      0      0
proc                  /proc         procfs   rw             0      0
```

This file indicates that the `/var/spool` filesystem will be mounted with access time updates turned off. The syntax may vary slightly depending on the exact filesystem and operating system. It's important to understand the information available in the `mount` and related man pages to obtain appropriate results.

3.3.2 FFS Alternatives

The most popular Linux filesystem, ext2fs [CTT94], runs in asynchronous mode by default. However, it is an extremely bad idea to use this mode on a filesystem that will store email (or any other important data, for that matter). When a filesystem runs in asynchronous mode and the operating system supporting that filesystem crashes or otherwise suddenly halts, the system might not be able to reconstruct that filesystem when it comes back to life. Unfortunately, if ext2fs is run in synchronous mode, then *every* I/O request to that filesystem is performed synchronously, including every `write()` call. While this approach makes the filesystem very safe, it degrades performance enough to make this solution unacceptable for high-performance systems.

Equally dangerous is the default behavior of ReiserFS for Linux, which updates its metadata log asynchronously, thereby allowing file renames, creations, and deletions to become lost if the server crashes suddenly. Starting with version 8.12, `sendmail` works around both the ext2fs and ReiserFS problems by always being extra careful when it runs on Linux systems. On Linux, to ensure the integrity of a queued message when updating a `qf` file, `sendmail` will write its temporary data to the `tf` file, `fsync()` the file, rename the file to be the `qf` file, `fsync()` the qf

file (using the same file descriptor), and then `fsync()` the directory that contains
the file. The first `fsync()` commits the data to disk synchronously. The second
`fsync()` is for those filesystems where `fsync()` must be run on a file to synchronize its metadata, such as FFS with Soft Updates. On filesystems that perform file
metadata updates synchronously, such as FFS, this additional call won't add significantly to the latency of the I/O operations, as the system call should return immediately because no additional work needs to be done. The third `fsync()` commits
the ext2fs and ReiserFS directory metadata (including the file's name) to disk synchronously. This approach makes running `sendmail` mail queues safe on Linux,
but of course this safety is guaranteed only when running at least version 8.12. Not
every other piece of email software is equally conscientious. A running `sendmail`
process cannot easily determine what kind of filesystem is mounted in the queue,
so `sendmail` always performs these steps by default on a Linux system, even if
other filesystems such as XFS or IBM's JFS [BES00] are used. Finally, note that the
second `fsync()` call was introduced in `sendmail` version 8.10.

This is all very complicated, but unfortunately necessary to ensure that email
transport remains reliable in all environments. In all legitimate cases, we cannot
afford to sacrifice email reliability for the sake of performance. This requirement
makes the work more difficult, but it is a non-negotiable trade-off.

What we really want is to somehow match the safety of synchronous operations with the performance of an asynchronous filesystem. Much of the research in
filesystems conducted over the last 15 years focuses on how to attain this goal.

One way to provide I/O safety without performing synchronous data operations is to use a synchronous journaling filesystem. A journaling filesystem keeps a
log (called the journal) of filesystem metadata operations. This journal is updated
synchronously with events such as file creations and deletions, but the actual inode
operations are performed asynchronously. Thus, if the system crashes, the journal
can be replayed to put it in a consistent state. Updating the journal synchronously
is not nearly as expensive as modifying filesystem metadata synchronously, so a
significant performance win can result. Examples of journaling filesystems include
XFS [SDH⁺96], VxFS [VER], and ReiserFS [REI], although ReiserFS updates its
journal asynchronously. General background information on journaling filesystems
can be found in [RO92].

An updated version of the Linux filesystem, called `ext3fs` [TWE98], has
recently become available. In essence, it consists of `ext2fs` with the addition of
asynchronous journaling. As a result, `ext3fs` filesystems are backward-compatible
with `ext2fs`. That is, an `ext3fs` filesystem can be mounted as `ext2fs`, albeit
without journaling support. An `ext2fs` filesystem can be converted to `ext3fs`

simply by running `tune2fs -j /dev/diskdevice`. The journal is stored in a reserved inode in the same filesystem as the regular files themselves.

The `ext3fs` filesystem supports three types of journaling modes, two of which are potentially useful for email delivery. The first, `data=ordered`, is the default configuration for `ext3fs`. Using this method, filesystem metadata are journaled, but updates to file contents go directly to disk. In the second configuration, `data=journal`, both filesystem updates and metadata are written to the journal before being written to disk. Under most workloads, filesystem performance using `data=ordered` will be superior to that with `data=journal` because file contents are written twice rather than once in the latter case. File contents are written to the journal and then the appropriate blocks are updated on the filesystem itself.

As with ReiserFS and `ext2fs`, `ext3fs` metadata updates are asynchronous by default. The primary stated advantage of `ext3fs` is that recovery is much faster in case of a system crash. Only the journal needs to be reconciled to put the filesystem into a consistent state. On nonjournaling filesystems, the filesystem checker, `fsck`, must examine the entire filesystem to assure that its contents remain consistent.

3.3.3 Linux Filesystem Comparison

With so many filesystems available for Linux, which one is the best for use on email servers? This question cannot be answered simply and unequivocally. It is entirely possible to come up with plausible email scenarios in which each of the Linux filesystems performs best. For this book, I've run a set of comparisons that illustrates that the best choice for a given scenario can often be surprising as well as highlights the complexities involved in making generalizations.

We test on the I/O-bound Linux server introduced in Chapter 1. As in the tests mentioned earlier in this chapter, this server acts as an email relay. It runs `sendmail` 8.12.2 in `interactive` delivery mode, with `SuperSafe` set to `True`. On the load generator, the number of concurrent SMTP sessions that relay 1KB email messages off of this server will be increased until the I/O-bound server's queue disk becomes saturated. At the saturation point, the number of messages processed per minute are counted. This test is repeated using each of the three Linux filesystems already discussed in this section.

The results of the first test using `ext2fs` were documented earlier in this chapter. Employing this filesystem in the queue, the test server succeeded in relaying 1,500 messages/minute.

Next, we rerun the test using version 3.6 of ReiserFS as our filesystem. In this test, throughput drops substantially, to only 530 messages/minute. While ReiserFS is advertised as working efficiently for large numbers of small files, this would seem to refer to storage efficiency and directory lookups rather than the performance of synchronous writes. While modifications to ReiserFS after version 3.6 improve on these results, they aren't yet enough to make it competitive with ext2fs in this particular benchmark test. ReiserFS can efficiently store a large number of small files due to its "tail-packing" algorithm, which allows the storage of small files within the same disk block as its directory tree nodes. This option can be turned off using the notail mount option. In the preceding test, remounting the queue using this flag did not significantly improve performance.

In ReiserFS, directory elements are stored in B* trees. This directory storage format allows for fast lookups of files in directories with large numbers of entries. In this test, however, the number of files in each directory never reached 50, so this benefit was not realized.

As ext3fs is just ext2fs with the addition of a journal, we might expect it to offer worse queueing performance than ext2fs. In reality, in a test run using the default data=ordered journal mode, a throughput of around 2,020 messages/minute was achieved, representing about a 35% increase over ext2fs. Even more remarkable, if the journaling mode is changed to data=journal, throughput increases substantially. Under this arrangement, the machine sending email to the gateway test server became the CPU-bound bottleneck, while the iostat utility showed only about 40% disk utilization on the relay server. With extrapolation of these numbers (always very risky), this configuration could potentially relay 4,000 or perhaps even 5,000 messages/minute.

Why does ext3fs perform so well in this environment? Its performance almost certainly reflects the short lifetime of the queue files in this test combined with the way the journal works. Using data=ordered, file data are written to disk and the file metadata are written to the journal. Within a fraction of a second, the file is unlinked and a delete operation is recorded in the journal. Periodically, a checkpointer runs to migrate journaled data onto disk and thereby free up journal space. When the checkpointer encounters a "create/delete" pair, these entries are removed from the journal, the disk blocks to which they refer are freed, and no metadata updates need to be performed. Adding and deleting these entries from the journal, essentially one large file, works considerably more efficiently than removing them from the filesystem, making ext3fs perform better than ext2fs. When the filesystem is mounted with data=journal, the file data are also stored in the journal along with the metadata log. Thus, if the message is relayed quickly enough, every bit of information associated with a queue entry creation and deletion is written and deleted in the log without ever requiring data to be written elsewhere on the disk.

In this test, the disk head on the queue disk might never perform a single seek outside of the journal region during the duration of the test, explaining why the throughput is so high.

On a production server, performance may not be quite so good. Not all messages will be delivered within a few milliseconds of their reception. Any file that exists in the queue for more than a few seconds will be rewritten to the disk from the journal. Moreover, most environments have larger average message sizes than those in this test run, and larger messages will consume journal space and bandwidth. Also, because real-world message transfers occur more slowly, more concurrent files will reside in the queue at the same time, which also consumes journal space and bandwidth. In fact, if email relaying occurs so slowly that all relayed messages are written out of the journal to disk before they're unlinked, `ext3fs` would probably perform worse than `ext2fs`, as it would have to write everything out twice. Similarly, if the queue directories are very large, it's entirely possible that the cost of queue metadata operations on `ext3fs` would be so high that ReiserFS would perform best. A production server using `ext3fs` as the filesystem in a mail queue may still be a good idea, especially if the journal is configured to be especially large and enough RAM is available to hold its entire image in the buffer cache. Nevertheless, the spectacular performance numbers demonstrated in this test are unlikely to be achieved in the real world.

Clearly, evaluating filesystems for a particular purpose can be quite complex. This section has provided some insights into which filesystems might be most appropriate for which workloads, but there is no substitute for direct testing. Excellent information on Linux filesystems, including feature, design, and performance comparisons, can be found in [VH01].

3.3.4 Hardware-Based Acceleration

As has already been mentioned, a high-performance filesystem can greatly improve I/O performance in a `sendmail` message queue by removing the need for slow directory locking during file creation and deletion. A solution to this problem using hardware also exists—the use of nonvolatile RAM (NVRAM). With NVRAM, instead of file updates being immediately committed to disk, they are committed to battery-backed memory modules whose contents can survive a power outage or machine crash. For example, when a file is deleted, the deletion can be noted synchronously, but very quickly, in NVRAM (much as is done for a journaling filesystem), and the application can move on to its next operation. Meanwhile, the operating system can update the filesystem to reflect the change at its leisure. If the server crashes before these updates are committed to disk, the log in the NVRAM can be replayed when the server reboots to reconcile any discrepancies found on the disk itself.

Back in the old days, hardware cards provided this support. Legato made one called Prestoserve, originally for VME-based machines and then for Sun's SBus. Users of these cards on systems that did a large number of file creates and deletes typically described their performance improvements as nothing short of amazing. Along the same lines, owners of the Sun Sparc 20 server could add a product called NVSIMM, an NVRAM chip that was installed directly on the machine's motherboard and provided the same service.

Unfortunately, these products have vanished from the face of the computing industry. NVRAM remains in use, however, as part of most commercial RAID systems. Today's disk storage systems typically provide the option of adding RAM whose contents can survive a power outage or other catastrophe such that this RAM acts as a buffer to lower the latency of synchronous operations. It has the additional effect of assisting in the optimization of disk movement. That is, by aggregating disk operations the storage system could wait until several metadata update operations needed to be performed on the same directory and then commit them to disk at the same time.

On email servers, small messages are often received and written to the queue, sent on to their destinations, and deleted from the queue within a very short amount of time. The time it takes to deliver a message is logged by `syslog`, so one can see typical numbers for a given mail server. The following is a very inelegant but easy-to-follow script that will create a rough histogram-like list showing the frequency of certain delay times. The name and location of the log file may need to be modified.

```
#!/bin/sh

zcat /var/log/'maillog'.*.gz |\
        tr ' ' '\n' |\
        grep "delay=" |\
        grep -v "xdelay" |\
        sed 's/,//g' |\
        awk -F'=' '{ sum[$2]++ } END { for (i in sum)
         print i, sum[i] }' |\
        sort
```

Run on a sample machine, it produces the following output:

```
00:00:00 27
00:00:01 29
00:00:02 4
00:00:03 3
00:00:04 3
00:00:05 3
00:00:06 3
00:00:07 3
00:00:11 1
00:00:13 2
00:00:21 2
00:00:24 1
00:00:31 1
00:01:27 1
00:10:01 1
```

Approximately one-third of the mail touched by this machine was transmitted in less than a second (of course, much of it is local). Another one-third was transmitted in about one second.

Based on this information, we could see how NVRAM might assist the performance of a `sendmail` mail queue in a remarkable way. Because most messages spend a very small amount of time in the queue, if the messages are small they can often be written to and deleted from NVRAM before the NVRAM contents are ever written to disk! The elimination of actual disk movement for many, if not most, email messages while still fulfilling RFC 2821's integrity requirements is a remarkable proposition.

NVRAM has been understood to be useful for accelerating disk operations for quite some time. Even though it is quite old in computing terms, a paper written by Mary Baker and others [BAD+92] is no less relevant in demonstrating how much of an advantage NVRAM can provide.

3.3.5 Other Filesystem Strategies

In combination, many operating systems and filesystems try to improve performance by aggressively "pre-fetching" data. The basic idea behind this approach is that if an application `read()`s several contiguous disk blocks out of a file, it is likely to eventually request the next several disk blocks, or even the rest of the file. Therefore, the operating system can provide faster access by pre-fetching the extra data that are likely to be requested next and storing that data in the buffer cache. In this way, when the request comes, the extra data have already been cached in memory and can be immediately passed to the application without moving a disk head.

In general, this strategy is a reasonable one. Unfortunately, it helps very little on an email server. To some small extent, performing pre-fetching of the next set of consecutive disk blocks will result in more efficient use of the disk if it will eliminate a disk head seek to read that section, but there's no guarantee that this event will happen. In general, any form of pre-fetching results in a loss of I/O bandwidth and increased memory consumption to gain improved latency. To be precise, the OS consumes disk bandwidth by performing operations in the hope that it can answer a forthcoming query much more quickly that it otherwise would. Of course, if that query never comes, precious bandwidth has been consumed with no return on investment. Whether or not the read ahead occurs, almost exactly the same disk motion will be required to fulfill the request. Thus, even if applications use the pre-fetched data, only a small savings in total I/O bandwidth will occur.

If a server stores extremely large scientific data files, movies, or other files that are typically accessed sequentially, pre-fetching can offer an enormous benefit. When files are small and accesses are less easy to predict, the pre-fetched files are actually used less often by applications, resulting in wasted I/O operations. While reducing the amount of time an email application must wait for data is a good thing, overall I/O bandwidth to the disks is almost always a much more precious commodity than latency.

On an email server, after reading the first data block from the file, it's almost certain that the application will scan through to the end of that file. Therefore, some read-ahead capability usually doesn't hurt. On systems where the amount is tunable, a minimal, but nonzero, read-ahead policy usually will provide the best performance characteristics. Details concerning which systems support tuning this capability and how to do so vary greatly from system to system, so it is impossible to give more specific advice that is both useful and reasonably brief.

If an email server handles many sessions over slow network connections, filesystem pre-fetching can result in an especially insidious problem. Suppose that an email server supports hundreds or even thousands of concurrent POP sessions at one time. Suppose also that these connections take place over slow modems that allow 2.5 KBps of data to be transferred. Each mailbox download, and hence each POP session, might take tens of minutes to complete if the mailboxes are large.

With a large number of sessions and slow transfers, pre-fetched data pages may consume a lot of memory on the system. If the system runs out of free memory at this point, memory will be reclaimed by freeing memory consumed by the buffer cache using a Least Recently Used (LRU) or similar algorithm. In the worst case, data that have not yet been sent to the POP client will be flushed from the buffer cache and must be reread from disk. This is a horrible eventuality, because now the same data must be read from disk twice.

At this point, the overconsumption of disk bandwidth could potentially cause the system to slow down noticeably, making each session last longer. This delay will cause the number of sessions to increase, which causes increased memory consumption, which causes faster depletion of the buffer cache, which leads to a catastrophe.

Of course, this scenario assumes that pre-fetching is aggressive, the mailbox files are large, and the network connections are very slow. This confluence of circumstances is not entirely implausible, especially for an email server that serves POP clients over dial-up links, such as an ISP. On a server that experiences this problem, the only solutions are (1) to reduce the aggressiveness of the pre-fetching algorithm or (2) to add more memory to increase the size of the buffer cache. Both are reasonable courses of action to take.

Detecting this symptom is straightforward if you monitor the buffer cache hit rate. On many systems, this information can be viewed by running something like `sar -b 15`. More information about system monitoring and the `sar` command appears in Chapter 7. On systems without `sar`, other methods must be used to obtain this information. These methods will usually be system dependent. If the data show the buffer cache hit rate declining precipitously and disk I/O bandwidth consumption measured in megabytes per second rising noticeably while the total amount of network bandwidth moving in and out of the system changes very little, buffer cache thrashing might be the culprit.

3.4 File Space

Like any other types of data that can accumulate on disks, email queues come with their own data storage management issues. This section provides some advice on how to deal with these issues on busy email servers where many pending messages may be queued up for eventual delivery and where I/O performance is important.

3.4.1 Large Directory Issues

Two issues related to disk storage can affect performance of an email gateway: disk space and the number of files in any given directory. In almost all cases these days, disk space isn't an issue for mail queues. Large disks are cheap. Instead, for mail systems I/O bandwidth is a greater concern than storage capacity. For performance-sensitive systems, an entire disk is likely to be devoted to the mail queue, if not an entire RAID system to take advantage of the NVRAM. It would be quite a trick to fill one of the disks available today with queued email under normal operations without performance becoming a nightmare first. The one scenario where a little caution remains warranted regarding total queue capacity is if network connectivity goes away, even to only a restricted set of sites. In this case, large amounts of email may back up.

As an example, suppose that we are running an ISP with a single machine that aggregates all email sent by our subscribers to the rest of the Internet. Suppose also that we have 100,000 subscribers, each of whom sends, on average, 10 pieces of email to the Internet each day, and that each message averages 10KB in size. Further suppose that 30% of our outbound traffic goes to America Online email addresses, not an implausible supposition. In the unlikely event that AOL's mail system goes off the air for 24 hours, our mail queue may grow to about 3GB in capacity before it starts to drain. While this amount isn't enough to fill a disk, it's still a lot of email. If we increase the number of subscribers at this ISP to 1 million, then we can easily run into sizing problems with contemporary equipment.

Just a few years ago, large ISPs going offline were a much more common occurrence than they are now, and situations where mail queues filled up due to the volume of mail bound for downed sites were not unusual. While the reliability of ISPs and their network connections, as well as the capacity of typical disks, makes this scenario less likely with each passing year, it is not beyond the realm of possibility. Given the low cost of disk capacity, there's no good reason to leave oneself vulnerable to these sorts of situations.

A more likely scenario might involve a corporate environment in which Company A has a close strategic partnership with Company B, but the two have disjoint email systems. An average company's network connection is almost certainly much less fault tolerant than that of a large ISP, so situations in which a company is completely offline are, unfortunately, more common. In this environment, if employees from Company A and B are collaborating on refining PowerPoint presentations or are exchanging business projections created with Excel, CAD drawings, and other large data sets, it doesn't require thousands of people to fill up mail queues when individual messages can easily exceed tens of megabytes in size.

In either case, an email administrator would be well advised to check the log files to find out which domain is the most common destination for email from company servers, and to figure out how many messages and how much storage might be required if that site went offline for an extended period of time. Use experience as a guide for determining the duration of the outage to use in the calculations, but planning for a 24- to 72-hour event (depending on the site) may be a reasonable estimate for a worst-case scenario. If the quantities of email that might be generated during an outage of this magnitude would cause problems for an organization's system, adding capacity might be in order.

It's not just storage capacity that can pose a problem. On most email systems, the number of files in a directory will cause the system to bog down long before disk space is in danger of being exhausted. Therefore, during such a crisis, an email system administrator needs to remain vigilant about the depth of the system's email queues.

Besides space, deep queues can cause another, often overlooked problem. As more entries are added to a directory, the filesystem will obviously need to allocate more space to that directory to hold the information on all of its files. Afterward, even if the number of directory entries returns to a manageable size, the space allocated to the directory itself does not contract. The blank records that used to contain file information must still be scanned as a process walks through the directory looking for files. Certainly, it takes less bandwidth to scan a directory that once contained 10,000 files but now holds 100 files than it does to scan a directory with 10,000 files. However, scanning a large, albeit mostly empty, directory can itself contribute a great deal of overhead to the time it takes to perform directory operations. Therefore, if a directory has become uncommonly large at some point, once the number of entries in that directory has become more manageable it's a good idea to remake that directory to make future lookups more efficient.

Many of the advanced filesystems that use a hash or tree structure for their directory entries can speed lookups on large directories, but they remain adversely affected by large directory sizes. The effect is just not as pronounced. Silicon Graphics' XFS [SDH+96] filesystem uses B+ trees to store directory entries, and ReiserFS [REI] uses B* trees for its directory storage. On both of these filesystems, a lookup of a file in a directory at its maximum size with 1,000 entries will likely go faster than a lookup in a directory that currently has 1,000 entries but once contained 100,000 entries.

In advanced filesystems, directory lookups traverse a tree or hash table searching for their entries. The time it takes to perform a lookup operation is typically $O(\log(N))$, where N is the number of entries in a directory. Lookup time grows much more slowly than the time for a linear, $O(N)$, search as N increases. However, it's still expensive to list all entries in a directory, and searches on larger directories always take longer than searches on smaller directories. Therefore, smaller directories are always better—it's just that these advanced file systems mitigate the consequences of having larger directories.

3.4.2 Multiple Queues

Starting with `sendmail` version 8.10, mechanisms are built into the MTA that help keep queue sizes manageable—namely, the ability to create and manage multiple simultaneous queues. In the `sendmail.mc` file, one could add a line like

```
define('QUEUE_DIR', '/var/spool/mqueue/*')
```

that would specify every directory underneath `/var/spool/mqueue/` as an additional queue. Presumably, the email administrator had already created some number of directories, perhaps a dozen, over which queued messages will be divided. As one might expect, the directory path can be made more explicit—for example, `define('QUEUE_DIR', '/var/spool/mqueue/queue*')`. File types also can be split out by making subdirectories in these directories that begin with `qf`, `df`, and `xf`, which house each file type respectively, further restricting the number of files per directory. In this case, `sendmail` will automatically place the appropriate queue file types in the appropriate subdirectories. Each of these directories and subdirectories can be a symbolic link, which would allow smaller and more frequently modified `qf` files to be stored on a disk with a small amount of NVRAM or allow multiple disks to be used, for example.

Because the `xf` files contain information relevant only to the process that created the file, they may be safely written to a memory-based filesystem, such as a Solaris `tmpfs`. A symbolic link pointing from the `xf` directory to `/tmp` would be one way to accomplish this goal on Solaris, as well as on some other platforms. The `tf` files cannot be separated out in this manner, however, as they act as placeholders for `qf` files that are being modified. When a `sendmail` process has completed writing to a `tf` file, it is `rename()`ed to supercede its original `qf` file. If the `tf` file does not reside on the same filesystem as the `qf` file, this operation will not occur atomically. For this reason, `sendmail` always creates `tf` files in the same directory as the `qf` file it will replace.

If multiple queue directories are available, with each SMTP connection `sendmail` determines the queue in which any message will reside pseudorandomly. Starting with `sendmail` 8.12, it is possible to use rules to segregate traffic bound for a certain host or domain to a special queue. Mechanisms for doing so are discussed in more detail in Section 6.1.3. If multiple queues are used, the `mailq` command, which lists all entries in the mail queue, will list the queue name and its contents for each queue it can find from listings given in the `sendmail.cf` file.

While this mechanism might seem little more than a fairly minor workaround for some filesystem's directory deficiencies, multiple queues offer one other advantage:

One can gain effective parallelism from multiple queue runners. Recall that when `sendmail` starts, one parameter given to it on the command line (typically something like `-q30m`) specifies how often a queue runner should start. This parameter indicates that every 30 minutes, the master `sendmail` daemon will fork a child process; this child process scans the entire queue looking for messages to deliver, sorts the messages, and then sequentially tries to deliver them. With multiple queues, one queue runner process exists per queue directory. As most of the time during a queue run is spent waiting for responses from email servers across the Internet (or lack of responses—remember that most items encountered by a queue runner were undeliverable in a previous attempt), it may take as little as $1/N$ times as long to complete a queue run over N queues as it does to attempt to deliver every item in a single queue, a significant speedup. This effort helps keep the total number of concurrently queued messages to a minimum.

3.4.3 Queue Migration

One tactic that is sometimes used to speed up the processing of deep queues involves moving entries that aren't being processed out of the main queue(s) and into other directories. This process of queue migration may seem like a good idea, and in some cases it may help. Nevertheless, most of the time better ways exist to manage the situation. Further, queue migration can be a perilous operation.

Queue migration operates by moving files out of one directory and into another. In its most straightforward incarnation, the UNIX `mv` command is used to relocate `qf` and `df` files. A danger exists that one might try to move a message while a `sendmail` process is operating on it. The `sendmail` processes keep from colliding with each other by using an operating system call, usually `flock()`, to place an advisory lock on the `qf` for the message on which they are working. Migration can work on operating systems, such as FreeBSD, that provide a command such as `/usr/bin/lockf`, which can obtain a lock before executing another command. On many operating systems, however, such a utility doesn't exist. In these cases, unexpected results can occur while a queued message is being moved unless some other mechanism can guarantee that inconsistencies won't occur, such as killing off or at least sending a STOP signal to all queue runners before manipulating queue entries. Starting with version 8.10, the `sendmail` distribution comes with a utility written in Perl and located in the `contrib` subdirectory called `qtool.pl` that can be invoked from scripts to safely migrate items from queue to queue. Moving messages from one queue to another can prove problematic when using `sendmail` 8.12's queue group features.

As an aside, note that the FreeBSD `lockf` command uses the `flock()` system call to lock a file, not the `lockf()` library call. This situation is more confusing than it ought to be.

If the destination queue resides on a filesystem different from the queue where the message to be migrated resides, the files must be copied and then deleted. If the two directories are located on the same filesystem, then `mv` can create entries pointing to the old inodes in the new directory and `unlink()` the old entries, saving a data copy. In the former case, copying results in many unnecessary I/O operations. Copying the files requires more total I/O (on both disks) than delivering them. Further, even when both directories reside on the same filesystem, the migrator must still perform the same (synchronous) I/O operations in the queue directory that would need to be performed if the message were successfully delivered in its next attempt. Even after the migration takes place, the same I/O operations must occur on that same disk when the message is eventually delivered, resulting in no net savings of disk I/O. Therefore, the only savings from queue migration is a reduced number of directory entries in the queue on future queue accesses. On the downside, queue migration will save very little, or perhaps nothing, in aggregate disk I/O, is potentially risky, and won't result in faster message delivery. Thus moving messages from one queue to another is rarely beneficial. Instead, queue rotation should be used to achieve the same goal.

3.4.4 Queue Rotation

In migrating entries out of a queue, the goal is to not have current and future messages encumbered by having to perform their operations in a large, slow-to-drain queue. Queue rotation is a safer and less I/O-intensive mechanism by which this end can be achieved. In queue rotation, one renames a queue (or queue hierarchy) by running a shell script similar to the following example:

```
#!/bin/sh

# Set my umask to match what I want on the queue directory.
umask 077


# Make sure the old queue directory name isn't currently in use.
if [ -d "/var/spool/mqueue.old"]
then
        echo "$0 : Old queue directory exists."
        exit 1
fi
```

```
# Make the new queue directory.
mkdir /var/spool/mqueue.new
# If multiple queues are being used, then subdirectories need
# to be made:
# cd /var/spool/mqueue.new
# mkdir qf df xf


# Quickly move the old directory out of the way and remake it.
# A real script should make sure the mkdir and mv commands
# succeed.
mv /var/spool/mqueue /var/spool/mqueue.old
mv /var/spool/mqueue.new /var/spool/mqueue


# Restart the master sendmail process.
kill -HUP `head -1 /etc/mail/sendmail.pid`


# Start a queue runner to drain the old queue.
/usr/sbin/sendmail -oQ/var/spool/mqueue.old -q30m
```

This script will work with multiple queues under the /var/spool/mqueue directory, but it may not be sufficient if several sendmail 8.12 queue groups have been defined. At the very least, the script must be altered to create the extra directories. Once the mqueue.old directory is empty, its queue runner can be killed. If the machine reboots, a queue runner must be started for every queue that still contains email. Also, note that once queues have been rotated, the mailq command won't display the contents of queue directories that aren't explicitly listed in the sendmail.cf file. This display can be done explicitly: sendmail -bp -oQ/var/spool/mqueue.old. Finally, if this script is used with sendmail prior to version 8.10, a queue identifier might be reused, which could make parsing the log files more difficult.

When sendmail starts, it changes its working directory to the mail queue, /var/spool/mqueue, from which it performs all of its operations. If this directory is renamed, the process remains associated with the directory's inode, not the logical directory name. Thus, after the earlier script executes, all currently running sendmail processes would continue to operate normally in the /var/spool/mqueue.old directory. We then restart the master sendmail process, which will operate in the newly created queue directory. While preexisting sendmail processes will continue to operate in the old queue, once they finish their queue runs, they will exit, leaving mqueue.old unprocessed. For this reason, we start a queue runner specifically to continue processing the old queue. Note that new message processing is not affected by the size of the old queue, already queued messages are processed just as quickly as they were before the rotation, and our cost in terms of I/O operations is a single rename() system call in the message queue's parent directory.

Examining the script closely reveals a race. Between the two mv commands, there exists a window where there is no queue directory. If a sendmail process starts from the command line during this interval, it will fail, giving the following error: can not chdir(/var/spool/mqueue/): No such file or directory. Of course, new sendmail processes spawned due to SMTP connections will not have this problem, as their parent process sits happily in the renamed directory. This problem will generally arise under only two circumstances: (1) if the master sendmail daemon is killed and restarted for some other reason while this script is being run, and (2) if someone interactively sends email from a shell or other mail-related application. The first situation is easy to avoid by policy—that is, by making sure nobody restarts this daemon while the rotation script is run. The second case is either easier or more difficult depending on the circumstances. If people log on to the email server to interactively send email, this scenario could manifest itself. If no one sends email from the command line on this machine, then very little risk arises. Generally, it's good policy not to let people log on to an institution's mail gateway. If this is unavoidable, then any queue rotations should occur only during idle hours or in an emergency. Note that the window for this race condition is extremely short, almost certainly much less than one second, so even someone who was looking for this phenomenon would be unlikely to find it under normal operation. Finally, this last problem disappears under the default installation of sendmail 8.12, as a different queue is used when sendmail is invoked from the command line—one that isn't being rotated.

Renaming the queue directory is straightforward only if the directory itself is not a filesystem mount point. This consideration is important in setting up an email server. Generally, mounting the queue filesystem on /var/spool/ is a better idea than mounting it on the /var/spool/mqueue directory. On a busy email gateway, not much else should be using general spool space, and this approach allows for rotation of the queue.

Alternatively, an entirely different mount point can be created, such as /queue, to be used solely for email queueing. Subdirectories, such as /queue/current, can be set up and defined in the appropriate .mc file as follows:

```
define('QUEUE_DIR','/queue/current')
```

It is also possible to mount the queue somewhere else—on /queue, for example—and to use a symbolic link to accomplish the queue rotation without changing the sendmail.cf file. Under this directory one could put in a number of subdirectories, perhaps creating one for each day, such as 2002-02-23. Then create a symbolic link pointing from /var/spool/mqueue to the appropriate directory. This link could even be automatically rotated by cron each day. The following script accomplishes this goal by using some command options specific to the FreeBSD operating system:

```sh
#!/bin/sh

# Define directories.
yesterday=`date -v -1d +%Y-%m-%d`
today=`date +%Y-%m-%d`

# Make today's directory.
mkdir /queue/$today

# Rotate the symbolic link.
# Race condition possible between the rm and the ln.
cd /var/spool
rm queue; ln -s /queue/$today queue

# Restart the master daemon.
kill -HUP `head -1 /etc/mail/sendmail.pid`

# Start a queue runner for yesterday's queue.
/usr/sbin/sendmail -oQ/queue/$yesterday -q30m
```

Some more work remains to be done. Something will need to eventually clean out and eliminate empty queues. Also, queue runners for the old queues need to be started when the server reboots. This script should suffice as an example, however.

This technique has the same window of vulnerability as the mv and mkdir technique. This problem is unavoidable, as no operating system allows the atomic repointing of symbolic links. Also, on the downside, the use of symbolic links generally indicates a kludge of some sort. The upside is that one no longer needs to have the rest of /var/spool reside on the same filesystem as the mail queues, an appealing idea. Either of these methods can be used in practice, and preference is largely a matter of personal taste.

With the symbolic link method, it might be tempting to perform disk house-cleaning by simply deleting directories older than the largest `Timeout.queue-return.*` value in the `sendmail.cf` file, perhaps plus a couple of days to provide a margin for error. This deletion should not be done blindly. If the directory contains any `qf` files, the Internet mail standards require that a "bounce message," a special type of Delivery Status Notification (DSN), be returned for each undelivered message. If an old directory that is not being accessed by any `sendmail` processes which may receive new messages to handle has no `qf` files in it, then it can be safely deleted. If one runs `sendmail -q` on a directory in which all files are older than `Timeout.queuereturn.*`, and `qf` files remain after the process completes its queue run, then something that shouldn't happen has happened and a person should investigate. Thus, a script written to clean up and remove old queue directories under these circumstances should perform the following steps:

1. Make sure the last file created in that directory is older than the largest `Timeout.queuereturn.*` value in the `sendmail.cf` file.

2. Make sure no `sendmail` process is currently operating on the directory (using the `fuser` or `lsof` utility). If a process is operating on the queue, it should be killed.

3. If the directory still contains any `qf` files, run `sendmail -q -oQ`*`DirectoryName`* to make sure bounce messages are sent for all messages in that queue.

4. If, after the queue runner has completed, `qf` files remain in that directory, inform a person who can investigate. The script should then exit, reporting an error condition.

5. If no more `qf` files appear in that directory, the directory may be safely removed.

3.5 Networking

Handling file I/O efficiently is the most significant area for performance tuning of email servers. Second on the list is examining the system's networking. Anyone who has been an Internet email administrator for any length of time has experienced the effects that network slowdowns or outages can have on an email server, so the fact that networking is important in email will come as no surprise. What may be more surprising is that less obvious networking issues may significantly affect service performance.

At one site, I spent a great deal of time talking with a customer about ways to improve email system performance. We discussed many of the issues mentioned in this book concerning improving the system's I/O capability and such. Then the client mentioned something that really caught my attention: The company was experiencing about 10% packet loss rates on the LAN that connected its email server to its customer base. This rate shocked me, but in retrospect I'm at least partially to blame for not exploring the fundamentals of the system before spending time talking about NVRAM, advanced file systems, and efficient queue rotation.

When building a house, it makes no sense to expend effort on exquisite interior craftsmanship if the foundation won't hold up. The same principle is equally true in providing networked computing services, as it is in any endeavor. The first thing to provide is a solid physical foundation for the systems, which means quality facilities. The machines need clean power, appropriate environmental regulation, a clean location, and physical safety. One cannot build reliable services without providing these basic necessities, and one cannot build high-performance systems without first providing reliable services. For a large ISP, clearly this effort entails building a quality data center. For a smaller company, an office converted to a machine room with tile floor, extra cooling, and a UPS may suffice, but these conditions are all too often neglected even though they are the very foundation of providing dependable computing services.

The next step is to provide quality networking. This does not mean over-engineering. For any mail server experiencing performance problems, at the very least I'd recommend a switched, full-duplex solution. Of course, 10 Mbps might be sufficient, if that's enough to handle the load. It's also not adequate to just check the local LAN(s) on which the server resides. Instead, one must thoroughly understand the entire network between the server and the Internet, as well as between the server and whatever internal machines with which the server communicates, whether that would be other email servers or end users.

Network load on all relevant networks should be monitored regularly. Setting up automated processes to gather this information is invaluable, and writing tools to analyze the data and look for warning signs *will* notify the alert email administrator in many cases before problems become severe. Any full-duplex or other reserved-bandwidth network (such as FDDI or Token Ring) that regularly runs at greater than 60% utilization for one hour per day represents a candidate for upgrading. Any shared bus network (e.g., half-duplex Ethernet) that regularly sustains 30% load also represents a candidate for upgrading.

Any shared bus network or any machine on such a network that sees 10% packet retransmission rates (whether due to error or collision) should prompt immediate concern. On a full-duplex network, packet retransmission rates of even 1% usually indicate that something is wrong with the network. If a large amount of packet loss occurs on a full-duplex network, then it may be better to let it run well at half-duplex than to perform badly at full-duplex, if it is an option. Ultimately, however, if a network operates poorly at full-duplex, it needs to be fixed. When configuring Ethernet network interfaces that should operate at full-duplex, usually it's best to configure them as full-duplex interfaces rather than to let them automatically configure themselves. Some devices from different vendors still have problems locking full-duplex; in some cases, if a transient network problem occurs, they'll renegotiate down to half-duplex mode and stay there. This result can cause difficult-to-diagnose problems if one isn't alert to the possibility.

3.5.1 Network Interface Cards

Network interface cards (NICs) can be a surprisingly important area of consideration in the design of email servers. Almost any 10 Mbps card is good enough for use. In fact, at the time of this writing, it's difficult to find a new 10 Mbps-only card to purchase. Certainly, quality 10/100 cards are cheap enough these days that one can't rationalize the use of an old 10 Mbps card to save money, especially if email performance might be an issue.

The quality of 100 Mbps Ethernet cards has increased markedly over the last several years. In terms of Internet service, the primary difference in quality between cards relates to the amount of memory available on the card for buffering data. Lack of buffer space can mean more work for the processor and more packet retransmissions, which can affect performance. Typically, cards that carry a "server" designation have more buffer space than cards designed for workstation use, which in some cases can't even sustain their peak data transfer rate. It's difficult to get information about the real difference between a vendor's regular offering and its "server" card, but physical inspection of the NIC will often reveal more physical memory via the quantity and capacity of the chips on the card. If so, the marginal difference that the extra cost of the server card adds to the total cost of the server would likely be worthwhile.

The contrary view is that (1) these days it's easy to turn out a good 100 Mbps Ethernet card that can easily fill its available pipe, so there's no reason to overbuy, and (2) even if the card doesn't have adequate buffer space, it primarily costs the server some of its CPU capacity to compensate for this shortfall, and the average email server has more CPU capacity than it knows what to do with anyway. These are valid arguments. If an inexpensive card works well, I would be the last person to recommend a change. Some of the cost of a "server" card may be diagnostic capability, which is worthwhile if it can be used. If this extra information cannot be accessed, then clearly it isn't worth the extra cost.

One area in which I still regularly see subpar Ethernet NICs are the interfaces that come built into the motherboard of systems. Unless the system's networking will not be taxed or the on-board interface is of especially high quality, I recommend the use of supplemental networking cards for Internet service and relegate the on-board NICs to monitoring or command-and-control networks.

These days, good 100 Mbps cards are fairly routine, but NIC quality remains very important for Gigabit Ethernet interfaces. In cases in which a server handles enough email to at least occasionally saturate a full-duplex Fast Ethernet connection, gigabit networking is a necessity. Unfortunately, as recently as three years ago, few Gigabit NICs could be driven at their claimed speed by any computing platform in a test lab, much less under real-world conditions. Of course, few email servers need this sort of speed. Anyone pushing beyond the 100 Mbps barrier must be very concerned about how much CPU effort it takes to drive the card, no matter how large a SPECint rate2000 number the server might be able to generate. Quality of cards in this regime is critical, and careful tests should be performed to find one that will deliver the needed performance with minimal effects on the server's processing capability.

One feature of Gigabit Ethernet that reduces network overhead in a great many situations is the use of the optional jumbo frames feature. It allows large packets, around 9,000 bytes in size, rather than the traditional 1,500-byte Ethernet packets. Increasing the packet size can greatly reduce the amount of processing needed to transfer a fixed number of bytes between two servers. In an email context, if the client, the server, and all intermediate networks support jumbo frames, it can reduce the processing overhead of moving the data considerably. Unfortunately, this is rarely the case. In the real world, few POP clients can trace a Gigabit Ethernet path all the way to their POP server. Certainly, we don't expect an SMTP server connecting to the general Internet to handle frames of this size, either.

3.5.2 Different MTUs in the Network

The problem of different networks having maximum packet sizes on the Internet is handled in two ways. First, packets can be fragmented by routers as needed along the way. This is easy on the sending host, but requires a router to perform extra work. Second, one can determine the maximum packet size that all networks between the two hosts can handle by sending large packets and receiving messages back from intermediaries that can't handle those large packets. This process, called "Path MTU Discovery," is documented in RFC 1191 [MD90]. The benefits of this method versus the alternatives are eloquently stated in the RFC. However, every packet that is sent to a remote host that is larger than the maximal MTU of an intermediate network must be re-sent at least once. This extra overhead might be avoided by setting the network interface's MTU to a more modest size, such as 1,500 bytes.

A big downside associated with Path MTU Discovery bears mentioning. Servers using this protocol typically send IP packets with the "don't fragment" bit set. Then, when a router cannot deliver the packet to the next hop, it will return an ICMP "Destination Unreachable" message to indicate that the packet cannot be processed. RFC 1191 specifies that the MTU for the next network hop be encoded in this ICMP packet. That way, the originating server will know the size of the packet when it is re-sent, and it can iteratively determine the largest packet size that can be transferred without fragmentation.

A problem occurs when a router between the two communicating hosts blindly discards ICMP packets. In this case, the sending host doesn't know what to do. It never receives an acknowledgment for the packet it sent, yet no ICMP Destination Unreachable packet is returned to inform it that something went wrong. A common manifestation of this problem is the successful transmission of very small email messages, while larger messages (perhaps totaling more than some "magic" size, such as 536 or 1,500 bytes) can't get through.

This situation is not as uncommon as it ought to be. In the name of security concerns, a significant number of sites have configured packet filters on their routers or firewall boxes to reject all ICMP packets. While this cure might seem worse than the disease, and certainly I don't endorse this strategy, it's not surprising that some sites choose this course of action. Many fears concerning ICMP-based network attacks, especially distributed denial-of-service (DDoS) attacks, are justified. Path MTU Discovery is a relatively esoteric part of the IP protocol, and a large percentage of the people responsible for implementing network security policy at sites around the Internet have likely never heard of it. Consequently, they don't understand why they need to support it. This policy may be wrong, but in this day and age it's understandable.

If an organization experiences problems getting email through to other sites, and Path MTU Discovery is the culprit, it's probably best to disable this feature on the affected servers. Of course, if a site's own network causes the problem, then the obvious fix is to allow ICMP Destination Unreachable packets through to the email servers. While offloading the effort involved in packet fragmentation may decrease the load on email servers, any benefit will be very slight, if it's even measurable.

3.5.3 Kernel Networking

Beyond a certain tuning threshold, once bottlenecks in filesystems, storage, and networking have been removed, email service largely comes down to just moving ones and zeros as fast as possible. Essentially, providing email service (like all Internet services) is a matter of taking bits off the network and putting them on disk, then taking them off disk and putting them back on the network. The faster this transfer occurs without sacrificing integrity, the better. After tuning the I/O system, another significant factor in determining how rapidly data can move is the number of copies performed on each piece of data as it moves through the system. Clearly, much less overhead is associated with writing the data into memory once and then passing it around by reference than with making copies of the data as it moves between applications, different parts of the kernel, and between main memory and devices.

Zero- and one-copy IP implementations within operating systems have represented a rich area of research in recent years, a good example of which may be found in [RAC97]. Running on the same hardware, the operating system that performs the fewest number of data copies for each network transaction would be expected to move data faster. Even if the operating system works relatively efficiently in this manner, email applications run in user space. Thus data moving from user to kernel space are typically copied rather than mapped, as the kernel doesn't want to give applications a lot of access to its data buffers, and for good reasons. Each user/kernel space boundary transition generally requires a copy. For example, if we're sending data between two programs via a pipe, the data are not typically mapped between the two applications. Rather, data are copied from the user space of the originating process into the kernel, then copied again into the buffers of the target process, resulting in two data copies rather than the expected one copy (between processes) or zero copies (as would be the case if the applications used mmap() and shared memory to communicate the same data).

Note, however, that if the tall tent pole when it comes to email server performance tuning is kernel data copying, then tuning of the system has already gone above and beyond the call of duty. Nevertheless, even on the same piece of hardware, email applications running on different operating systems may perform differently. All operating systems are not created equal when it comes to moving data quickly. It's more than fair to consider success at raw data-moving tests a significant factor when evaluating which operating system should be used for email, or any other high-volume Internet service.

Data copying between applications and the kernel, and between the kernel and NICs, generally consumes very little of an email server's overall effort. Nonetheless, some research efforts and products aim to minimize this effort, and they're worth mentioning. Data copies occur not merely between an IP stack and a NIC, but also within the kernel and between applications and the kernel. Thus eliminating just one of these sources of copies is merely part of the battle. For this reason, doing work on network I/O systems that reside in userland and have direct access to both NICs and applications is increasing in popularity. With this method, data coming in to a network card are written directly into a reserved section of memory, then passed around by reference. No kernel/user space boundary issues arise, because this threshold is never crossed. The most widely known solution along these lines uses Myrinet [BCF+94]. It provides an ultra-high-speed, ultra-low-latency network plus software that interfaces with an application to eliminate many of the data copies in an application. Another promising area of research along similar goals is the Virtual Interface Architecture (VI) [VI97]. The principal downside of these solutions is that they must be available to servers on both sides of the network link, an unlikely event in a general-purpose internetwork. Nonetheless, the key ideas underlying these intriguing technologies are slowly working their way into traditional solutions.

3.5.4 Bandwidth and Latency

One argument that nearly always surfaces when discussing network performance tuning is the question of bandwidth versus latency. Briefly, *bandwidth* measures the total capacity of a network between two given points without regard to anything else. *Latency* measures the amount of time consumed in the transmission of a single message (which can be a packet, a three-way TCP handshake, or an email message) from the time the initial connection is made to the time the destination receives the last bit of data.

In the context of an email server, bandwidth is nearly always what we're interested in; latency is of lesser concern. This is not to say that delays in email are not a cause for alarm, but rather that the sorts of network-induced latencies that email server tuning can influence almost never result in a measureable delay.

For example, in any except the most geographically dispersed or heavily loaded corporate network, the IP packet round-trip time between an email gateway and the gateway router that links it to the network service provider's network will be less than 5 ms, and probably no more than 1 ms. The round-trip time between my email server and a "random" selection of three large ISP mail servers, one large university email server, and two *Fortune* 500 corporate email servers (all within the United States) varies between 20 ms and 90 ms, with a median of about 70 ms.

Clearly, the latencies that are under my control are dwarfed by those that are not. Moreover, even if the latency between my email server and my gateway router grew to 100 ms, this interval would still be too small to cause a person to notice the extra delay that the message took to reach its destination. On the time scales here, the consequences of latency/bandwidth trade-offs are consequential only in a performance context. They remain essentially negligible from a human interface standpoint, unless an email server becomes so badly overloaded that the delays are measured in seconds or longer time scales. Of course, the noticeably high latencies are then themselves a symptom, rather than the root problem.

In terms of Internet services, as long as delays remain short enough to avoid notice by people, increasing latency on email gateways primarily means that individual SMTP sessions take longer, which means that more processes run on that machine and more memory is consumed. Typically, these items are not tall tent poles when it comes to improving the performance of an email server, but they can be important. This topic will be revisited from another angle in Chapter 8.

This section has stated that bandwidth is far more important than latency. Other parts of the book say a great deal about methods to reduce latency. This might at first seem contradictory, but there is a consistent strategy here. Increasing the mail server's throughput is almost always more important than reducing latency. If bandwidth is not diminished as a consequence, then latency should be reduced as much as possible. An example of sacrificing latency for bandwidth is turning off aggressive filesystem pre-fetching. Eliminating unnecessary DNS lookups or lowering the overhead of each request reduces latency without affecting overall bandwidth.

3.6 Summary

- Most email servers end up being I/O bound. On email gateways, the primary source of I/O contention involves the mail queue.

- Email I/O is (1) write-intensive, (2) synchronous, and (3) characterized by small and random accesses. Using a high-performance filesystem that gracefully handles directories with many entries and efficiently but safely handles synchronous writes can be an enormous win.

- Storage space rarely emerges as an issue in an email queue unless something goes wrong. A disk's suitability for this purpose should be determined by how many operations per second it can perform.

- For email performance, we're primarily interested in increasing the amount of email that can be moved on and off a machine per unit time. While the latency of the transaction represents a secondary concern, reducing latency remains a good idea, as long-lived connections consume resources.

## Chapter 4

Tuning Email Reception

Besides relaying email by passing it in and out of the mail queue, email servers receive and store messages in the message store for later access by users. Many of the same issues we find in email relaying apply here: The systems are still likely to be file I/O bound, and message deliveries remain synchronous. However, the data moved tend to be less temporary and less transactional. Storage volume requirements are higher, and access mechanisms, such as POP and IMAP, have some different characteristics than SMTP. This chapter discusses these similarities and differences.

4.1 What Happens During Email Reception

Just as we walked through an SMTP relay session in the previous chapter, let's examine what happens when a message is received by an email server and stored in its message store. For the purposes of this example, let's assume that we run `sendmail` version 8.9 as our MTA in `background` delivery mode on a typical operating system, we use `/usr/libexec/mail.local` as our LDA and Qualcomm's `qpopper` as our POP daemon, and the message store uses the familiar 7th Edition mailbox format [SHO94] to store email. We'll discuss the particulars of various mailbox formats later in this chapter, but for now note that 7th Edition mailbox format is just a fancy name for the default format in which email messages are stored on almost every UNIX or UNIX-like system. Much of the session remains the same:

1. The originator machine opens an SMTP connection with the server.
2. The server accepts the connection and spawns a new instance of the `sendmail` daemon to handle this connection.

3. The new `sendmail` process inspects the SMTP envelope to determine whether the message should be accepted by policy.

4. If the message is acceptable to the gateway, a `qf` file, which will eventually contain the message's header along with delivery information, is created in the queue, typically the `/var/spool/mqueue` directory. Next, the remote machine receives permission to send the message itself, and then the gateway creates the `df` file, which will hold the message's body, also in the queue.

5. The originator sends the message's header, which the server stores in memory temporarily, followed by the message body. As the body is received by the server, it is buffered and written out to the `df` file.

6. Once the originator indicates that the message has been completely sent, the gateway adds its own "Received:" line to the header, modifies the message headers if necessary, and writes out the contents of the `qf` file. It then issues an `fsync()` command on the still-open `qf` and `df` file descriptors, closes the files, and acknowledges receipt of the message to the originator.

7. Another `sendmail` process is spawned that examines the `qf` envelope and message headers to determine what to do with the message. It creates an `xf` file to store any error messages regarding this delivery attempt.

8. The originator closes the SMTP connection if no other messages will be transferred in this session.

Until this point, the session has been identical to that for relaying. Here the tasks performed by the email server diverge.

9. If the local machine is identified as the final destination for the message, the `sendmail` process spawns the LDA that will complete the delivery. The LDA is passed the list of local user names for which the message is to be delivered.

10. The LDA opens a temporary file in which it will store the message. A line beginning with "From " that contains the sender's email address and the current date and time is written to the file. The message is written out to this file, and a blank line is appended to the end of it. The message is passed from the MTA through the LDA to the temporary file.

11. The LDA opens and then locks the first mailbox on its list of recipients by using `flock()` (or `lockf()`, if the system doesn't support `flock()`) and creating a temporary lock file in the mail spool. For example, if the email user's login name is `npc`, then the file created would be `/var/mail/npc.lock`. Acquiring the advisory lock and being able to create the lock file indicate that the LDA can safely proceed with message delivery.

12. The contents of the temporary file are appended to the first mailbox. The mailbox file is then closed, which also clears the advisory lock, and the lock file is deleted.

13. The LDA goes on to the next recipient and repeats the last two steps. If this recipient is the last recipient, then the temporary file is unlinked and successful delivery is indicated to the MTA as the LDA exits.

14. After the LDA reports a successful delivery, the MTA can unlink the `qf` and `df` files in the queue.

Some of the details of this transaction are worthy of special mention. First, `sendmail` writes the message to the queue regardless of whether the destination is local or remote. If a system is running `sendmail` 8.12 in `interactive` mode with `SuperSafe` also set to `interactive`, then the SMTP session may be held open while the message is passed to the LDA, bypassing writes in the queue, just as in relaying. Second, the LDA writes the message out to a temporary location before appending it to mailboxes. Thus a message will get written three times, including twice with `fsync()`, to effect a single delivery. From a pure efficiency standpoint, one would hope that the message would have to be written out only once. Third, the LDA uses two mechanisms to ensure that the mailbox is locked, including creating lock files in the spool during message delivery. Many filesystems will perform these additional metadata operations synchronously. Both locking mechanisms act as safeguards against email reading programs that might use only one or the other. For example, if the LDA can be assured that every program which accesses mailboxes respects the `flock()` advisory locks, then the creation of this lock file would be unnecessary.

In the email relaying procedure list presented in Chapter 3, it was documented that in `sendmail` versions 8.10 and 8.12 some items in the procedure list changed somewhat. These changes, mostly in the order and nature of queue operations, also apply to email reception. Because the nature of those changes was thoroughly discussed in Chapter 3, they won't be repeated here. Instead, this section focuses on the events that happen beginning with the spawning of the LDA.

4.1.1 The Local Delivery Agent

On the question of efficiency, at the very least it would make sense to modify `mail.local` so that a message bound for a single recipient would not create the temporary file. This effort requires modification of the LDA source code. It would also be possible to force `sendmail` to never attempt local delivery to multiple recipients at one time by removing the F=m flag from the local mailer definition in the configuration file. While this step would normally not be advisable, in conjunction with the other modification, it would mean that the temporary file would never need to be written. It's possible to alter the LDA's behavior in this way by adding the following line (no "m" is included to the list of flags) to the `sendmail.mc` file:

```
define('LOCAL_MAILER_FLAGS', 'Prn9')
```

A better approach is to use the `MODIFY_MAILER_FLAGS` option, which became available in `sendmail` version 8.10, to remove this flag:

```
MODIFY_MAILER_FLAGS('LOCAL', '-m')
```

Not having the temporary file written to disk will reduce the total number of writes performed by the email server. For multiple recipients, however, the file must be read from the queue multiple times. After the first copy occurs, the message likely will reside in the operating system's buffer cache, making successive read operations inexpensive; on most systems, the cost of several in-memory data copies (which consume only CPU resources) will be much lower than the cost of a single disk write. Without eliminating the need to write out the temporary file for a single recipient delivery, this approach would require writing the temporary file out for each recipient, which would increase the amount of I/O performed in the filesystem where the temporary files are stored. If the temporary file is stored in a memory-based filesystem and the files are small, then writing out the temporary file or files probably wouldn't be terribly expensive.

If `sendmail` does not spawn the LDA with multiple recipients, then one separate LDA process must be created using the `fork()` and `exec()` system calls for each recipient of the message. While this process will consume CPU resources, UNIX-style operating systems have become quite efficient at spawning new processes (`sendmail` does it quite often). Again, these actions consume only CPU resources, which are typically abundant on email servers. Besides the extra processes, each time the LDA is invoked, `sendmail` performs "canonification." Within the context of `sendmail`, *canonification* means making sure addresses and headers are complete and correct. In this specific instance, it means confirming that all host names are proper—that is, all exist in DNS, all are fully qualified, and all have a "." or perhaps other character in them if the canonification rules have been redefined or modified in the configuration file. On most systems, this step will require DNS lookups to the name server. If the name server resides on the local host, the cost consists of CPU time, two context switches, and one network round trip across the loopback interface. If the name daemon isn't located on the same server, this approach can be more expensive.

Overall, we might want to know the following: Would it be cheaper for the system to write out a temporary file but send the message from the MTA to the LDA only once, or would it be better to recanonify the headers but save I/O involved in the creation of the temporary file? Unfortunately, no simple answer to this question exists. It depends entirely on the cost of each operation performed in each case on any particular email server. If DNS lookups to the name server are local (and they should be), then almost any amount of CPU overhead that avoids a write to a real disk is a price worth paying as long as the server isn't already CPU bound. If the temporary file write never moves a disk head (because it is written to a memory-based filesystem and the messages are smaller than the amount of RAM available to this filesystem), then writing out temporary copies of the message costs very little.

The default location for the temporary message file created by the LDA is typically /tmp, although the system's mkstemp() library call governs the precise location. On many systems, /tmp is a memory-based filesystem, which means that writes to this filesystem are merely written into the virtual memory system. Thus writing files here will result in disk I/O only if main memory fills and the OS pages the extra data out to swap. Using a memory-based filesystem to store files is a safe procedure as long as all files written to it are truly temporary, as in mail.local's case. The files have no value if the invocation of the LDA that created the file stops running, and consequently no data in these files must be salvaged if the machine crashes. Not writing these files to disk can produce a significant performance savings. On those servers that deal with very large messages, /tmp may be called upon to store a lot of data, filling available memory. If the temporary files will be written, this effort would result in disk operations under any circumstances, because as the system runs out of main memory it will be forced to write the extra data to swap space. Nevertheless, on most machines that support it, using a memory-based filesystem for storing the LDA's temporary files is a good way to mitigate the cost of the extra message write, at least most of the time.

If a memory-based file system isn't an option, then turning the LDA's temporary file storage area into a separate filesystem mounted asynchronously may be a good idea. While storing real message data in an asynchronous filesystem presents an unacceptable risk, it isn't necessary for these files to survive a system crash, so the performance gain obtained by making the filesystem asynchronous is worthwhile. In such a case, the temporary file storage area should be a separate filesystem. If mkstemp() creates files in /tmp, and /tmp is just another directory under the root filesystem, then making the / filesystem asynchronous to speed up writing the LDA's temporary message files is not appropriate.

4.1.2 Multiple-Recipient Performance Example

Let's examine this issue in some detail by using the CPU-bound email server that was introduced in Chapter 1. In this test, the target server runs `sendmail` 8.12.2 in `background` (default) delivery mode. It uses a very generic configuration file, accomplishing final delivery with the `mail.local` LDA that came with that `sendmail` distribution. The `/tmp` directory, where the LDA will write temporary files, is mounted as a `tmpfs` filesystem. We bombard 50 test accounts on that server with email messages that are about 1KB in size, each of which is bound to five randomly selected recipients. In the first test, we leave the "m" flag defined as a flag in the local mailer definition. With this setup, we see successful injection of 84 messages per minute (which translates to 420 messages delivered to mailboxes per minute). In the second test, we modify the configuration to remove the "m" flag from the local mailer definition. Under the same circumstances, we see only 50 messages injected per minute (250 messages delivered to mailboxes per minute), or about 60% of the throughput with F=m.

This result shouldn't be surprising, as we already know that the server is CPU bound, not I/O bound. We expect some reduction in throughput due to the extra data copies, canonification, ruleset parsing, and `fork()`ing if the LDA won't deliver to multiple recipients. Further, because we use `tmpfs` to store the temporary files, these writes don't cause disk movement. This example is especially contrived, as the LDA wasn't modified to not create temporary files, even in the single delivery case.

Most real-world numbers would be less dramatic. For instance, most email servers probably won't see an average of five recipients per message. At many sites, email is primarily a one-to-one communications medium. However, organizations that use email primarily as a one-to-many or many-to-many communications medium may experience results similar to our test case. The conclusion is that delivering to multiple recipients results in a significant CPU savings over delivering the message to each recipient individually.

4.1.3 LMTP

Even on reasonably sized email servers with well-tuned I/O systems, a system can become CPU bound. In these cases, reducing the number of `fork()`s performed by the system is certainly a good thing. With an appropriate LDA, this goal might be accomplished by making the LDA become a persistent process, perhaps by multithreading it, and passing messages between the MTA and a LDA via Local Mail Transfer Protocol (LMTP) rather than through the use of `fork()` and a one-way interprocess communication (IPC) channel, as is traditionally done. Unfortunately, no currently available Open Source solutions behave this way. Even so, using LMTP to communicate between `sendmail` and the LDA offers some benefits.

LMTP is defined by RFC 2033 [MYE96]. In essence, LMTP is a subset of the SMTP protocol designed to allow mail transport over very short and reliable networks, such as between two processes on the same host or, at the extreme, over a very reliable LAN. The RFC specifically states that this protocol should not be used over a WAN, and I wouldn't expect to ever endorse the use of LMTP between two hosts separated by a router.

The `mail.local` LDA that comes with the Open Source `sendmail` package includes support for LMTP. To enable it in the MTA, add FEATURE (`local_lmtp`) to the `.mc` file from which the `sendmail.cf` is generated. In terms of operational differences, some DSN information will change, and the z and X flags are added to the F= equate in the configuration file. These flags indicate, respectively, that the LMTP is supported and that the "hidden dot algorithm," as defined in Section 4.5.2 of RFC 2821, is used to encode lines beginning with a ".". Why might it be beneficial to use LMTP for communication between the MTA and LDA? For common `sendmail` installations, LMTP permits the elimination of one of the most pervasive and misunderstood email system errors without removing the F=m flag from the `sendmail.cf` file.

Suppose that `sendmail` invokes `mail.local` with three local recipients for a message, and that the first two deliveries of this message succeed but the third one fails due to some temporary problem. The LDA has no way of communicating the details of the failure back to the MTA; it must either signal success or failure for the entire delivery. Taking its delivery obligations seriously, the LDA reports a failure code. As it is also required to err on the side of caution, the MTA must assume that delivery failed for all of the recipients. The next time it tries to deliver the message, it is sent to everyone again. As a consequence, two of the recipients end up with duplicate messages. This duplication takes up I/O capacity, consumes disk space, and annoys the users. By using LMTP, the MTA can learn about the success or failure of delivery to each individual recipient, and it can then attempt redelivery to only those users for whom the initial attempt actually failed.

Because LMTP specifies a protocol in addition to the raw data transfer, we might expect to pay a mild CPU cost as a consequence of enabling LMTP support. In fact, if we return to our CPU-bound email server, we will see that this is, indeed, the case. In both tests, we use `sendmail` version 8.12.2 with the version of `mail.local` that ships with that distribution. We configure `sendmail` to deliver messages using background mode and test it by repeatedly sending one approximately 1KB message to one of 50 randomly selected recipients. In the first test, we use regular IPC delivery. We measure a throughput of about 242 messages/minute. After adding the following line to the `.mc` file

```
FEATURE('local_lmtp')
```

and resetting the server, we can deliver about 236 messages/second, a decrease in throughput of less than 3%. This is a small price to pay to avoid extraneous deliveries.

RFC 2821 specifies that an email message traveling between two hosts should have each line in the message terminated with both a carriage return character and a line feed character. In the notation of the C programming language, this would be denoted by both \r and \n. In the RFCs, it is often referred to as CRLF (usually pronounced "CUR-liff") or "wire" format, as the message has this format when it is sent out over a network wire. UNIX-like operating systems, however, tend to terminate lines in files with just a line feed. Thus, every time a message is received from the Internet, it must be converted from CRLF to UNIX format when it is written to disk; every time it is sent back to another host, each \n is changed to \r\n.

If the only processes that access mailboxes on a given email server are the LDA and POP daemon, for example, it might seem tempting to store messages on the server in CRLF format to eliminate the need for these translations. Unfortunately, `sendmail` makes these translations when it writes the messages into the queue, so if the messages will be stored in the mail spool in CRLF format, the LDA must make the changes when the message is written to the spool, which largely defeats the purpose. The source code modifications required to change `sendmail`'s behavior would definitely be nontrivial. Unless future versions of `sendmail` support storage of messages in this format, it would probably be wise to not venture down this road, especially given that it would likely result in very small performance gains.

4.2 Recipient Verification

Unless it has been configured not to do so, when `sendmail` is told that a message is bound for a recipient in a local domain, it will look up the user name to make sure that the recipient actually exists on the server before it attempts to deliver the message. This step allows a misaddressed message to be rejected during the portion of the SMTP dialogue where the envelope is exchanged. If a message can be rejected during the envelope exchange, the server won't have to expend resources associated with processing and queueing the message itself. High-performance email servers often store very large numbers of individual mailboxes. Operating systems sometimes don't perform very well, or even correctly, if the /etc/passwd file contains hundreds of thousands, much less millions, of entries. Furthermore, for some large systems, it would be better to not locally store any email account information.

If an alternative authentication system is used and bypassing the system's normal authentication mechanisms becomes necessary, four ways of dealing with this issue in the MTA exist:

1. Don't have the MTA check for account existence upon delivery.
2. Modify the sendmail source to make the check using the new mechanism.
3. Use Pluggable Authentication Modules (PAM) or some other operating system-supported mechanism to make the traditional system-provided user lookup calls access the external information source.
4. Use the sendmail Mailbox Database (mbdb) API.

4.2.1 Don't Check

The first case is the easiest to accomplish. Simply exclude the "w" flag from the local mailer definition. Note that this step also disables checking for .forward files. This is necessary because sendmail cannot gain information about the location of a user's home directory. Removing the user lookup can be effected using the MODIFY_MAILER_FLAGS macro in the same manner as in an earlier example:

```
MODIFY_MAILER_FLAGS(`LOCAL', `-w')
```

This flag isn't modifiable using the LOCAL_MAILER_FLAGS variable, so if the MODIFY_MAILER_FLAGS macro didn't exist, we would have to make some major changes to the M4 files that come with sendmail to accomplish this goal without hand-hacking the sendmail.cf file.

The downside to this method is that a message must be received and handed off to the LDA before we might discover that its recipient isn't valid.

4.2.2 **sendmail** Source Modification

Modification of the sendmail source to use an alternative authentication method isn't terribly difficult for an experienced programmer. Simply create a routine that provides an interface to the authentication system that mimics the UNIX getpwnam() library call, and then make the appropriate insertion into the

definitions of `sm_getpwnam()` and `sm_getpwuid()` in the `sendmail/`
`conf.c` file in the source distribution. These routines have remained remarkably
stable over the last few major revisions of `sendmail`; only the directory in which
the source code for the MTA resides in the distribution has changed, from `src` to
`sendmail` during the change from version 8.9 to version 8.10.

Of course, once these changes are made they must be maintained, applied,
and tested against future versions of `sendmail`. A major advantage of a widely
adopted Open Source software package such as `sendmail` is the comfort that
comes from knowing that many experienced programmers analyze the significant
changes made to such a package, and that many more people are involved in the
thorough testing process that results from its wide use. Once a site starts modifying
the source, it can never again be completely certain that the global testing that the
package constantly endures will remain entirely applicable to the code being run.
A considerable amount of time will be required to keep one's changes in sync with
a package that changes as often as `sendmail`. This issue should provide a strong
incentive to avoid making site-specific changes to the source code unless absolutely
necessary. When changes are necessary, a minimalist approach is best.

4.2.3 Alternative Authentication Method

The third possibility for using an alternative authentication scheme with `sendmail`
is to alter the way the system performs its authentication. The mechanism by which
this goal is most easily achieved is by writing one's own Pluggable Authentication
Module (PAM) and configuring the system so that this module handles `sendmail`'s
authentication requests. Of course, not all operating systems support PAM, but this
strategy is a reasonable option for those that do. A nice side benefit with PAM is that
other applications may use the new module without modification. The modules
should also be straightforward to create for an experienced software developer.
Many already exist that may be used or modified for use at a given site. A useful list
of many modules that can be adapted to various systems is available [PAM].

4.2.4 mbdb

The fourth method, using the mbdb interface, was introduced to `sendmail` starting with version 8.12. The mbdb interface avoids the necessity of modifying arbitrary
pieces of the `sendmail` code. Of course, code modifications remain necessary, but
now the authentication mechanisms have been abstracted out to make this new
code more maintainable, and to allow a site to configure this parameter in the
`sendmail.cf` file.

The `sendmail` version 8.12 source tree, in the `libsm` directory, contains a file called `mbdb.c`. This file holds a set of authentication routines: `sm_mbdb_initialize()`, `sm_mbdb_lookup()`, and `sm_mbdb_terminate()`. Support for two different authentication models are coded into this file: (1) support for authentication via the default `getpwent()` family of library calls, and (2) a sample Lightweight Directory Access Protocol (LDAP) authentication implementation. A "NULL" authentication method is also defined, but it is presumably intended just for testing. It should not be used in actual practice.

The `sm_mbdb_initialize()` and `sm_mbdb_terminate()` routines perform any pre- and post-authentication configuration activity required by a particular authentication system. When using `getpwent()`-style authentication, `sm_mbdb_initialize()` does nothing, and `sm_mbdb_terminate()` calls `endpwent()`, which merely closes the `passwd` file. However, LDAP requires some setup before an authentication request can be made. The database needs to be contacted, parameters need to be defined and passed to it, and so on. These actions would be performed in `sm_mbdb_initialize()`. Also, after processing the authentication request, the connection to the database needs to be closed. These actions would be performed in `sm_mbdb_terminate()`. The actual authentication request(s) occur within `sm_mbdb_lookup()`.

Suppose we wanted to add a new user lookup interface—for example, assume we wanted to continue with delivery if a 7th Edition mailbox already exists for that user in the `/var/mail` directory and refuse the message if it doesn't. For the sake of argument, let's call this authentication mechanism "me," which stands for "mailbox exists." Here are the steps needed to activate this mechanism in the `sendmail` 8.12 source for the FreeBSD operating system version 4.5. Someone attempting to thoroughly understand this example may want to have a copy of the `mbdb.c` file available while reading through this code.

As we plan to use the `stat()` system call to determine whether the mailbox exists, we include the following header file at the top of `libsm/mbdb.c`:

```
#include <sys/stat.h>
```

Next, also at the top of the `mbdb.c` file, we need to define the new authentication functions. We take our cue from the LDAP example already there, and add the following lines:

```
static int  mbdb_me_initialize __P((char *));
static int  mbdb_me_lookup __P((char *name, SM_MBDB_T *user));
static void mbdb_me_terminate __P((void));
```

Just below the LDAP function definitions, the various authentication methods are defined. The ones already present are "pw," "ldap," and "NULL." Between the #endif terminating the "ldap" method and the "NULL" entry, we'll add our new one with the following line:

```
{ "me", mbdb_me_initialize, mbdb_me_lookup, mbdb_me_terminate },
```

In our case, mbdb_me_initialize and mbdb_me_terminate will do nothing, so we can blatantly steal the code from the "pw" functions, modify the "terminate" routine slightly, and add them to the file:

```
static int
mbdb_me_initialize(char *arg)
{
        return EX_OK;
}

static void
mbdb_me_terminate()
{
        return;
}
```

Next, we write a very simple module for the "lookup" function that checks whether /var/mail/*username* exists. It takes two arguments: the user name and a pointer to a structure in which we're supposed to fill in information such as the user's full name. We can't know this information for certain without looking it up with getpwent(), which would defeat the purpose of this module. However, we can obtain the proper UID and GID of the file and assume that they are set correctly by the system, so we'll partially fill in the structure:

```
static int
mbdb_me_lookup(char *name, SM_MBDB_T *user)
{
  char path[MAXPATHLEN]; /* MAXPATHLEN defined in sm/conf.h */
  struct stat sb;        /* Status structure               */
  errno = 0;

  /* Form the path to the file to be stat()ed    */
  /* _PATH_MAILDIR defined in sm/conf.h          */
```

```
if (sm_snprintf(path, sizeof(path), "%s/%s",
        _PATH_MAILDIR, name) >= sizeof(path))
{
        return ENAMETOOLONG;
}

if (stat(path, &sb) < 0)
{
        /* Can't stat mailbox file.                    */
        switch (errno)
        {
          /* It doesn't exist.                         */
          case ENOENT:
                return EX_NOUSER;
          /* We can't stat the file.                   */
          default:
                return EX_TEMPFAIL;
        }
}
else
{

        /* Mailbox exists!                      */
        user->mbdb_uid = sb.st_uid;
        user->mbdb_gid = sb.st_gid;
        (void) sm_strlcpy(user->mbdb_name, name,
                sizeof(user->mbdb_name));
        /* But home directory, etc., don't.     */
        user->mbdb_homedir[0] = '\0';
        user->mbdb_fullname[0] = '\0';
        user->mbdb_shell[0] = '\0';
        /*
        * We can do other things here, such as define a
        * quota and check sb.st_size against it if we
        * want.
        */
        return EX_OK;
}
}
```

Finally, we need to tell `sendmail` to use the new authentication procedure. It's also a good idea to turn off `.forward` file lookups, as no home directories exist.

We add the following lines to our `.mc` file:

```
define('confFORWARD_PATH','')
define('confMAILBOX_DATABASE','me')
```

Recompile `sendmail` to include these source code changes, reinstall the new `sendmail.cf` file, and this mechanism should work.

Much more should be done in this code before it goes "live," such as checking whether the mailbox file is a plain file and not a symbolic link or a directory, and making sure that the LDA is aware of this authentication mechanism (the `sendmail` 8.12 `mail.local` uses mbdb). Nevertheless, this suffices for a quick-and-dirty example. In this case, creating an email mailbox for holding mail for the user "npc" would be as simple as running "`touch /var/mail/npc`" and properly setting ownership and permission.

I'm not advocating the use of this mechanism as a real email authentication, as it makes no provision for a user to retrieve email. The purpose of this exercise is simply to provide a trivial example of how to use mbdb; in that sense, it meets its goals.

All of these methods of modifying how `sendmail` performs its authentication involve considerable risk. If any of these mechanisms is adopted, exhaustive testing is an absolute requirement before the system goes live. None of these strategies (except, perhaps, removing the "w" from the local mailer flags) should be considered as a quick hack by any means. Regardless of the extent to which a new authentication system has been tested, once the new system goes live, it must be monitored vigilantly, and a rapid backout strategy should be prepared just in case.

In examining the `mail.local` code (or the code for `/bin/mail` or other LDAs), it becomes apparent that, like `sendmail`, the LDA validates a local user before continuing with email delivery. On a dedicated email server with only administrative user accounts, if we set "`F=w`" in the local mailer flags, then this step really shouldn't be necessary, as the MTA has performed the same check. If `sendmail` determines that the user is valid, then the LDA really shouldn't have to do so, too. On servers authenticating against small `passwd` files or larger files stored in a hashed format on local disk, the cost of the LDA performing the extra lookup will be small, so this sort of optimization probably isn't necessary. If the authentication database is large or is stored on another system, however, this extra delay in delivering messages might not be completely benign. If the LDA can figure out from the user name where the message should be delivered, then it would be safe to assume that the account is supposed to receive email. In this case, the second authentication check becomes unnecessary. If all recipient mailboxes have the same UID, the LDA simply would be run as this user. Otherwise, the LDA would be run as root and change its EUID to that of the owner of the file, assuming that ID is set correctly on the system.

4.2.5 Mailbox Quotas

On systems where disk space is scarce or where mailboxes may grow to very large sizes, it's often advantageous to set a quota limit on mailbox sizes. The most common way to do so is to use the operating system's quota mechanism on the mail spool disk system. The quota mechanism available will likely differ from system to system, but generally running `man quota` will provide information on where to start. On large systems where the users don't have direct access to the server and must read their email via POP or IMAP access, all email may be stored under the UID of a single user responsible for the entire message store. In this case, an operating system's quota mechanisms won't be useful as they are universally based on tracking data storage via UID. Instead, it's often easiest to build quota-checking functionality into the LDA. The MTA could also perform quota checking using the mbdb interface discussed earlier, but this tactic requires more work. If this functionality is added to the LDA, then it becomes the LDA's responsibility to determine whether an email account is over quota, and, if it is, to refuse to deliver more email until this situation is rectified. This problem breaks into two parts: (1) determining what quota is associated with which mailbox, and (2) determining whether a user is over quota.

The easiest solution to the first problem is to force a universal mailbox quota limit and to code this value into the LDA. This option might be a reasonable response at many sites. The other possibility is to do a table lookup with a default value if the user name doesn't appear in the table. These tables can be simply constructed, for example, in two columns with the user name on the left and the quota (in megabytes, for example, on the right), such as the following:

```
npc      100
jim       10
scott     10
philip    20
```

If this file is large, it can be stored as a database. The most straightforward way to do so is to use the same sorts of Berkeley Database files that `sendmail` uses for its maps, such as the `virtusertable` or the `access` table. Berkeley DB is an Open Source product from Sleepycat Software [OBS99], and some version of it typically comes with most UNIX-like operating systems. These database files can be constructed from "flat" text files using the `makemap` utility that comes with the `sendmail` distribution. For example, on a system whose DB library supports the btree format, we'd run the following command on a flat file called `emailquota`:

```
makemap btree emailquota < emailquota
```

On a FreeBSD system, or any other operating system with a recent version of Berkeley DB, this command will create a file called `emailquota.db` in the current directory that stores the same information as the text file from which it was generated, except in a btree format readable by the Sleepycat libraries. It's easy to write programs that perform simple queries against these database files. Besides the documentation at the Sleepycat Web site [SLE], a good place to start to understand how this interface works is to run "`man db`".

Regarding the Sleepycat DB package, serious advances have been made in terms of this package's functionality. However, few operating systems have incorporated the latest versions into their releases. Sleepycat DB version 3 has been in wide use for several years. It's rock-solid and provides considerable improvements over earlier versions. Sleepycat DB version 4 recently came out, but is still relatively new. Many operating systems ship with Sleepycat version 2 or even later releases of version 1. It is worthwhile to consider upgrading a system that uses Sleepycat DBs extensively.

At those sites where the email system performs user authentication requests against remote data repositories, such as LDAP, that repository would be a natural place to store quota information. As an LDA will check whether an account is valid before completing a message delivery, having it request quota information from this database is a logical way to accomplish both tasks at once.

The second aspect of quota enforcement is to verify that a mailbox isn't over quota. For a one-file-per-mailbox storage method, such as the 7th Edition mailbox format, the quota conformance can be checked by the `stat()` system call to verify the file's size, after a lock has been established on the mailbox but before delivery begins. If the mailbox uses a one-file-per-message format, this task becomes trickier. In this case, each file in the directory (or directory tree) must be found and a `stat()` performed on each file. These sizes are then summed to see whether the quota has been exceeded. This task involves much more work than in the single-file mailbox case, but it's basically the same amount of work that's performed if one were to run "`ls -lR`" in the mailbox directory, which will also `stat()` every file in a directory hierarchy. To expedite this process, some commercial email servers that provide quota support keep a separate database containing the sizes of the email messages in a given mailbox, updating this record if a new message is delivered or an old one deleted. It's more work to keep this extra data repository in sync with the actual mailbox, and this database must be made available to both the LDA and the POP and/or IMAP daemons. Overall, it is probably not necessary to keep such a database, but it would be straightforward to implement one if necessary.

One final comment on the LDA and quotas: One of the big questions that many people ask concerning email quota implementation is, What should be done with the next message if a user's mailbox is over quota? Specifically, should the delivery be rejected with a temporary or permanent error status? If the error reported back to the MTA indicates a permanent error, the message will be bounced as undeliverable. If it's a temporary error, the message will be queued for redelivery. At first glance, the temporary error might seem to achieve the best result, but this may not be the case, especially if the system struggles with performance issues. A mailbox that is over quota takes up too much space because of either somebody's carelessness (not cleaning out email or forgetting to deactivate unused accounts) or somebody's malice (sending larger email messages than are appropriate, such as mail bombing). In either case, if we don't want to store that email message in the message store, then we certainly don't want it (and its cousins) clogging the mail queue, especially if the server is the target of a mail bomb. In either case, the only way to make sure an overfull mailbox doesn't turn into an overfull mail queue is to bounce the message by indicating a permanent delivery failure. Of course, if the server in question is lightly loaded or if a user's quota might be exceeded due to files not related to email, returning a temporary failure may indeed be more appropriate. This book focuses specifically on those systems with heavy use, where resources are specifically in short supply. This policy may seem unkind or even draconian, but it's almost certainly the lesser of two evils under these circumstances.

Unfortunately, the `mail.local` LDA that ships with the `sendmail` source distribution has historically considered mail quota violations to be a temporary failure condition. In older source distributions, one can easily patch `mail.local` to change this behavior by removing the following lines from `mail.local.c`:

```
#ifdef EDQUOT

        case EDQUOT:          /* Disc quota exceeded */

#endif
```

In the source code, this case is part of a list of error conditions that will result in the LDA returning a temporary failure. After removing it from that list, a filesystem error condition of EDQUOT will implicitly result in `mail.local` returning a permanent error.

Starting with `sendmail` version 8.10, this behavior can be mandated more easily by having `sendmail` invoke `mail.local` with the -b flag. For a system such as FreeBSD, simply add the following M4 code to the appropriate .mc file:

```
define('LOCAL_MAILER_ARGS','mail.local -d -b $u')
```

Under the sendmail source distribution, look at the files in cf/ostype to find out which flags are appropriate for various operating systems. The flags can also be changed here, but it is probably more appropriate to make these changes in a domain-specific file.

To accomplish this task, go into the cf/domain directory under the top-level sendmail source distribution directory. In this directory, create an appropriate domain file—for example, example.com.m4. Place the change given earlier in this file, and include it in the configuration by replacing the line

```
DOMAIN(generic)
```

with

```
DOMAIN(example.com)
```

4.2.6 Other LDAs

Some sites use delivery agents other than the traditional mail.local or /bin/mail. One common LDA replacement is procmail [PRO], which is used by default in many Linux distributions. It provides a great deal of functionality, especially in the realm of email filtering, that other LDAs don't possess. Despite its large feature set, procmail performs remarkably well as an LDA.

We can configure sendmail to use procmail as the LDA by adding the following line to a .mc file:

```
FEATURE('local_procmail')
```

Returning to the CPU-bound email server introduced in Chapter 1, we can rerun our standard test case (sendmail 8.12, background delivery mode, delivery over IPC, sending many messages, each about 1KB in size, to one randomly selected recipient out of 50) using mail.local and procmail as delivery agents. Recall that using mail.local we achieved a delivery rate of about 242 messages/minute. Under the same conditions using procmail version 3.22, about 247 messages/second are achieved. This rate represents a 2% increase in throughput, although this number is probably within the margin of error for this particular measurement. Nonetheless, it is a respectable showing for procmail.

Recent versions of procmail can be compiled to deliver via LMTP as well. To do so, uncomment the #define LMTP declaration in the conf.h file that comes with the source code bundle. However, procmail's LMTP implementation suffers in the performance department. Using the same test methodology as in the previous experiment, we achieved a delivery rate of 236 messages/minute using mail.local and LMTP. With procmail using LMTP, the delivery rate is highly variable, but on average it drops to 183 messages/minute, a decline of more than 22%. To configure procmail and LMTP together, use the following code:

```
FEATURE('local_lmtp', '/usr/local/bin/procmail')
define('LOCAL_MAILER_ARGS', 'procmail -Y -a $h -z')
```

I wouldn't recommend taking this step on a performance-sensitive email server without first improving procmail's LMTP delivery performance.

Another LDA worth mentioning is the deliver LDA used by the Cyrus IMAP [CYR] system. The Cyrus mail server software is discussed in more detail later in this chapter. On a system running Cyrus IMAP, one must use the LDA provided with this package, deliver, as the LDA because Cyrus's message store has a unique layout. Cyrus IMAP is a good example of a system with a one-file-per-message message store in which all mailboxes are owned by the same UID. It's unlikely that someone would want to use deliver in a non-Cyrus context.

4.3 Storage Systems

Compared to most common file benchmarks, the I/O operation mix that typically takes place in email message stores is write-heavy, synchronous, and nonsequential, just as it is in the queue. Disks spend a lot of time writing data to random locations in the message store, and modifications to these files are followed by fsync()s. Unlike in the mail queue, however, file creates in the message store are less likely to be followed by immediate deletes. Files in the message store are significantly less temporary. Further, the amount of storage required in the message store is at least one and probably two or more orders of magnitude larger than space in the queue. For any performance-sensitive email system, use of a Redundant Array of Independent Disks (RAID) system for the message store will be mandatory.

RAID systems are quite complex, and an entire book easily could be written discussing even the user-visible features and administrative issues. Even though this information might seem like a long diversion from the book's primary topic, storage systems are an important enough factor in evaluating an email server's overall performance to justify this discussion. A RAID system provides two advantages over single disks, redundancy and striping. Redundancy aims to provide data integrity, although usually at a cost of some reduction in performance, in case a disk in the storage system fails. All RAID systems, except for RAID Level 0, which is pure disk striping, provide data protection in the event of a single disk failure. Striping aims to divide the I/O load over several disks. The RAID system provides the illusion of a single large virtual disk to the operating system. Behind the scenes, I/O requests for different virtual disk locations are parceled out to different physical disks.

4.3.1 Disk Concatenation

The most simple form of disk striping is concatenation. With concatenation, multiple disks are aggregated sequentially into one large virtual disk. In the worst case, disk blocks will be allocated such that once the first disk fills, the next write will occur on the following disk. As an example, assume that three 4GB disks are concatenated together. If we start writing out a huge file, the first 4GB will reside on the first disk in the aggregation. Once this disk fills, the next byte, at an offset of 4GB + 1B, will occur on the second disk. Once 8GB have been written, the next byte will live on the third disk. Once 12GB have been written, the disk system is full. To applications, this system looks like one 12GB disk. Some filesystems handle concatenation better than this example does. That is, they do not allocate storage in a strictly sequential fashion, but make use of all disks, even if the aggregate stores data representing only a fraction of its capacity.

The other way to aggregate physical disks into a larger unit is to stripe them. Instead of addressing the space on the disks sequentially, each disk is divided into "stripes" and the first stripe on each disk is addressed sequentially. Assume that we start with the same set of three 4GB disks mentioned earlier with no data on them and a stripe width of 1MB. If we write out a 4MB file to the disk system, the first 1MB would go on the first disk (filling the first stripe on the first disk), the second 1MB would go at the beginning of the second disk, the third 1MB would go at the beginning of the third disk, and the fourth 1MB would begin at the 1MB + 1B position on the first disk. (As an aside, another way of looking at disk concatenation is that it is a special case of disk striping, where the stripe size is equal to the disk size.)

It's important to consider the application when deciding on a RAID stripe size. Consider, for example, storage systems that store extremely large files that are manipulated by a single application. To obtain sufficient performance, smaller stripe sizes are generally beneficial to achieve as much I/O throughput as possible by having many disk heads in motion for a single data transfer. With email systems, the opposite situation arises: Several I/O streams will be occurring between the server and their storage systems at any one time, so each access to a single file should affect only a single disk if possible. This approach reduces the total number of disk heads that need to move to satisfy a particular I/O operation. As moving disk heads is the most expensive operation performed by a disk, obviously any way it can be minimized will improve performance.

An email server will almost always contain a very large assortment of file sizes. Files may range from hundreds of bytes up to very large file sizes, depending on several factors. In many environments, single files in message stores can easily run into the tens of megabytes. A stripe size of two times the size of the largest file would minimize the chance that more than one disk head movement will be necessary to access that file. Of course, the stripe need not be larger than all of the files on the server. For some email servers, the optimal stripe size will be larger than the maximum allowed by the storage system used. In this case, the largest available size should be selected. In fact, for email server use, my advice would generally be to set a RAID system's stripe size to be the maximum configurable.

An argument against disk concatenation, and against very large stripes in general, goes as follows: The typical filesystem stores new files by allocating the first group of sequentially numbered disk blocks that it expects can hold the given file. Some filesystems are not so naive, however. Even on those that are, this serves only as an approximation of what happens. If a filesystem does use a sequential allocation policy, then if only the first 50% of the disk system becomes filled with data, one cannot use the bandwidth provided by the last 50% of the disk spindles in the array.

Non-uniform file distribution can reduce the available disk bandwidth on striped disks as well. As an example, consider the three disk array considered earlier, and assume an extreme case in which each stripe width is half of a disk's total capacity. Then, using 33% of the available disk space may result in using, effectively, 67% of the disk system's total I/O capacity. Of course, this example assumes that the access to the data is uniform and random, but it is a good approximation when dealing with an email message store. Only 67% of the capacity is used because only the first two of the six available stripes would be filled with data if we used three disks. Of course, if we lower the stripe size to 10% of a disk's capacity, this problem effectively vanishes. Using nearly 50% total space utilization on the array, the load on one spindle will be no more than 20% greater than the load on any other spindle, even in the worst case, again assuming a random distribution. This variation isn't terribly large, and no RAID system can practically be built with a stripe size this large. The lesson here is to not be afraid of extremely large RAID stripe sizes for email applications. Conversely, going to the extreme of concatenation is probably not a good idea unless the filesystem will evenly distribute files across all spindles, even if the filesystem is nearly empty.

4.3.2 RAID Levels

The trade press abounds with descriptions of RAID Levels, and it's important to understand at least roughly what they mean. While the information presented here doesn't describe all the intricacies of RAID systems, it will suffice for the purposes of this book.

RAID Level 0 refers to data that are striped across multiple disks without any redundancy. RAID Level 1 consists of mirrored data. Mirroring means that two disks will contain exactly the same contents and be kept completely in sync. No RAID Level 2 systems are commercially available, so we won't consider them here. RAID Level 3 introduces the concept of *parity*. Parity is the use of extra disk space to store additional data that allows the information from a failed disk to be reconstructed just from data on the other disks in the array. By allocating a single disk to hold this parity information, we can protect against any single disk failure regardless of the number of disks in the array. In RAID Level 3, each disk in an array operates in lockstep; that is, the disk arms on all disks move in unison. In a RAID 3 system, one disk is allocated to act as the parity disk. RAID Level 4 is the same as RAID 3, except that data are stored independently on every disk, so that reads and writes do not involve accesses on every disk. These disks do not operate in lockstep, so data from different parts of different disks can be read simultaneously. A single disk holds parity information. RAID Level 5 is the same as RAID 4, except that parity data are striped across the entire array, not stored on a single disk. RAID 6 is the same as RAID 5, except that one extra disk per RAID group is added, and a second checksum algorithm ensures that the system can survive two disk failures. These RAID Levels are defined by the RAID Advisory Board. Much more information on RAID can be found in *The RAID Book* [MAS97], among other sources.

RAID 1, mirroring, provides the most fault protection and has excellent performance characteristics, as no parity calculations are performed. Even though email storage is relatively write-heavy, serious performance gains can be obtained from RAID 1 systems that balance their reads between both disks storing any particular datum. When purchasing a RAID 1 system, the ability to balance reads over the mirrored pairs should be a requirement of any product under consideration.

While RAID 1 consumes a great deal of disk space, with fully 50% of all disk storage being devoted to redundancy, it is the recommended solution when a single disk or small number of disks need to be aggregated and protected, as is the case for an email queue, temporary file storage, or small message store.

Although not recognized as an official classification by the RAID Advisory Board, many storage vendors offer a RAID 0+1 option. With this system, the disks are divided into two groups. One becomes a RAID 0 system, and the second group mirrors the first group. Thus disks are striped together, and then the group is mirrored. Again, this very good high-performance strategy works efficiently for relatively small numbers of disks.

Because any particular data operation requires accessing all disks for RAID 3, it is far more suitable for single-application solutions such as scientific computing or Hollywood-style special effects work than for email applications. The single parity disk often becomes a bottleneck for write-intensive applications (like email) for RAID 3 (and RAID 4) systems. Some vendor implementations of very-high-performance RAID 3 and 4 configurations should not be immediately discounted as storage systems for email applications, however. Typically, these systems have large amounts of NVRAM to buffer writes and RAM to act as a read cache, thereby masking the potential limitations of these two solutions. I've used both RAID 3 and RAID 4 solutions from specific vendors as part of high-performance email solutions, and these products are near the top of my personal list in terms of what they provide for the money. Nevertheless, unless the storage system is specially designed to perform well in write-heavy, random access environments, it is best to avoid RAID 3 or RAID 4 configurations for email applications.

Once we consider disk systems that are too large to be built economically using RAID 1 or 0+1 systems, the most common and appropriate RAID Level for email applications will be RAID 5. As indicated earlier, it's almost universally true that the quality of the RAID solution is more important than the RAID Level. Assuming a quality implementation, RAID 5 is usually the most appropriate RAID Level for large-scale transactional storage. For RAID Levels 3, 4, and 5, one needs to allocate a certain number of parity disks or disk space for a given amount of data storage. Typically, I'd recommend allocating in the range of 1 parity disk (or equivalent space striped across all disks for a RAID 5 system) for every 5 to 13 data disks, depending on the system in question. The storage vendor should be able to help by providing some specific recommendations. In general, being conservative and sacrificing 20% of the total available disk space to avoid parity-induced slowdowns should be viewed as an investment, and a modest one at that.

What is the threshold for a large-scale storage system? For storage requirements of 10 or fewer disks' worth of data storage, RAID 0+1 solutions usually make the most sense, as the number of disks is so small that the extra expense of mirroring isn't especially high. If 36 disks will be aggregated into a single storage system, then dividing these into six 6-disk RAID 5 groups probably would be recommended. Between these two limits, I would be loathe to provide any specific recommendations. However, disks are generally cheap, so taking a conservative stance typically will not be as costly as being wrong in the other direction.

4.3.3 RAID Implementation

RAID systems can be classified as two distinct types: hardware RAID and software RAID. With software RAID, knowledge of which physical disk stores which data and how the data are protected is maintained by software that is part of the server's operating system itself. On a hardware RAID system, the operating system is merely aware of a large virtual storage device, and the device itself maintains the details of how the data are divided over the disks.

The primary argument in favor of a software RAID system is its inexpensive nature, requiring no additional hardware other than the disks and an enclosure to hold them. Further, on an email server the system's CPU is rarely heavily taxed, so it should have capacity available for performing RAID duties. These arguments often lead to an acceptable solution, but one should be very careful before blindly embarking along this path. First, using the main CPU to stripe and mirror data usually doesn't impose an enormous burden. On the other hand, requiring it to perform more complex parity calculations and handle the extra writes necessary for parity storage, such as those required for a RAID 5 system, is almost always a mistake. These calculations on I/O-intensive systems can be considerable and can result in noticeable performance degradations even on servers with very powerful processors. Offloading these calculations to a special-purpose processor on a controller card or RAID array is a good idea.

Second, while one might expect software RAID systems to be well-tuned applications that were implemented by their vendors with performance considerations of paramount importance, often this is not the case. Almost all vendors that sell RAID software also sell large, and expensive, storage systems. Carefully tuning RAID software solutions might reduce the amount of money they can make on these storage systems, so it might not be too surprising to find that the performance of their RAID software is not as strong as one might at first expect. This is not to say that these products are bad, just that the performance of systems running software RAID systems can prove disappointing. Improving the speed at which it runs might not be the vendor's top priority.

Hardware RAID systems come in two varieties: self-contained storage systems and controller cards to which a set of separately purchased disks are attached. Essentially, both are RAID controllers, but one sits inside the server and the other comes with a bunch of disks. As with most other computer systems, the quality of both types of products and their suitability for any particular purpose vary wildly. While the cliché "you get what you pay for" largely applies here, one occasionally stumbles across a system that defies its price tag, most commonly in the wrong direction. Nearly all "dirt cheap" RAID systems perform poorly, but not all expensive systems perform well.

As an example, not too long ago I hooked up a RAID system provided by a major UNIX server vendor with NVRAM and six disks into a 3 + 3 RAID 0+1 configuration to do some performance testing. Running mail queues on this arrangement delivered about 1.5 times the throughput of a single disk working alone, with the disk system and not the controller representing the bottleneck. This result is simply unacceptable: Anything less than 3 times the single disk performance would be embarrassing, and a very good RAID system should exceed that level. Under most circumstances I tend to purchase brand-name computer peripherals, usually from the server vendor, but RAID systems are often an exception to that rule. The "best bang for the buck" often comes from third-party equipment.

Of course, not all third-party RAID systems are good—in fact, quite the contrary. As science fiction author Theodore Sturgeon once said, "90% of everything is crud." This rule of thumb certainly applies to RAID systems. In any event, before embarking on a project requiring high-performance storage, allocate plenty of time to try out several pieces of equipment from several vendors before the project needs to go live. Don't expect to find a top-notch solution in the bargain bin, and test, test, test in as close to a real-world environment as possible. Chapter 8 describes testing considerations in more detail.

4.3.4 Evaluating RAID Systems

While no substitute for direct testing exists, one can use some objective measures to begin to evaluate RAID systems. Each storage system capable of hardware RAID must have a processor to perform parity calculations and move the data from the disks to the computer. The same processor may carry out both tasks, or one or more specialized processors may be devoted to each task. As in other areas, an apples-to-oranges comparison of clock speeds means little, but learning that one system uses a processor that another vendor reserves for a higher-end model can be telling. A vendor might also use special-purpose processors for parity calculations and other more familiar or general-purpose processors for data transfer. A system with generally more horsepower available for data movement is a good thing, although of course it is not sufficient to indicate a quality product.

Every quality RAID system should contain its own RAM for data caching and NVRAM to accelerate writes. How much of each the system can hold may be an indicator of its expected capabilities in terms of total throughput. At the very least, expansion capability can provide a potential upgrade path if disk I/O becomes a performance constraint again in the future. NVRAM is indispensable if RAID 3, 4, or 5 solutions are considered, because writes for these RAID Levels are much more resource-intensive than those for RAID Levels 0 and 1.

Other considerations include the following: How much thought has gone into eliminating throughput bottlenecks in the RAID system? Are all internal pipes large enough to deliver the projected maximum sustained throughput? Finally, don't overlook the obvious need to make sure that the connection between the storage system and its host is fast enough to handle the load. No matter how good the components are, no one can get 50 Mbps of throughput from a RAID system connected by a SCSI-2 interface.

Evaluating RAID controller cards requires the same sort of careful testing as total RAID systems do. The quality of the processor, the amount of memory on the card, the types of caching performed by the card, and the protection of the data stored on the card if the machine crashes are all important factors that one should be able to evaluate from a specification sheet. The company's data sheet might list information such as how much CPU loading is required per megabyte transferred per second and actual sustained throughput numbers. However, real data need to be determined by testing, and ultimately these numbers are the ones that matter. Overall, RAID controller cards can prove useful for small disk systems, but if one plans to support more than six disks, then a complete RAID system will usually be a better solution.

Whether one uses RAID controller cards or regular SCSI cards to attach hardware RAID systems, there's always a danger of providing more disk I/O than a controller can handle. To prevent this problem, one can use any of several approaches. First, each RAID system, disk pack, or solid state disk (SSD) should have its own disk controller card on the host. It's almost always worthwhile to make sure this card is the best-performing piece of hardware that one can obtain. Second, do not mix high-speed, performance-sensitive storage and low-speed devices on the same SCSI bus. Even if the bus has plenty of I/O to handle both the disk that stores an email queue and a tape drive used to back up the system, this mixing is usually not a good idea. For some buses, the whole chain will sync down to the speed of the slowest device, even if it's never used, which can have disastrous consequences. Most controllers are smart enough to converse at different rates with different devices. Even in this case, however, the slow device will take up more than its fair share of the total available bandwidth when it runs, as it cannot take advantage of the bus's maximum speed. Therefore, data transfers involving this device will consume the bus's resources for a greater amount of time than desired.

Sometimes even a single RAID system or bus does not have enough I/O capacity to satisfy the demand. In these cases, multiple RAID systems must be used, and the application can be made aware that the data in question reside on multiple filesystems that are accessed through different directory paths. As a trivial example, this goal can be accomplished by modifying a POP daemon and LDA to look for mailbox names that begin with the letters a–m under the /mbox1 directory, and locating the n–z mailboxes under /mbox2. As an alternative, one can use software RAID striping to mask the fact that these multiple mount points exist. If each storage system uses RAID Level 5 to protect its data, then striping several of these systems together using software RAID is commonly called RAID 50, even though this RAID Level is not recognized by the RAID Advisory Board. Many variations on this theme are possible.

As already mentioned, the use of software RAID to perform operations such as striping and mirroring will often provide a reasonably well-performing solution, so this solution is recommended for those storage environments in which a single filesystem image is required, yet the I/O bandwidth to the devices exceeds that of a single high-end I/O controller, such as Fibre Channel or Ultra-SCSI 160. In the email application realm, this case will arise only with truly mammoth systems.

4.4 Disks

When setting up an email storage system, it's important not to overlook the most critical component—the disk drives themselves. The disks that work best for email storage have fast platter rotation rates and very low seek times. Disk capacity is far less important. In fact, it's difficult to find appropriately *small* disks for most email systems. For very high I/O environments, there's no substitute for having large numbers of spindles. In general, buy the smallest and fastest (especially as measured by seek time) disks available. This choice isn't cost-effective in terms of megabytes per dollar, but it is cost effective in terms of I/O operations per dollar, the really important metric. These days, no matter how small the disk, expect that its entire capacity won't be effectively used for email storage, especially on systems such as an ISP's POP-based system, where mailbox storage is fairly transient.

4.4.1 ATA Versus SCSI

Most high-performance email servers should use SCSI disks, even if the server is implemented with hardware that supports ATA (Advanced Technology Attachment; also called IDE) disks. Even though they're more expensive, manufacturers typically quote longer mean time between failure (MTBF) numbers for their SCSI disks than their ATA disks, and robustness is a key feature when it comes to email servers' disk drives. Also, accessing data on SCSI disks requires fewer server CPU resources than accessing the same data on ATA disks. ATA controllers require the server's CPU to handle the transfer of data on and off the disk. With SCSI, the SCSI controller performs these operations. At the present time, the fastest SCSI controllers can transfer data at 160 Mbps. The fastest form of ATA, known as Ultra-ATA/133, can transfer data at a maximum rate of 133 Mbps.

In tests of single disks with otherwise identical characteristics, ATA disks may mildly outperform SCSI disks. This result may reflect the ATA disk's ability to take advantage of the system's fast CPU while the SCSI disk uses its own more modest processor to move the data to and from the disk. On a system whose CPU is used for tasks other than raw data movement, the test results might be quite different. If a test reveals that an ATA disk greatly outperforms its SCSI counterpart, the operating system or disk in question is likely treating the data differently. To give the illusion of better performance, some ATA-based systems will acknowledge a write before it has actually been written to the disk. Clearly, this behavior is unacceptable on an email server, and ATA storage should be avoided unless one can be certain that this behavior will not happen. One clear indication of this behavior is an ATA disk that performs impossibly well on a test using relatively small data sizes, on the order of a few megabytes or less. As with most things, if the numbers seem too good to be true, they probably are.

ATA disks are limited to 2 per channel, whereas even older SCSI-2 controllers can address 7 devices, more modern Wide SCSI controllers can address 15 devices, and Fibre Channel allows a maximum of 127 distinct devices on a single loop. The limitation in the number of devices per channel may not pose a problem for email queues, but the message store on a high-performance system should almost certainly be based on SCSI. Of course, it's rare that in a high-performance environment 15 SCSI devices, or even 7, will be connected to the same SCSI controller. Nevertheless, having the option for more than 2 devices is useful.

4.4.2 Stupid Disk Drive Tricks

Another trick is worth mentioning, even though it rarely justifies the effort required to implement it. Some filesystems will allow the formatting of just part of a disk. If one can make sure that just the outer cylinders (those that reside near the outside edge of the disk) are formatted, then some additional performance increases are possible. Let's consider an example. Pretend that we format an 18GB disk drive to only 9GB using just the outer cylinders. By cutting the disk storage capacity in half (roughly proportional to the area of the disk), we cut down the distance that the disk head must seek along the radius of the disk to about 30% of the original distance it would have to cover, because more of the disk's area occurs near the edge of the disk than in the center. This approach results in a considerable savings in terms of the amount of distance the disk head has to seek, thereby reducing the latency of disk operations. Moreover, the linear velocity of the disk underneath the heads at the outer edge of the disk is much faster than the linear velocity near the center of the disk, meaning that more data pass underneath the heads in any given time period, which also increases throughput—a double bonus.

Even on systems where it isn't possible to format just the outer cylinders, a disk may be partitioned—for example, into two equally sized parts. Once it has been determined whether the inner or outer cylinders belong to a given partition, one can use just the outer partition for email storage and ignore the rest, or use it for less frequently accessed data, such as log archival.

Generally, this sort of optimization should be reserved for true speed freaks. Most folks with the expertise to set up, document, and maintain a system in this manner would achieve a better return on their investment by just buying more disks, as these devices are cheap by almost everyone's standards, especially as compared to the value of the time spent by people with this sort of expertise. Further, most of today's filesystems start their storage on the outer (faster) cylinders anyway, so much of this benefit happens "by default," at least early in a disk's life, before data become scattered across the platters. Also, it's easier to configure a system by formatting the whole disk, and having the extra space as a "buffer" against mail bombing, network outage, or other unwelcome events can be very useful. Some data and additional considerations may be found in the literature [MET97].

The principal lesson is that on a very transient mail spool, if it will be necessary to access 100GB of email, don't buy three 36GB disks or even six 18GB disks and think that's enough. Disk space bears very little relation to server performance. Making sure a system can keep up with the transactional demands of the service is more important and difficult than finding space in which to store the data. Additional disks are purchased primarily to provide additional operations per second, and only secondarily to increase storage.

4.5 Solid State Disks

Although Gordon Moore's law postulates that CPU power for the same amount of money doubles every 18 months, disk access speeds have not kept up with this torrid pace. In 1994, a state-of-the-art disk had a capacity of about 2GB, the platters revolved at 5,400 rpm, and the disk had an average seek time of 10.4 ms. Larger disks were available, but they were fairly error-prone and not suitable for mission-critical work. In 1997, disk capacity was about 9GB, rotational speed was 7,200 rpm, and seek time averaged about 7.4 ms. In early 2002, a state-of-the-art disk for email systems means 36GB, 15,000 rpm, and 3.8 ms seek time. Larger disks are available, but at this time, these configurations are the disks of choice for email systems. While these improvements are remarkable, over the last eight years, storage capacity for disks has gone up by a factor of 20, rotational speeds have tripled, and seek times have been cut by a factor of 3. On a related front, I/O bus speeds—specifically, SCSI speeds—have increased over the same period by a factor of 8. Over the same time period, CPU speeds have increased by a factor of 40. In relative terms, CPU progress has left disk access in the dust. This trend has been one of the main drivers for the use of parallelism to achieve high I/O performance. This point, combined with the equally rapid reduction in the cost per megabyte of SDRAM, explains why the solid state disk has become a cost-effective storage mechanism on the high end.

To the host computer to which it is attached, an SSD appears as just another disk drive on the end of a Fibre Channel or SCSI chain. It has a stated capacity and permanently reads and writes data sent to it, just like a regular Winchester disk. An SSD, however, has no moving parts (except, perhaps, a cooling fan). It consists of several or many banks of RAM and a bunch of batteries. The RAM stores the data just as the disk does, but because no delays ensue while the disk heads move or platters rotate, latencies are typically around 0.5 ms, an order of magnitude better than the times for state-of-the-art Winchester disks. Reducing "seek" time is especially beneficial for applications such as email, where small operations are performed randomly scattered across the disk. In fact, SSDs are often even fast enough to mask deficiencies of older FFS-based filesystems. When operations occur so quickly, it's much less expensive to perform directory operations synchronously than it is on slower disks. Of course, no matter how fast the disk is, substantial benefits will accrue from running a high-performance filesystem.

Some manufacturers ship a sort of hybrid SSD/Winchester disk. The enclosure will contain both a regular Winchester disk and RAM equal to a significant percentage of the disk's capacity, typically in the range of 2% to 10%. The writes are written into memory as a persistent cache and, ideally at a leisurely pace, committed to stable storage on the disk. Largely, this arrangement represents a compromise between a pure SSD and a small amount of NVRAM sitting in front of a small disk array—it's merely a matter of degree. It's not difficult to envision an environment where a few megabytes of NVRAM are not enough to achieve the desired throughput, but gigabytes of SSD space are not necessary either, so these hybrid solutions fill a valuable niche.

If RAM loses power, its contents will be lost. This result is unacceptable for email storage, and SSDs need to account for this possibility. At the very least, they include batteries to keep the RAM chips continuously powered. These batteries can range from the same kind of lithium ion batteries that power a personal camera or the clock on a PC motherboard, to full-fledged uninterruptible power supplies (UPSs). Many systems also contain a Winchester disk, so that once the battery level falls below a critical threshold, the remaining energy can be used to commit the memory contents safely to disk. This feature is very useful, but represents a substantially different strategy than the hybrid SSD/Winchester disk. In the hybrid case, under normal operation data are routinely written to the hard disk. In the case just mentioned, data are written to the hard disk only if the unit loses power and the batteries are about to fail; the feature is never used during regular operation. If an SSD unit contains a Winchester disk, it's important to understand under which circumstances it will be used.

Several very large ISPs have used SSDs for their `sendmail` queues. This strategy is cost-effective because of the nature of the queue operation and the relatively small volume of data stored at any one time. Message Stores typically require much higher storage capacities, and any system's transactional volume is likely not so high as to justify storing all of the data on SSDs. However, SSDs can still play an important role in the acceleration of these large filesystems' operations.

Recall that with journaling filesystems, metadata updates are written first to a special journal, and then the journal is efficiently updated on the "real" disk system. To achieve reasonable performance, it's usually advisable to put the journal on a different disk system than the data it updates, so that the disk heads do not have to constantly seek between the journal and persistent areas. In fact, a disk is often dedicated for the journal itself. Moreover, this disk does not have to be large. Journaling filesystems rarely require a journal area even as large as 100MB. Clearly, a small SSD could very effectively store the journal (acting, essentially, as NVRAM) for a very large disk storage system. Being able to concentrate the bulk of the transactional overhead of a filesystem onto a small, and therefore relatively inexpensive, device represents the most fortunate sort of meeting of elegant hardware and software solutions. In many situations, a comparison of the I/O capability per dollar of this solution against other options will show a remarkable bias toward this architecture, one compelling enough that this solution should never be lightly dismissed.

In general, though, the use of SSDs represents a fairly extreme solution. Although the prices of these devices have dropped substantially over the last few years, they remain relatively expensive. In many, perhaps most, situations, adding more spindles or upgrading the filesystem provides sufficient performance improvements for a fraction of the price. Everything else should be very well tuned before one seriously considers purchasing an SSD, but these devices can deliver a remarkable I/O acceleration for those situations that really need it.

One final word on SSDs: Despite the high cost of these devices and the fact that they're not directly manufactured by any of the large computer vendors (or, perhaps, because of it), customer satisfaction among those who have purchased SSDs is often higher than for almost any other computer-related product, hardware or software. Perhaps this satisfaction reflects the fact that these devices are not cheap, so the vendors can spend extra time understanding their clients' solutions and making sure the delivered products meet their needs. Almost certainly it has something to do with the substantial performance increase delivered by these systems. Also, these devices are highly reliable, chiefly because they contain very few moving parts. I have never felt the need to make a specific recommendation to a potential customer for or against any of the SSD vendors because I've heard so few harsh words about any of the products on the market. Whatever the reasons, I find this situation truly remarkable.

4.6 POP Tuning Specifics

At this point, we'll cover some specifics for providing high-performance POP service. The POP protocol is defined in RFC 1939 [MR96]. Even though it is possible to configure most POP clients to leave copies of all messages on the email server, a POP server is intended to act as a temporary repository for email that will be periodically downloaded to another machine. While not all users will operate along this model, in most environments a majority of them will.

Although we restrict our field of interest here to Open Source email solutions, the email administrator can choose from many packages. These POP daemons differ in their feature sets, such as whether they support APOP, POP over Transport Layer Security (TLS) [NEW99] (formerly called SSL), and other bells and whistles. Despite the fact that each distribution uses its own code base, each POP daemon that implements a certain feature must perform the same tasks, and there are only so many ways that these tasks can be implemented. Therefore, performance differences between various POP daemons due to coding choices tend to be relatively minor, and only the rare POP server ends up being CPU bound. When it comes to decisions regarding the layout of and interactions with the message store, differences become more apparent.

4.6.1 The 7th Edition Message Store

All programs that come with standard UNIX distributions that interact with a user's mailbox assume that email will be stored in the 7th Edition mailbox format. This format entails a single file per user, with each message concatenated after the other within this single file. Some programs and systems use slightly different mechanisms for determining when one message ends and the next begins, but generally the LDA marks the beginning of a new message by writing a special line in the mailbox file beginning with "`From`". The LDA makes sure that messages naturally containing "`From`" at the beginning of any line in the body of a message are not interpreted as the beginning of a new message by escaping the potential header. This result can be seen by sending oneself email on a UNIX system with a line in the body that begins with "`From`". Here is what happens when I send myself email with such a line:

```
From: Nick Christenson <npc@acm.org>
Message-Id: <200109192258.f8JMwBxD016945@gangofone.com>
Subject: Test
To: Nick Christenson <npc@gangofone.com>
Date: Wed, 19 Sep 2001 15:58:10 -0700 (PDT)

>From the mountains to the prairies...

--
Nick Christenson
npc@acm.org
```

When the LDA writes a message to a 7th Edition mailbox, it first writes the "`From`" line, then writes the message header and body, and finally appends a trailing blank line at the end, just to be sure.

The LDA and POP daemon, as well as other programs, may both wish to modify a mailbox at the same time. It is imperative that such simultaneous changes be prevented by the use of some form of locking, and every program that modifies a mailbox must agree to use the same locking mechanism. When selecting email programs, it is vital to understand how they lock mailboxes and messages and to ensure that everything will cooperate so that mailbox corruption cannot occur. This point cannot be stated too strongly.

Two of the most common locking mechanisms are the `flock()` system call and the creation of a lock file, such as *mailboxname*`.lock`. Although either works, `flock()` does not rely on synchronous filesystem operations and so is more performance friendly. A few UNIX flavors still do not support the `flock()` system call. On these versions, `lockf()` or, rarely, `fcntl()` can be substituted, but `flock()` is preferred.

Let's walk through the steps of what happens on the email server during a typical POP session operating on a 7th Edition mailbox:

1. The client Mail User Agent (MUA) connects to the `pop3` port of the email server (port 110).

2. The master POP daemon, or `inetd` as appropriate, receives this connection and spawns a process to handle the session.

3. The client authenticates its user to the POP daemon. The POP daemon verifies the authentication credentials and authorizes access to a single mailbox. As an example, suppose that the user's name is `npc` and the mailbox is the file `/var/mail/npc`.

4. The POP daemon locks the mailbox, either by creating a `/var/mail/`*mailboxname*`.lock` file or by calling `flock()`, or both, just to be extra careful.

5. The POP daemon makes a temporary copy of the mailbox with which to work. Assume this file is named `/var/mail/.npc.pop`. While creating the temporary mailbox, the POP daemon has the opportunity to scan the mailbox, assembling information about how many distinct messages are present, what their sizes are, who sent each message, and so on.

6. Once the temporary mailbox is created, the POP daemon unlocks the mailbox.

7. The POP daemon signifies to the POP client that it is ready to handle requests regarding the mailbox.

8. The POP client will likely request a list of the messages. It may also request unique identifiers or header information about each message.

9. If the reader intends to leave the messages on the server, then as each message is read, it will be individually downloaded on demand and the POP session will stay open for the whole session. More likely, the client will simply download every message.

10. In the typical case, all downloaded email will be marked for deletion on the server. It's possible that all, some, or none of the email in the POP mailbox will be marked for deletion.

11. The client disconnects.

12. The POP daemon needs to reconcile the POP session mailbox with the system mailbox, as new email may have come in or the mailbox may have otherwise been modified. During this process, the POP daemon locks the mailbox.

13. If no new email has arrived and all messages were deleted in the POP session, then the reconciliation is an easy task, the main mailbox is truncated, the .pop file is unlinked, and the lock is released. If not, all messages in the mailbox will be deleted, then the POP daemon constructs a new temporary file containing the modified mailbox. Messages themselves may be modified. For example, the POP daemon may add a `Status:` header in messages to mark that they are old or have been read. In the reconstructed mailbox, some messages may have been deleted, and some new messages may have arrived. Once the temporary mailbox is constructed, it is renamed to the mailbox name, the `.pop` file is deleted, and the mailbox is unlocked.

14. The POP daemon handling the session exits normally.

The POP protocol does not include provisions for allowing two POP sessions to operate on the same mailbox at the same time. If a POP daemon is active for a given user, and someone attempts to open a second POP connection as that user, then the second daemon will notice the `.pop` file and disallow the second session. This proper POP procedure is required to ensure that the mailbox does not become corrupted. The `.pop` file acts as a lease on the mailbox for potentially competing POP daemons. It may be left around if a POP daemon exits abnormally without having a chance to clean up. Therefore, any `.pop` file that exceeds a certain age threshold safely can be assumed to be stale and deleted. While a POP daemon remains active, it must periodically refresh this file by updating its `mtime` timestamp using the `utime()` call.

Historically, some POP daemons have had bugs whereby if the daemon becomes busy, it might not finish its current operations before the lease timeout expires on the .pop file, leading to mailbox corruption. In most POP daemons, this problem has been fixed by having an alarm handler wake up to perform the update periodically regardless of what the daemon is working on. However, a process cannot respond to an alarm signal while it is within kernel space. On an unsaturated email server, a process should never be unable to refresh its lease for an amount of time greater than the lease timeout on the .pop file, which is typically a few minutes. Unfortunately, on filesystems that are overwhelmed by the load, this may happen. One must strike a balance between how long a user should wait before being able to reestablish a new POP session after a daemon crashes and the risk of mailbox corruption under the circumstance that the server runs extremely slowly, especially given that these two events (processes dying abnormally and horribly slow file access) often are correlated activities. This problem can't be resolved simply, but clearly any email server on which this situation might arise under any except the most extreme circumstances needs to be tuned or upgraded to avoid this possibility.

If we can be absolutely certain that the only processes that might edit the mailbox will respect the lock mandated by the .pop files and that the LDA will only append messages to the mailbox, then we can reduce the I/O that the POP daemon performs. We do so by creating a .pop file, but not putting data in it until or unless the POP daemon needs to edit the file. If all of the messages in a mailbox are typically downloaded, and no new email arrives during this session, then most of the time the mailbox can be truncated without having to be rewritten, which can result in a large I/O savings. Within the context of qpopper (the most commonly used Open Source POP daemon [QPO]), this form of operation is called SERVER_MODE. This technique provides considerable performance advantages, but it is totally incompatible with standard UNIX email readers, such as mailx, elm, or other programs that can be used to perform arbitrary edits of a mailbox and don't check for .pop files.

4.6.2 The `maildir` Message Store

While 7th Edition mailbox is the default format used on UNIX systems, it is not the only option. After having the mailbox be a single file containing all messages, the next most common format is to represent the mailbox as a directory with one file per message in it. Several variations on this theme exist, although the most frequently cited one is the qmail format (named after the MTA that popularized it). The qmail documentation calls it the maildir format.

The maildir message store works as follows: Each user has a directory under his or her home directory for receiving email, typically named Maildir.

In this book, we want to focus on centralized email servers, so the directory that contains email messages will more likely reside in a centralized message store, such as /var/qmail/npc. This directory contains three subdirectories: tmp, new, and cur. Delivery of a message occurs via the following procedure:

1. When a new message comes in, a file is created in the tmp subdirectory with the name *time*.*pid*.*host*, where *time* is the traditional UNIX time returned by the time() library call (the number of seconds since the beginning of the year 1970), *pid* is the process's PID, and *host* is the host name. If this file cannot be created uniquely, the delivery agent sleeps for a while and tries again. For a file name collision to occur, two unique delivery agents with the same PID would have to try to deliver a message to the same user within the span of one second. As long as the operating system assigns PIDs sequentially, it is difficult to imagine a single email server capable of this sort of performance outside of a contrived example.

2. Once the file exists in the tmp directory, the message contents are written to this file. An extra "From " is not written at the beginning of the file, nor is an extra blank line added at the end. Lines in the message beginning with "From " do not need to be specially escaped. Once all the data are written out, the program uses fsync() to commit the file to disk.

3. The file is moved using rename() to the new subdirectory. The file's name is not modified.

4. The message delivery is completed, and the MTA is informed of a successful delivery.

As with all commonly used MTAs, there's a great deal to understand about how qmail operates, far too much to describe completely here. Further information can be found at the qmail Web site [QMA] or books on the subject [BLU00] [SIL01]. However, some additional notes bear mentioning. The cur directory is available to be used by programs such as the POP daemon as a place to store old messages. A POP daemon that recognizes maildir-formatted mailboxes may end its session by unlinking all messages to be deleted, and then using rename() to move all saved messages from the new directory to the cur directory.

Because the number of inodes consumed by maildir (one for each file and directory) is much larger than for 7th Edition format, it is even more important that a filesystem containing a maildir email spool support large numbers of small files. A cautious rule of thumb would be to divide the total unformatted capacity of the disk by the expected average message size to get the number of inodes that the filesystem should support. Multiplying this number by 1.5 might not be a bad idea, just to be safe, as the directories themselves will consume additional inodes. The quantity of inodes available to a filesystem is specified at file creation time as a parameter to the `newfs` command (or the equivalent command on other systems). Some advanced filesystems have the capability to add more inodes after creation, but this feature isn't common. In general, this issue should be carefully planned out before the first email message is delivered, as the problem might be difficult to fix later. If one isn't aware of it, running out of inodes on a disk can be tricky to diagnose, because many applications will report that the filesystem is out of space when, in reality, it has plenty of space but is out of inodes. Use `df -i` to inspect inode utilization on a machine's filesystems.

Even though the `maildir` format arose as part of the `qmail` email system, no part of it is incompatible with a `sendmail`-based email system. If mailboxes are stored in `maildir` format, whether running `qmail` or `sendmail` as the MTA, the POP daemon and the LDA will need to understand this format. Two options are to use the `qmail-pop3d` that comes with the `qmail` distribution or to patch `qpopper` to respect the `maildir` format. At least one patch to the venerable but obsolete `qpopper` version 2.53 is floating around the Internet, as is a patch for CUCIpop. Of course, because `sendmail` itself never touches the message store, it does not need to understand the message store format; only the LDA (defined by `Mlocal` in the `sendmail.cf` file) does. It's possible to use `procmail` [PRO], which understands the `maildir` format as the LDA, or it's a straightforward procedure to modify the `mail.local` LDA that comes with the `sendmail` distribution.

4.6.3 The Cyrus Message Store

The Cyrus message store also uses a one-message-per-file storage mechanism. All messages in the message store are owned by the user `cyrus` and the group `mail` by default. This setup precludes the mechanism's use by local mail reading programs, such as `mailx` or `elm`, without substantial modification of the software and its authentication mechanisms.

The root of the Cyrus message store is set in a master configuration file called `/etc/imapd.conf`. For example, `/var/spool/imap` might be a common location for the message store. Personal mailboxes are directories named `user/`*username* under the message store root. This mailbox is visible to an IMAP client as the special "INBOX" mailbox. Other mailboxes names are appended to this naming convention. Thus, if a personal IMAP mail folder was called `book-reviews`, it would appear on the file system as `user/npc/book-reviews` under the `/var/spool/imap` directory, or whatever top-level directory is defined in `/etc/imapd.conf`.

Each message is named via a number followed by an ASCII period (" . ") in the mailbox directory: `1.`, `2.`, `3.`, and so on. Unlike most other email systems, Cyrus stores its messages in CRLF (wire) format. Several other files found in each mailbox directory are used by the Cyrus IMAP software for various purposes:

`cyrus.cache` This file contains header information for every message in the mailbox. It is a performance optimization for IMAP clients, where requests for headers from a given mailbox are common. To satisfy this request, the Cyrus IMAP daemon can open and read from just one file rather than having to read every message file in a mailbox.

`cyrus.header` This file contains information about the mailbox in which it is stored. It includes the IMAP Access Control List (ACL) as well as the IMAP user-defined flags for the mailbox along with other information.

`cyrus.index` This file contains information about the mailbox as a whole as well as information about individual files. The last message number assigned to each mailbox and the date and time when the last message was added to the mailbox are some of the global information recorded in this file. For each message, information such as the contents of the `Date:` header and the message's size are stored here as well.

`cyrus.seen` This file contains information about which messages have already been read and which messages have arrived since the mailbox was last read.

The `cyrus.cache` and `cyrus.index` files need to be updated upon each message delivery. Other information repositories may need to be modified on delivery as well, including a database containing quota information. Cyrus supports a number of optional complex features (single-instance message storage, duplicate message suppression, SIEVE mail filtering support, and so on). A person is not expected to keep this entire system working by making file changes by hand. Rather, a powerful administration client, called `cyradm`, is available to make this job much easier.

Overall, this message store format is much more complex than either the 7th Edition or `maildir` format. Consequently, deliveries and simple retrievals are much more CPU- and I/O-intensive than they would be on the more basic formats. Of course, the Cyrus system is tuned for the demands that IMAP clients place on it. No other email packages use this message store format. If a site needs IMAP, then implementing Cyrus and its message store is a fine choice to meet those needs.

If IMAP support isn't necessary, then the extra overhead of associated with Cyrus is wasted.

There is a lot more to Cyrus than has been covered here. For more information, read the `overview.html` document that comes bundled with current Cyrus source code distributions in the `doc` directory. Another excellent source of information is the book *Managing IMAP* [MM00].

4.6.4 Comparing Message Store Formats

When evaluating message store formats, we'll disregard the Cyrus message store. Either a site will need Cyrus for IMAP support or it won't, and evaluating this criterion should simplify the decision-making process.

Comparing the other two message stores discussed here, using the `maildir` message store offers some compelling advantages. The exclusive creation of the message file in the `tmp` directory is as close to explicit locking as this protocol gets, yet it remains completely safe on most filesystems. Therefore, lock files are unnecessary and the `.pop` file timeout problem cannot occur. Further, I/O is reduced because no second copy of the mailbox at the beginning of a session is required. Also, when the POP session starts, the mailbox does not need to be scanned to determine where each message begins and ends and how large it is. Instead, this information is available trivially from each message file.

On the other hand, `maildir` has its disadvantages. If the LDA should enforce mailbox size quotas, a 7th Edition LDA can determine a mailbox's quota status from a single `stat()` of the file, which is fairly inexpensive. With `maildir`, each file in at least two directories needs to be `stat()`ed, one needs to ensure that a message isn't double-counted (it might be moved while quota is being checked), and the results of each check must be added together. These operations are not terribly expensive by themselves, but they can add up when a mailbox contains a large number of messages. Also, while the same number of bytes is typically read or written in each case, a POP session operating on a `maildir` mailbox typically requires quite a few more (usually synchronous) metadata operations. Each message read requires an `open()`, and each deleted message requires a separate, usually synchronous `unlink()`. A file system's predictive read ahead, which doesn't help much for 7th Edition mailbox systems, is even less effective on servers using `maildir`.

Moreover, it is *not* safe to use `maildir` on a filesystem using Soft Updates without first patching the software. Using Soft Updates is often desirable to reduce the cost of the metadata operations. Soft Updates isn't safe because `maildir` relies on the file being renamed between the `tmp` and `new` directories to indicate a completed delivery. If a server running Soft Updates crashes after the rename occurs, it's possible that this rename will be rolled back because it isn't performed synchronously; in such a case, the file may sit in `tmp` forever, as every new process will ignore files in `tmp` that it did not create. This problem will result in the loss of the message. Software using `maildir` could fix this flaw by performing another `fsync()` on the open file descriptor after the rename occurs, as `sendmail` has done for queue operations since version 8.10. Indeed, an unofficial patch to `qmail` 1.03 does just that. For the same reasons, the `maildir` message store format is not supported for use on filesystems that don't perform metadata updates synchronously, such as `ext2fs`, `ext3fs`, and ReiserFS. As with `sendmail`'s operations in the message queue, patches that `fsync()` the directory after file rename will solve the problem for these filesystems on Linux. Note that this fix is mandatory, not optional. Because these systems perform so many metadata operations, and because running unpatched code on a filesystem using Soft Updates isn't an option, it's usually a good idea to either use NVRAM or a journaling filesystem with a synchronous journal for high-performance `maildir` systems. Fortunately, either is usually easy to obtain.

It's hard to beat the performance of 7th Edition mailboxes if complicated mailbox edits are rare, lock files need not be created, and the system runs in SERVER_MODE. In this case, an entire session can occur with only the `fsync()` after the mailbox truncation needing to be synchronous. If deleting some but not all messages is a typical occurrence in a session or the system cannot be run in SERVER_MODE, however, `maildir` may be much faster. Also, anywhere except on a Soft Updates system, `maildir`'s locking is generally safer—no small comfort. It is entirely possible to run high-performance email systems using either message store format. In the end, the email administrator must decide which format to use based on expected I/O patterns, the kinds of filesystems that are available, and the software used to access the message store.

4.7 Message Store Hashing

As mentioned earlier, many filesystems perform a linear search for file or subdirectory names in a directory. With large numbers of users, this search can present a real performance problem in the `/var/mail` directory. Even using filesystems that perform hashed directory lookups, having hundreds of thousands, or even millions, of files or subdirectories in a single directory will not work well, or at all. For this reason, it's a good idea to subdivide a large message store by hashing it.

Support for a simple way of performing this task is provided in the `qpopper` distribution. One sets a variable called `HASH_SPOOL` to a numerical value at compile time, and qpopper will use that value and the mailbox name to construct a set of directories under which a mailbox will be stored. For example, a HASH_SPOOL value of 0 leads to the default mailbox location for the user npc of /var/mail/npc. With HASH_SPOOL set to 2, the mailbox location becomes /var/mail/n/p/npc. Of course, the LDA must be similarly modified.

While this approach generally works fairly well, it has a tendency to bunch up many of the mailboxes. On most very large email systems, the contents of the t/h directory tree might be numerous while the q/x tree contains very little. Of course, this issue may not be a major problem, but whether it's a good idea or not, there exist email systems where a sizable fraction of the email addresses have the same first letter(s).

One general solution to this problem would be to always use the entire user name as the hash; for example, npc's mailbox might be located in /var/mail/n/p/c/mbox. Of course, the directory with this mailbox may contain several subdirectories representing the beginnings of other names, but as long as no programs that operate on mailboxes use single-character names for files, no collisions will occur. While the SMTP standard leaves it up to each local email server to decide whether the user name portion of an email address is case sensitive, sendmail is not case sensitive by default when it comes to locally delivered email. Unless this behavior is explicitly changed, email sent to NPC@example.com and npc@example.com will therefore end up in the same mailbox on a typical sendmail system. In such a case, no more than 50 ASCII characters could be used as part of an email address; thus, including files used by the POP daemon, no directory would ever have more than 55 or so inodes in it, which is a very manageable number.

Such a scheme uses up inodes fairly quickly, so it would be wise to consider this issue before adopting this mechanism. A very conservative estimate can be obtained by multiplying the number of users times the maximum number of characters in a user name and allocating that number of inodes to the system. This approach is conservative because it assumes that no portion of the directory namespace will be reused from one user name to another, which won't be the case.

Although not at all tricky to code into most existing applications, this system has its share of disadvantages. Traversing a large number of directory levels causes a large number of directory lookups. Within the operating system, the function that converts path names to inodes is called namei(). For namei() to resolve the mailbox for the user npc using this hashing scheme, it must sequentially search the contents of the /, var, mail, n, p, and c directories before arriving at the desired mailbox. Much of this information, probably the first few levels of directory lookup, will be stored more or less permanently in the filesystem buffer cache, as these items will be accessed so frequently. On an email system with a very large number of users, more directories will be present than can be cached, so many of these lookups must happen on disk. While these lookup operations aren't expensive, they do consume resources and, more important, cause the disk heads to move. While disk heads are moving, they're not reading or writing, which slows down the aggregate number of disk operations that can be performed.

Another problem with this scheme is the challenge involved in extracting the complete list of mailboxes with mail on the system. It can be done with something like the following:

```
#!/bin/sh
find /var/mail -type f -name mbox -print | \
    sed 's:^/var/mail/::
        s:/mbox$::
        s:/::g'
```

This code is hardly an elegant solution and is much more cumbersome than `ls /var/mail/*/*/`.

Another solution is to use one or two directory levels (as appropriate) but to run some numerical hashing algorithm over the user name to determine the location of a mailbox. Here's an example of an algorithm that is likely to be effective: Pick a prime number (roughly equal to the square root of the maximal number of users we expect to support on this system). Let's assume we might support 58,000 subscribers. We then might select PRIME=241 as our number of bins, so we create the directories `/var/mail/0` through `/var/mail/240` inclusive. Now, when it comes time to locate a particular mailbox, we run HASH(*username*) % PRIME, where HASH() is some hashing function and % denotes modular division. This function defines the location of each mailbox on the system.

The hashing algorithm could be something well known such as MD5 [RIV92]. We don't need a cryptographically secure hashing algorithm, however, and MD5 is much more computationally expensive than is necessary for these purposes. Take the following C code, for example:

```
# define BIGPRIME 241

int
hash(char *username)
{
        char *s = username;
        int x = 7;
        int y = 19;
        int prime = BIGPRIME;
        unsigned int n;
```

```
        for (n = (unsigned int) strlen(username); *s != '\0'; s++)
               n = ((n << x ^ (n >> y)) ^ *s);

        return (n % prime);
}
```

In this algorithm, a string representing the user name is passed in and an integer representing the hash bin to which that user name corresponds is returned. Internally, `prime` is the number of hash bins, and `x` and `y` are arbitrarily selected small primes.

This algorithm will do almost as good a job of balancing user names over a set of hash bins as MD5 but in a much less computationally expensive manner. With this method, one would need to write a small program that, given a user name, would produce the path to any particular mailbox so that individual mailboxes could be located. This task represents an inconvenience, but not a major one, and `ls /var/mail/*/*` still provides a complete mailbox list (as long as there aren't too many mailboxes). Essentially, the same mailbox hashing scheme is described in [CBB97].

On email systems with up to, say, 10,000 accounts using a high-performance file-system, hashing the mailboxes may not be necessary. Even if the message store isn't hashed, putting the `.lock` files (if necessary) on another disk can reduce the number of files in the spool and, at the same time, spread out the I/O load over more spindles. In fact, because the `.lock` files don't have any consequence after a reboot, placing them in a `tmpfs` filesystem would be entirely appropriate. For `.pop` files, they should reside on the same filesystem as the mailboxes they represent so that they can be replaced atomically with the `rename()` call. Of course, that doesn't mean that they can't also reside in a different directory. Creating a `/var/mail/.pop` directory for these files certainly would be acceptable, but make sure that `.pop` isn't allowed as a valid user name!

4.8 IMAP Tuning Specifics

Three popular Open Source IMAP server solutions exist: the University of Washington (UW), Cyrus, and Courier IMAP solutions. Each has its own niche and characteristics that makes it the best choice under certain circumstances. In this document, we will only briefly consider the performance implications of these services, as a truly in-depth analysis would require an extra book. IMAP is a very complicated protocol, much more so than any other aspect of email service, and its intricacies also will not be discussed here in any depth. For an understanding of the issues involved in running an Open Source IMAP server, check out *Managing IMAP* [MM00].

Generally, IMAP access differs from POP access in several ways. First, IMAP processes tend to be comparatively long lived. While the typical interaction with an email server using POP is to log on, download all new email, and then log off, a typical IMAP session might be to log on at the beginning of the day when one arrives at work, and then log off at the end of the day when one leaves, staying connected the entire time. On a POP server that provides service for 200,000 concurrent users, no more than a few thousand POP connections are likely to be active at any one time, and perhaps many fewer. With IMAP, however, a majority of the server's users may be connected at once. This setup creates some serious problems if an IMAP server uses one process per connection. Many operating systems don't even provide 100,000 unique process identification (PID) numbers, much less function adequately when nearly this many processes are active simultaneously. All of the Open Source solutions require one process per open connection, so supporting many tens of thousands of concurrent IMAP users on a single server running any of these Open Source packages simply will not work very well.

One might decide to adopt a commercial solution based on a multithreaded IMAP server, but a problem still exists. Even though one could theoretically hold millions of simultaneous socket connections open on a single server, each open file consumes a file descriptor, each session consumes some amount of memory, some practical limit usually restricts the number of concurrent threads an operating system will support, and other tables may become filled or lookups may become so inefficient that the whole system can't run. Therefore, under any except the most extreme circumstances, any single server is unlikely to be able to support more than a few tens of thousands of concurrent active IMAP connections at once. Consequently, dividing the user base over several servers will be necessary. In any case, both commercial multithreaded IMAP daemons and handling of multiple servers are beyond the scope of this book.

Aside from the long duration of connections, IMAP differs radically from POP in the duration one expects a message to remain on the server. With POP, messages will likely be downloaded to a local machine for storage, processing, editing, and response. With IMAP, all of these actions may take place on the IMAP server itself. As a consequence, the amount of disk space consumed by the average IMAP user will be much larger than that used by the average POP user, often by several orders of magnitude. While message sizes will not change just because of the protocol, the frequency of access to each message will. Even though disk access patterns will still remain synchronous, small, and randomly located, a much lower percentage of the total available disk space will be accessed during any given time period. Therefore, fast I/O channels, NVRAM, journaling, and fast metadata updates will all be just as important as they are in the POP case, but disks generally should be larger. In addition to the POP-like workload, they will be carrying a large amount of infrequently accessed data.

In populating RAID systems for IMAP service, mirroring (RAID Level 1) is typically not feasible, as too much disk space will be required for it to be cost-effective. RAID Level 5 or RAID 50 will be the preferred way to go. Also, instead of buying the smallest, fastest disks available, buying the largest, fastest disk will generally yield the best results. Total RAID system storage capacity then becomes important. In the POP case, I/O bandwidth would almost certainly become saturated long before the RAID system was completely populated with disks. With IMAP, it's even more difficult to give hard and fast rules on how much space each user will need; rather, the answer will depend very much on the user's workload, sophistication, environment, and types of messages typically sent in the organization. Count on this, though: No matter how much space one provides, it will eventually get filled. Usage of IMAP message store space is much more like a user's home directory than POP server space. An email server that is deployed with the maximal amount of disk space available will need to be replaced in short order, regardless of the users' access patterns.

Another feature of IMAP is that the user has available a great deal more information about and options concerning the messages stored by the server. Requests for header information from a range of messages, shared mailboxes, and message searching capabilities are just some of the myriad commands supported in the IMAP protocol. Many IMAP message stores try to at least partially optimize for these requests, but if a large percentage of a server's user base performs searches over a large number of messages, I/O bandwidth will be exhausted and the machine will run slowly. Not much can be done about this problem, but it makes capacity planning difficult. Expect that even with a stable user population, as time goes on, mailboxes will grow, people will handle more email per capita, and users will increasingly resort to more demanding options on the server. IMAP servers will constantly need to be upgraded over time, and it would be wise to plan for that eventuality up front.

UW IMAP is the reference implementation of the IMAP protocol. It can flexibly be adapted to a wide variety of message store formats, although most often it uses a slightly modified version of the 7th Edition folder format. For smaller servers, UW IMAP performs adequately, but it lacks some of the feature sets of other IMAP systems. Due to its relatively poor performance characteristics, this package is rarely used in demanding environments.

Cyrus is probably the most commonly deployed Open Source IMAP solution. It is built around its own message store format, which uses a one-file-per-message layout as described earlier in this chapter. Cyrus comes with its own LDA, called `deliver`, which replaces `mail.local` when used with `sendmail`. Cyrus has reasonably good scalability characteristics, but I don't know of an Open Source-based IMAP server that supports more than 100,000 total users. At such a scale, it's doubtful that more than 10% of the subscriber base is active at any point in time. At the time of this writing, the most current version of the Cyrus IMAP software is 2.1.5, but many sites continue to run the latest release of version 1.6 due to concerns about Cyrus 2's stability. The Cyrus folks have been making real progress in increasing the stability of Cyrus 2 (it's already more stable than several commercially available IMAP servers), so watch progress on this version carefully.

Courier is a complete email solution based on the `maildir` format. Courier has logged less field time than the other two solutions mentioned here. Nonetheless, quite a few sites are using it. Its performance characteristics seem fairly good, but a head-to-head performance comparison between Courier and Cyrus would clarify this issue. I'm not aware of any really large-scale Courier installations, but that lack doesn't mean that it wouldn't be straightforward to scale.

4.9 Summary

- Email reception, storage, and access are very I/O-intensive processes.
- Both the LDA and the MTA contribute to email peformance when delivering email. The POP and IMAP daemons contribute to email performance when email is being accessed.
- For large message stores, some form of RAID system will probably be necessary. RAID Levels 1 and 0+1 are best for relatively small volumes. RAID 5 or RAID 50 is usually most appropriate for very large message stores. Good hardware RAID is usually superior to software RAID, and is mandatory when running RAID 5.
- Small, fast disks usually are best for email applications, especially if the email is stored transiently.
- Good RAID systems can be very difficult to find. There is no substitute for rigorous testing.

Chapter 5

Tuning Email Sending

A large number of legitimate organizations send out enormous amounts of email to happy subscribers every day. However, it can be difficult to provide information on how to better accomplish this task without also providing information that is valuable to spammers, people who send out vast amounts of unsolicited email, typically advertising shady or illegal products. One key difference between the legitimate bulk-email houses and spammers is that the bad guys don't care if some of their messages get lost along the way. In contrast, those organizations providing a service that people actually want are more likely to make sure that their information reaches its intended destination. Spammers tend to "fire and forget" email messages, whereas large, beneficial mailing lists want to `fsync()` messages as they're queued to ensure that they don't vanish. Therefore, by focusing on "safe" outbound emailing, we can provide information of value to legitimate mass-mailing houses without fear that the spammers will benefit significantly from it.

In general, the problem of sending out mass email can be divided into three categories:

- Mailing lists
- Generating and sending email from a UNIX command line
- Draining preconfigured email queues

Each has its own characteristics and will be dealt with separately in this chapter.

5.1 Mailing Lists

In their simplest form, mailing lists are single email addresses that represent more than one actual recipient, sometimes as many as hundreds of thousands of unique individuals. A mailing list server can never be certain when the next message for a given list might come in, but its goal will be to take a single incoming message for the list and send it out to all subscribers as quickly as possible. Messages might come in a flurry or a great deal of time may pass between them, but the server must be able to handle a large volume of messages in short order during times when the list heats up.

A mailing list server largely functions as a mail relay, as described earlier in this book, except that it sends much more outbound email than it receives. The same issues with queue performance arise here. We want cheap metadata operations, the safety of synchronous writes with asynchronous-like performance, and parallelism of as many operations as possible.

When a message is sent to multiple recipients, sendmail usually creates only one df file and one qf file for the whole lot of them. Under some circumstances the envelope will be split, but these instances are relatively rare and don't affect general performance. If we can expediently handle the qf files with large numbers of recipients, then the few single-recipient qf files won't pose much of a problem. Consequently, it takes far fewer directory operations to send a message to 10 people than it does to send 10 messages to one person each. This works in our favor.

With sendmail 8.12, one can force the envelope to split after a specified number of users by setting the "r" option for the default queue group and assigning an appropriate value to it. Here is an example in which we limit the maximum number of recipients per envelope to 10 for the default queue:

```
QUEUE_GROUP('mqueue', 'P=/var/spool/mqueue, r=10')
```

See the *Sendmail Installation and Operation Guide*, section 2.3.1 [ASA], for more information about setting up queue groups.

It is somewhat ironic that for very large mailing lists, the creation of *more* qf files will speed up delivery, because the DNS lookup, connection, and delivery for several recipients at once can be performed in parallel. Of course, achieving parallelism requires multiple concurrent queue runners, but that is straightforward to implement. It does require more operations in the queue, but the increase is not directly proportional to the number of times the envelope is split. Multiple distinct qf files will exist, but there will be only one df file with multiple names (hard links). The same number of metadata operations are performed as if all the split envelopes concerned separate messages, but the contents of the (common) message body are written only once.

Finding the optimal number of recipients for splitting the qf files is tricky. With large numbers of queue runners and small numbers of messages, we want to set the number of recipients per message as low as possible. This choice creates a large number of qf files in the queue, which we can process in parallel to obtain the maximum message throughput. Obviously, as the message rate increases, the number of concurrent messages in the queue will go up. At some point, we will run out of I/O bandwidth in accessing the queue, and the number of qf files will pass the threshold at which we can speed up delivery through increased parallelism. Instead, the overhead caused by the sheer number of qf files will start to slow throughput down; at this point and beyond, fewer queue entries would be better. This is a delicate act to balance, and no simple formula will yield the optimal number of recipients per message. Instead, this metric must be determined by observation.

As a method to determine what the "sweet spot" might be in terms of the number of recipients per message, we might start with a relatively aggressive maximum number of recipients—the number 10, used in the configuration example, is quite aggressive—and see how it works. If the queue starts to back up, as represented by large numbers of qf files and slow access times in the queue, then raising this number is probably appropriate. Of course, this choice requires careful monitoring of the system, but scripts that count the number of qf files sitting in the queue are straightforward to write and are part of any vigilant server monitoring effort.

After making an adjustment, we want to make sure a sufficient amount of time has elapsed so that we have a representative feel for the loading of the server. If queue processing hasn't slowed down due to the number of concurrent messages in the queue, perhaps an even more aggressive envelope splitting strategy would be appropriate. I wouldn't recommend setting this value any lower than 10 unless it takes longer to process each message than is tolerable for that list.

Another modification to the sendmail.cf file that can help directly is raising the value of the CheckpointInterval variable. As a sendmail process tries to deliver messages to the recipients listed in the qf file, after a certain number of successful deliveries it will update the qf file to reflect the delivery status of the message to those users. By default, the value of CheckpointInterval is set to 10. This number can be raised—for example, by adding the following line to the .mc file:

```
define('confCHECKPOINT_INTERVAL','100')
```

Updating the qf file requires metadata operations. A tf file is created with the updated information and then rename()ed to replace the existing qf file. Therefore, raising this parameter will lower the number of operations needed to be performed during processing of a single message bound for many recipients. There is a downside to this strategy, of course. If a message is sent to a set of recipients but the machine crashes before the qf file is checkpointed, then when the server comes back up those subscribers who were sent the message after the last checkpoint will receive the message a second time. Of course, as inconvenient as receiving the same message twice might be, duplicates are not the same caliber of evil as lost messages are.

Of course, if the checkpoint interval exceeds the envelope splitting parameter, altering it further in that range will change nothing.

As noted earlier, the multiple queues introduced in `sendmail` version 8.10 can help ease the congestion on busy email relays. On mailing list servers this ability isn't quite as useful. Instead of having many different queue entries over which one may parallelize the delivery load, we have a much smaller number of files with multiple recipients. However, some benefit can still be obtained by frequently rotating queues so that recently spawned queue runners don't have to work through a lot of temporarily undeliverable messages. The queue rotation interval might be quite frequent. In some cases, rotating the queue every few minutes might prove optimal. On servers that handle infrequent messages to very large numbers of recipients, one might even want to rotate the queue after each message. Some experimentation will help to strike the right balance.

A danger with frequent queue rotation for busy mailing lists is that if a clogged queue is rotated, it may take a very long time to drain. In the meantime, new messages coming in to a new, fast queue may be processed very quickly. As a consequence, mailing list messages will be delivered out of order. One cannot completely avoid this hazard, and anyone who has subscribed to an email mailing list for any length of time will have observed this behavior. This unavoidable problem is an intrinsic part of the email medium. Nevertheless, recipients may become confused if email messages that are part of a dialogue arrive out of order, so one should avoid this phenomenon to the extent possible. Usually, paying a little bit in performance to substantially reduce subscriber confusion is worthwhile. Does this mean that busy queues on mailing list servers shouldn't be rotated? No, it doesn't. However, every time a queue or a mailing list server becomes busy, a risk arises that the list's messages will be delivered out of order. Even though many smart MUAs will present the messages to the user in their proper order, this issue should be viewed as just one more reason to make every reasonable effort to avoid letting queues get badly clogged.

Many people have struggled with the prospect of improving mailing list performance. Descriptions of the trials and tribulations of managing a mailing list server using older versions of `sendmail` can be found in papers by Rob Kolstad [KOL97] and the crew at GNAC [CHK+98].

5.2 Command-Line Message Generation

A collection of messages to be sent may reside in files on local storage, or the messages may be generated on the fly by a UNIX process that then hands them off for delivery by `sendmail` via a socket or a pipe. Sometimes the latter approach is called "interactive" email delivery. While it technically has nothing to do with `sendmail`'s "interactive" delivery mode, starting with version 8.12, this mode is generally preferred for performing mass mailings of this variety. In general, interactive mail delivery greatly resembles the processes involved in relaying email messages, so almost everything said so far about relaying applies to this situation as well. The main distinction is that not only is the relaying server under one's control, but the message originator, often called the "injector," is as well. This ability to control message creation and injection works to our advantage.

Running in interactive delivery mode with SuperSafe also set to interactive can vastly reduce disk operations. When these variables are set, the sendmail 8.12 process that accepts the connection attempts immediate redelivery, writing the message to disk only if the first redelivery attempt fails, assuming the message is short. Because the sending side knows the size of these messages, no good reason exists not to make sure that the buffering threshold of the MTA exceeds the size of all messages involved in this transaction. For mass mailings, the messages tend to be relatively compact for the obvious reasons. The details of this configuration were chronicled in Section 3.2.

Recall that the downside for interactive delivery mode is that it might cause the SMTP (or pipe) connection from the injector to remain open longer while delivery is attempted. When the injector resides on a local network and under our control, this issue shouldn't be a problem. On the client side, a single injector process must simply wait a little longer for the connection to close. In the meantime, a well-written injector should consume no CPU resources and almost no memory. The exception arises when the injector process must be serial—that is, if we can't run more than one injector per machine at any one time. In this case, the duration of the connection between the injector and the relayer should be made as short as possible under almost any circumstances, and total system throughput certainly will increase if sendmail runs in background mode. As long as the requirement is in place, the relaying machines are unlikely to act as the bottleneck.

If the injector supports SMTP, why not have it make the connections with the email servers of the intended recipients directly? The answer is that while it is straightforward to write a program that hands email via SMTP off to a well-understood program such as sendmail for relaying, sending Internet email involves much more than implementing code to correctly handle a client SMTP session. Just scratching the surface, the injector would have to understand SMTP's DNS requirements and DSNs, implement a queueing mechanism for failed connections, and deal gracefully with other email servers' flawed SMTP implementations. Once one has accounted for these requirements, one has written half (the sending half) of an entire MTA. I can't recommend going to all of this trouble. It's a lot of work, and it's even more difficult than it first seems.

Whenever possible, the injector should sort messages by the destination domain so that a minimum number of SMTP connections and a minimal amount of qf file rewriting take place on the sending machine. Starting with sendmail version 8.12, the MTA may sort a list with multiple recipients by recipient domain before the message is queued, but it's always cheaper if this step occurs before the messages are handed off to sendmail. Also, it should be fairly obvious that if a single message will go to 9 recipients at a single domain and 11 recipients at another domain, it would be better to send the 9 bound for the single domain in one batch and the 11 bound for the other domain in another than to send the messages in two groups of 10 in any combination.

If a site runs sendmail version 8.12 using the default installation, the sendmail binary will not have been installed as set-user-ID root, but the main mail queue, /var/spool/mqueue, remains writable only by the root user. In these environments, if sendmail is invoked from the command line, the message will first be queued in a special queue, usually /var/spool/clientmqueue, and then the message will be sent via an SMTP session to the master sendmail daemon listening on port 25 of that machine. This daemon will also queue the message (typically in /var/spool/mqueue) before sending it to its final destination.

From a performance standpoint, this double-queueing of outbound email is inefficient. Where the performance of sending email from the command line is important, it will be desirable to eliminate the writes into clientmqueue. Version 8.12 of sendmail will attempt to contact the recipient's email server directly via SMTP, queueing the message only once, as long as two conditions are met:

1. sendmail must not find the submit.cf file, usually stored in /etc/mail.

2. sendmail must still be able to queue messages.

It is straightforward to make sure that the first condition is met. The second condition can be met in several ways. The sendmail program can be run by the root user, the binary can be installed as set-user-ID root, or the program can be run by naming a special queue to which the user invoking sendmail can write. For example:

```
/usr/sbin/sendmail -oQ/home/npc/mqueue npc@acm.org
```

Of these three options, I'd recommend adopting the last one in most mass-mailing environments. The root user could also bypass the clientmqueue directory even if the submit.cf file exists by using the -Am flag on the sendmail command line:

```
/usr/sbin/sendmail -Am npc@acm.org
```

5.3 Draining Queues

At the outset, I should point out that this third strategy for the mass mailing of files is the one I recommend least. It would be very easy to get a little sloppy with this method and cause a considerable amount of heartache, either in terms of work that needs to be redone or in the creation of an email mess for the intended recipients of the messages. The reader should consider this method to be included primarily for completeness.

Another option to consider for mass mailing is to precreate sendmail qf and df files in directories (queues) and, when the appropriate time to send comes, run sendmail -q -oQ*/path/to/directory* to drain the queues. This strategy requires a solid knowledge of the format of the qf files, which isn't too difficult to determine. Much of the information is available in Costales' *sendmail* book [CA97]. More up-to-date but terse information can be found in a comment inside the sendmail/queue.c file. Good prototypes for these files can be generated using the following method:

1. Start sendmail on a test machine in queue-only mode: sendmail -odq -bd.

2. Send several pieces of email to the test machine with the destination of addresses that belong to the sender. We don't want to spam anyone in case we make a mistake.

3. Shut down sendmail, and then move the messages out of /var/spool/ mqueue for inspection and use as templates.

Here's an example qf file that we might use as a prototype. It was sent from a machine using sendmail version 8.12.0.

```
V6
T1001371039
K0
N0
P120381
Fbs
$_root@localhost
${daemon_flags}c u
Snpc
Anpc@discovery.gangofone.com
C:npc@acm.org
rRFC822; npc@acm.org
```

```
RPFD:npc@acm.org
H?P?Return-Path: <<\081>g>
H?x?Full-Name: Nick Christenson
H??Received: (from npc@localhost)
        by discovery.gangofone.com (8.12.0/8.12.0/Submit) id
        f8OMbJVu087571 for npc@acm.org; Mon, 24 Sep 2001 15:37:19
        -0700 (PDT)
H??Date: Mon, 24 Sep 2001 15:37:19 -0700 (PDT)
H??From: Nick Christenson <npc@discovery.gangofone.com>
H??Message-Id:<200109242237.f8OMbJVu087571@discovery.gangofone.com>
H??To: npc@acm.org
H??Subject: test
.
```

Let's take a closer look at some of these lines and what they represent.

The first line begins with "V", which denotes the version number for the format of the file. The version number for sendmail 8.12 files is 6. This file cannot be parsed by sendmail 8.11 or earlier releases.

The second two fields, "T" and "K", denote the time that the message was created and the time that it was last processed, respectively. Because the qf file in this example was never processed, the file includes K0. These times are written in the UNIX time_t format, so they represent the number of seconds since the beginning of 1970. This number is used when determining whether a message is too old for delivery. If a sendmail process fails to deliver this message, and the current time minus the T value is greater than the Timeout.queuereturn value in the /etc/mail/sendmail.cf file, the message will be bounced. If the current time minus the T value is greater than the Timeout.queuewarn value, then a warning message will be sent. For mass mailings, such a warning message is probably undesirable. The sender can easily determine which messages haven't been sent yet by inspecting the queues, so Timeout.queuewarn should be set to 0 and Timeout.queuereturn should be set either very high or to 0. In pregenerated qf files, T should be very close to, but not more than, the actual time at which the message will be sent. The K value should be set to either T or 0.

The "N" value indicates the number of times delivery has been attempted for this message. It should be set to 0 as in this case, or the line should be omitted.

The "P" value is the message's priority. Priority isn't quite as useful a parameter as its name might imply. Under most circumstances, it's a good idea to set the priorities of all messages in a single queue to the same integer, such as 1, or to omit the field from the file.

The "S" line is required; it contains the sender's email address in RFC 2821 format. In this case, because the message was set from the command line, it has not yet been canonified. Once canonified, it will be used as the argument to the MAIL command in the SMTP envelope of the message transmission.

The "r" line contains the original recipient. This information provides the address to which DSNs would be sent. The "R" line contains the recipient address in RFC 2821 format. One of these lines should appear for each recipient of the message. The second letter "P" in this field stands for "primary," which is usually the appropriate choice. The "D" indicates that this message requests delay DSNs, if appropriate. An "F" indicates that this message requests failure DSNs.

After the "R" line come the message headers, in the formats specified in the `sendmail.cf` file. Take special care when altering these lines, as changes to them can have side effects. More information on headers can be found in Appendix B of the *Sendmail Installation and Operation Guide*.

If pregenerated `qf` files will be used, one may as well sort the recipients to optimize delivery. If multiple recipients of a message reside in a single domain, put as many of these recipients as is practical in a single message. This clustering will save resources on both the sending and receiving server, as the message will need to be transmitted only once for all of these recipients. To discourage spammers, some sites will set the `sendmail MaxRecipientsPerMessage` parameter in their configuration files. After this threshold is exceeded, the receiving server will issue temporary failure codes for succeeding recipients of the message. These messages will have to be re-sent. This threshold will differ for each site, but on servers that have it set, it typically does not exceed 100, but rarely is set to less than 10. Therefore, it should be safe for the time being to construct messages to be sent to 10 simultaneous recipients. With these sorts of numbers, if some recipients are initially rejected, the duplicate effort will be minimized. If information on the policies of each domain can be compiled, it would make sense to use it when pregenerating messages in the future.

Pregenerating `qf` files offers the advantage of allowing one to finely control numbers of recipients per message, queue sizes, and numbers of queues, although this level of granularity is rarely necessary. Going through these gymnastics makes sense only when one has a lot of email to send, interactive delivery mode with `sendmail` 8.12 isn't realistic, a considerable amount of preparation time is available before the messages need to go out, and the messages must be sent out very quickly when that moment arrives. In fact, pregenerating `qf` files is a dangerous business in general. Before going live with such a scheme, messages should be carefully tested to make sure their results are sane. It is easy to get wrong, so it's not recommended that email be sent this way at all.

5.4 Another Mailing List Strategy

A strategy that several sites have used to expedite email delivery deserves some mention, and this is as good a place to do it as any. The idea is to split up the reception of email messages and queue processing tasks with the notion that sending email can become more efficient by aggregating messages in the queue bound for a given destination rather than trying to send out email as it arrives. Basically, the sendmail daemon listening to port 25 will run in queue-only mode. That is, as messages come into the server, they are accepted and written to the queue, but no immediate delivery attempt is made. At the same time, several sendmail processes run that simply process the queue. Instead of initiating a sendmail daemon at start-up that does both,

```
/usr/sbin/sendmail -bd -q30m
```

two sets of processes would be started:

```
/usr/sbin/sendmail -bd -odq
/usr/sbin/sendmail -q30m
```

As part of this strategy, when a queue run starts, the queue is sorted by recipient, which is QueueSortOrder=host, in the .cf file. Therefore, when the queue run starts, all of the qf files whose first recipient is bound for the same domain will be processed at the same time, ideally minimizing the number of SMTP sessions required to deliver all queued messages. The intent is that spawning the minimal number of SMTP sessions will minimize the amount of effort expended by the server to get messages to their destinations.

When using this strategy, several other parameters are often altered so as to further improve performance. First, MinQueueAge is usually set to ensure that queued messages sit in the queue for some period of time before being sent. This idea is exactly the opposite of the strategy usually advocated in this book. The rationale is that we *want* messages bound for the same domain to accumulate in the queue before they are sent, so that all can be transferred in one connection. In this example, we might fire off a new queue runner every few minutes, maybe even every minute. To accomplish this task, we can invoke sendmail with

```
/usr/sbin/sendmail -q5m
```

but set up the configuration file in the following manner:

```
define('confQUEUE_SORT_ORDER', 'host')
define('confMIN_QUEUE_AGE', '30m')
define('confMAX_QUEUE_CHILDREN', '100')
```

At the rapid rate that queue runners are started, it's possible that a sudden flurry of messages will lead to delays in queue runners finishing their queue runs. This problem might cause more processes than optimal to work on the queues to operate at the same time. Therefore, we cap this number by using confMAX_QUEUE_CHILDREN, just to make sure things don't get too far out of hand.

Using sendmail 8.12, another optimization uses the queue groups features—namely, SplitAcrossQueueGroups—to split envelopes such that qf files with multiple recipients tend to have all of those recipients at the same domain placed within the same qf file. A good example of how this approach might be used is available in the file sendmail/TUNING in the 8.12 source distribution. If the recipient list in a qf file contains nine email addresses from a popular domain such as aol.com and one recipient from the domain very-obscure-smtp-site.com, but the latter recipient is listed first in the qf file, a queue runner won't know that associating this message with others bound for aol.com might be a good idea. Therefore, this strategy will suffer if none of the following conditions are met:

1. Each message is bound for a single recipient.
2. The messages are grouped by destination when injected into the machine.
3. sendmail can use queue groups to split up the recipients by domain.

In its totality, this strategy runs counter to just about everything mentioned so far in this book. Let's look at it more closely and see what it is really designed to accomplish. First, because messages will always sit in the queue for some time before being progressed, this strategy will by no means minimize the amount of time needed to deliver the message to its final destination. In fact, if lowering the average or maximum transit time of the email is a critical factor, this strategy should absolutely not be used. Second, every message will sit in the queue for some period of time before its first delivery attempt is made. If a delivery attempt has never been attempted for a message, then the first time a queue runner encounters a message in the queue it will attempt to deliver the message regardless of whether confMIN_QUEUE_AGE is set. In any case, we'll still have more queued messages at any one time—possibly orders of magnitudes more—than with the other strategies advocated in this book. While using version 8.12 queue groups with a large number of queues and envelope splitting based on recipient domain can reduce this number, this strategy will almost certainly result in relatively deep queues, something the rest of this book warns against as being a tremendous hazard.

So, what is being saved? This strategy reduces two things. First, the number of SMTP sessions that need to be spawned in total is drastically reduced. This change decreases the number of DNS lookups that need to be performed as well as likely minimizing memory consumption, the number of `fork()`s that need to occur, and so on. Second, the total number of write operations in the queue is minimized. While queues may be deep, a fairly small number of writes will occur in them, as each `qf` file should never need to be rewritten; rather, it will be written and then unlinked. The number of reads of `qf` files shouldn't increase much, as the files need not be opened to determine when they entered a queue. The creation time (`ctime`) of the file can be discerned by `stat()`ing the file.

If larger numbers of queued messages don't pose a problem, no real need for rapid message delivery exists, but the number of total SMTP connections should be minimized, or queue runners using another policy get through their queue runs slowly, this technique might be effective. On the busiest email servers, this strategy likely would not be useful. The large number of queued messages would tend to be too high a price to pay for any optimization in SMTP connections. Instead, in those circumstances, aggressive envelope splitting, rapid queue rotation, and multiple queue runners sorting by `random` will usually achieve higher throughput than the methods described above, although some systems do use this method effectively. Finally, note that this strategy will usually be more effective for outbound email sending. In most cases, it would not be a useful way to handle inbound email.

5.5 SMTP PIPELINING

Starting in version 8.12, `sendmail` implements support for SMTP PIPELIN-ING. A complete description of this feature appears in RFC 2920 [FRE00]. A brief description will be given here. Basically, PIPELINING allows the sending of multiple SMTP commands without having to wait for a response from the server. Some commands can be sent in this manner, such as the transmission of SMTP envelope information. Some SMTP commands may not be pipelined, such as DATA, QUIT, and NOOP.

Let us consider a sample SMTP conversation without the use of PIPELINING. In the following examples, the client side of the conversation is prefaced with a "`C:`" and the server side of the conversation is prefaced with an "`S:`". Lines preceded by neither an "`S:`" nor a "`C:`" are continuations of the previous line. A short horizontal line denotes a separate request or response sent by the client or server:

```
S: 220 discovery.gangofone.com ESMTP Sendmail 8.12.2/8.12.2;
   Tue, 9 Feb 2002 18:04:55 -0800 (PST)
--
C: EHLO streaker.gangofone.com
--
S: 250-discovery.gangofone.com Hello streaker.gangofone.com,
   pleased to meet you
S: 250-ENHANCEDSTATUSCODES
S: 250-8BITMIME
S: 250-SIZE
S: 250-DSN
S: 250-ETRN
S: 250-STARTTLS
S: 250-DELIVERBY
S: 250 HELP
--
C: MAIL FROM:<npc@streaker.gangofone.com>
--
S: 250 2.1.0 <npc@streaker.gangofone.com>... Sender ok
--
C: RCPT TO:<jim@gangofone.com>
--
S: 250 2.1.5 <jim@gangofone.com>... Recipient ok
--
C: RCPT TO:<scott@gangofone.com>
--
S: 250 2.1.5 <scott@gangofone.com>... Recipient ok
--
C: DATA
--
S: 354 Enter mail, end with "." on a line by itself
--
C: Subject: Hello!
C: [other headers omitted for the sake of brevity]
C:
C: Thinking about it, I've got nothing to say.
C: .
--
S: 250 2.0.0 g1PNlHLq032937 Message accepted for delivery
--
C: QUIT
--
S: 221 2.0.0 discovery.gangofone.com closing connection
```

Sending this message required 15 separate messages to be exchanged between the client and server.

    This is what the SMTP conversation would look like if both the client and server supported SMTP PIPELINING:

```
S: 220 discovery.gangofone.com ESMTP Sendmail 8.12.2/8.12.2;
   Tue, 9 Feb 2001 18:05:25 -0800 (PST)
--
C: EHLO streaker.gangofone.com
--
S: 250-discovery.gangofone.com Hello streaker.gangofone.com,
   pleased to meet you
S: 250-ENHANCEDSTATUSCODES
S: 250-PIPELINING
S: 250-8BITMIME
S: 250-SIZE
S: 250-DSN
S: 250-ETRN
S: 250-STARTTLS
S: 250-DELIVERBY
S: 250 HELP
--
C: MAIL FROM:<npc@streaker.gangofone.com>
C: RCPT TO:<jim@gangofone.com>
C: RCPT TO:<scott@gangofone.com>
C: DATA
--
S: 250 2.1.0 <npc@streaker.gangofone.com>... Sender ok
S: 250 2.1.5 <jim@gangofone.com>... Recipient ok
S: 250 2.1.5 <scott@gangofone.com>... Recipient ok
S: 354 Enter mail, end with "." on a line by itself
--
C: Subject: Hello!
C: [other headers omitted for the sake of brevity]
C:
C: Upon further reflection, I've got nothing to say.
C: .
C: QUIT
--
S: 250 2.0.0 g1PNlHLq032937 Message accepted for delivery
S: 221 2.0.0 discovery.gangofone.com closing connection
```

The same information is exchanged, but this time it required only seven network round trips to complete the session.

In situations where messages have a very large number of recipients, or on networks where the latency is exceptionally high, PIPELINING can provide a significant benefit. The same data move between client and server, which means the same bandwidth is consumed and the same disk operations need to be performed. Fewer TCP packets are sent, however, and we expect the total exchange to consume less time. This results in fewer concurrent processes running on the servers. The use of PIPELINING doesn't always produce a large improvement in performance, but in the case of sending large mailing lists, it may yield a significant positive effect.

Of course, for PIPELINING to effectively reduce the duration of SMTP sessions, both the client and server must support it. As of this writing, few large ISPs, which represent the destinations of a large percentage of large mailing list email, run MTAs that support this extension. Further, because it was introduced to `sendmail` fairly recently, there is not yet a large body of experience from which the overall effects of this feature can be evaluated. However, making sure a mass-mailing SMTP client can support this feature is a good idea. The benefits of doing so may not be significant at the present time, but the advantages will likely become more apparent as more sites run MTAs that support this feature.

5.6 More Notes on Mass Mailing

When using a message injector, this procedure can carefully track the success and failure of each message being sent, and can regenerate a given message if a catastrophe occurs. In this case, and probably only in this case, it wouldn't be unreasonable to turn the `SuperSafe` option off, so `fsync()`s won't occur and I/O would be sped up considerably. If `SuperSafe` is set to `False`, one must be able to detect and be willing to reconstruct incomplete message deliveries at the time of a server crash; in most cases, then, it's easier to keep `SuperSafe` on or set to `interactive`. This is especially true if the relay server runs 8.12 in `interactive` delivery mode, where most of those writes won't occur anyway.

It's obvious that several injector processes running on an email server and passing their email to `sendmail` via a pipe can operate at the same time, using a format such as `injector filename|sendmail -t`. It should also be apparent that if several `sendmail` processes are invoked from the command line, they don't all have to use the same queue:

```
injector filename1|sendmail -t -oi -oQ/var/spool/mqueue-a
injector filename2|sendmail -t -oi -oQ/var/spool/mqueue-b
injector filename3|sendmail -t -oi -oQ/var/spool/mqueue-c
```

These queues can be different directories on the same disk, or they may reside on different filesystems on their own disks. One should attempt to increase parallelism and reduce contention in shared file areas wherever possible on email servers. Many creative ways exist to achieve this goal, and these solutions are worth seeking out. However, it would be impossible to state generally what the optimal parameters are without a detailed understanding of a specific situation. A potential fix must be tried and iterated to realize as much parallelism as possible from multiple processes without thrashing the disk.

In the injector command line, the -oi flag tells sendmail that a "." on a line by itself in the message does not constitute an end of transmission. Instead, that line is "dot stuffed" to make sure it isn't interpreted that way. Of course, this occurrence is unlikely, but it can't hurt to be careful. Also, this example assumes sendmail 8.12 syntax. On earlier versions, it was appropriate to add the -U flag to the command line to indicate that this message was an initial submission. However, no other email program that I'm aware of actually did so.

The -t flag tells sendmail to get its recipient list from the To: line in the message header. By default, the message will be sent as the user that invokes the sendmail process. This choice can be overridden on the command line by using the -f user@example.com syntax.

One final thing to remember: When sendmail is invoked from the command line in this way, any errors it encounters will be printed to STDERR. This outcome can be altered by using the -oex command-line flags, where x is the ErrorMode. One especially useful variation under these circumstances is the -oem option, which generates an email message to return the error to the sender. All allowed values for these options are well documented in Section 5.6 of the *Sendmail Installation and Operation Guide* included with the version 8.12 distribution.

5.7 Summary

- A major difference between legitimate mass mailing and spamming is that the legitimate mass mailers are generally interested in making sure all of their email reaches the intended recipients, whereas spammers don't care.

- For messages with a large number of recipients, the most important factor for improving throughput is making queue operations efficient.

- For messages with a large number of recipients, splitting the qf file can result in faster delivery because several delivery attempts can occur at once. The downside is that it results in more files and often more I/O operations in the queue directory. Optimizing against these two factors can prove quite challenging.

- When sending large amounts of email, the sender has control over how and at what rate the email is injected into the system. This information can be used to improve throughput.

## Chapter 6

Configuration, Security, and Architecture

Until this point, this book's primary consideration has been the general nature and operation of email systems and ways to tune the machines on which `sendmail` and other email software run. This chapter examines the configuration of `sendmail` itself, the trade-offs involved in weighing performance versus email security, and overall email service architecture. *Service architecture* involves strategies for making several email servers running `sendmail` cooperate effectively to improve the overall performance of the entire email system.

6.1 Configuration

This section explicitly focuses on the options available within the `sendmail.cf` file to see how modification of various parameters can improve throughput in different situations. I've waited until this point to discuss these issues because tuning the system's file I/O is almost always more effective in speeding email server throughput, but some configuration options can result in significant changes.

6.1.1 Timeouts

One set of configuration parameters that can lead to performance speedups involves changes to `sendmail`'s timeouts, although altering some parameters in this area can prove perilous. RFC 2821 specifies some minimum timeouts for MTAs at different phases of an SMTP protocol exchange. While `sendmail` will allow timeout parameters to be changed to values below the RFC recommendations, this step is rarely advisable. Some of these parameters may seem rather long and archaic on today's Internet. For example, it may not seem necessary to have to wait for 10 minutes to receive a "250 OK" message at the end of a DATA phase. However, these are the rules by which we play on the Internet, and breaking them should not be undertaken lightly or, in almost every case, at all. Besides, most of these time-out situations happen rarely and therefore have relatively little influence on overall performance. If the goal is to improve the total throughput of an email server, it is important to focus on speeding up those situations that arise frequently, as large cumulative improvements can be made there.

Timeout.ident

As noted earlier, operations that result in disk movement or network round trips are likely to be the tall tent poles when it comes to the total amount of time required to process an email message. Therefore, if an opportunity presents itself to remove a network query to a remote host, then that strategy should be seriously considered. A network round trip can be safely eliminated by setting the `Timeout.ident` variable to 0 from its default, `5s`. `sendmail` waits this amount of time for IDENT information to return from a remote server during an SMTP connection. If the variable is set to zero, the IDENT query is never attempted.

IDENT is a security protocol designed to return information regarding which user owns the client-side socket used in an Internet connection. This protocol is defined in RFC 1413 [JOH93]. It has little use in today's Internet because (1) it is applicable only to email sent by a user logged into a multiuser machine, relatively few of which exist these days, and (2) one cannot trust IDENT information coming from a server administered by someone else.

Most email servers don't run IDENT servers; on those without user accounts, the information IDENT provides is meaningless. For example, on all UNIX-based email gateways or proxies, we would expect the user identified in an IDENT request to always be `root`, `mailnull`, `daemon`, or some other generic system account. Strangely enough, the real delays that `sendmail` sees due to IDENT problems don't relate to servers that choose not to run IDENT daemons. Rather, they come from servers that reside behind firewalls that don't return a "connection refused" response for protocol requests that aren't supported—IDENT is almost always on the "unsupported" list.

Here is how this scenario works. My email server receives an SMTP connection from another server. After the connection is established but before my server returns the "220" greeting message, signaling that I am willing to carry out an SMTP conversation with the connecting server, I send an IDENT request back to the host originating the SMTP session. The originating host's firewall, which sits between the two servers, intercepts this request. The firewall then silently discards the packet. I now wait until the timeout value has expired before allowing the SMTP session to proceed. At best, the firewall displays antisocial behavior. In fact, I would go so far as to say this behavior is flat-out wrong. It's not uncommon on today's Internet, however, and each time a connection is made to a remote site that behaves in this fashion the duration of the SMTP session will be lengthened by the timeout value plus the time it takes for a network round trip. I always set `Timeout.ident` to 0 on all my email servers:

```
define('confTO_IDENT','0')
```

Timeout.iconnect

Some sites that send out a great deal of email will set the `Timeout.iconnect` variable to be lower than allowed in the RFCs, such as 10 seconds, but then provide a FallbackMX host with the same timeout set to an RFC-compliant value, minimally 5 minutes. Section 6.3 discusses the advantages of using a FallbackMX host more thoroughly. With this mechanism, the first attempt to send the message either succeeds or fails very quickly. If it fails because the remote server runs slowly, the message is shunted off for a more leisurely delivery on a server running at a lower load, thereby freeing resources on the "fast" relay to attempt the next delivery. While this method technically violates the RFCs, it does adhere to the spirit of these documents by allowing the remote server to be appropriately slow while minimally penalizing the sending host for this fact. In general, these sorts of optimizations should not be undertaken without careful consideration of all their ramifications.

Queue Processing Timeouts

Another set of timeouts that can modified are `Timeout.queuewarn` and `Timeout.queuereturn`. In some cases, messages cannot be sent to any server for some period of time. After `Timeout.queuewarn` (default of 4 hours) passes, the system generates a DSN warning the sender that the message hasn't yet been successfully delivered, but the server will keep trying. While this result can be convenient, it's just one more piece of email for the server to process, which adds to its overall burden. Indeed, this message often ends up being more confusing than helpful to many email users, especially in an ISP setting where the customers may not have much experience in these matters. In my ISP days, I saw more than one piece of irate email sent to the mailer-daemon demanding that it expedite mail delivery after a warning message was sent back to the user. I've even received an occasional piece of mailer-daemon fan mail, thanking this kind person for trying to help the sender get a message to a family member or friend. Especially in this environment, but also in a legitimate mass-mailing endeavor, increasing `Timeout.queuewarn`, even to a value higher than `Timeout.queuereturn`, or setting it to zero is entirely appropriate. However, DSNs signaling that email has been delayed is a feature that may be missed in an environment with more savvy Internet users.

`Timeout.queuereturn` denotes the amount of time that a message will remain queued before being bounced as undeliverable. The default `sendmail` value for this parameter is 5 days. Each truly undeliverable piece of email represents one extra item in the queue that is processed with each queue run. Each time it is processed, it slows down the processing of the rest of the queue, because the connection to the remote server can't be made. Therefore, decreasing this number may be appropriate. I would rarely recommend shortening this period to less than 3 days (the amount of time a corporate mail server might be down if it fails on Friday and service is restored Monday morning). This value doesn't account for the fact that this outage would be noticed and someone would scream long before the weekend concluded at most places, nor does it account for longer weekends that include vacation days. Of course, one can also mitigate this problem in a straightforward manner by rotating queues more frequently than `Timeout.queuereturn`—for example, daily.

Good information on SMTP timeouts appears in the *Sendmail Installation and Operation Guide* [ASA] and RFC 2821 [KLE01]. The reader is strongly advised to peruse the pertinent information in both of these documents before altering queue processing timeouts.

Resolver Timeouts

As has already been discussed, the nature of `sendmail`'s interaction with DNS services can have a significant effect on an email server's performance characteristics. Few Internet services provide an interface to alter the resolver library's behavior in response to differing network or server circumstances. Parameters such as timeouts are usually hard-coded into the resolver library itself; even in cases where applications may override these numbers, few elect to do so. Because the interactions between DNS and `sendmail` are so important, beginning with version 8.10, it became possible to alter some of the resolver's behavior within the `sendmail.cf` file.

Because DNS requests typically take the form of UDP packets, the only indication to a DNS client that a server received its request is a response. It's generally impossible to know how to interpret the lack of a timely reply. It might mean that the name daemon is not running on the remote host, that the server itself is down or overloaded, or that the server is up and operating but the specific information requested isn't immediately available. Typically, a resolver library will try to make a DNS query some small number of times—two to five attempts is typical—and will space these requests in time. Every 5 seconds is a default value present in some recent versions of BIND, although much longer timeouts, often exceeding 60 seconds, have historically been commonplace on some versions of UNIX.

The `Resolver.retry.*` parameters control how many different queries will be made of each name server listed in the `/etc/resolv.conf` file, usually with a maximum of three name servers listed. The `Resolver.retrans.*` parameters control the interval between retransmissions. In `sendmail`, the default for all `Resolver.retry.*` parameters is four attempts, and the default for all `Resolver.retrans.*` parameters is 5 seconds. More fine-grained control of these parameters is available. Each comes in a `Resolv.*.first` and `Resolv.*.normal` variety, as well as the default `Resolver.{resolv,retrans}` mechanism. The distinction between "first" and "normal" refers to the message delivery attempt, not to the particular DNS request attempt.

On a typically well-configured email server, the `resolv.conf` file will probably list two name servers. The first will be `127.0.0.1`, referring to the locally running caching-only name server, and the second will be a dedicated name server with an interface on the local network, on the off chance that the local name server stops responding for some unforeseen reason. If the locally running name server stops responding, we expect that condition to be detected in very short order by locally running automated processes and that fact to be reported to a human being very quickly. In the usual case, we expect the local name server to respond to the first attempt, and to respond very quickly. If IP packets are getting lost on the `loopback` interface, then the server has bigger problems than slow DNS queries. Even for the locally attached "backup" DNS server, the server should generally respond to the first request, or at least one of the first two, so it's probably acceptable to lower `Resolv.retry` to 2. While this change may yield a slight performance improvement, it probably won't make a noticeable performance difference under most circumstances, so no harm arises from leaving the default values intact.

As soon as they have an answer, both the name server on the `loopback` interface and the backup name server on the local network will respond to DNS requests very quickly. Even if the local name server is running on a machine a few network hops away, the bulk of the time spent waiting for a general DNS resolver request would likely relate to the query across the Internet from the name server to the root name servers and then the appropriate top-level name servers, not to any local data connection. Just because especially fast name servers are available, it doesn't mean that decreasing the `Resolv.retrans` value is a good idea. On today's Internet, 5 seconds is a pretty reasonable yet conservative period in which to expect a DNS response. Note that if the value of `Resolv.retry` is cut from

4 to 2, it will halve the maximum amount of time a given `sendmail` process will wait on DNS requests for a domain that is not responding from 20 seconds to 10 seconds. Decreasing this value, which is fairly safe, will have a more beneficial effect than trying to trim the `Resolv.retrans` interval. Similarly, if all DNS servers listed in `/etc/resolv.conf` are fairly reliable, and they should be, dropping the number listed from 3 to 2 will decrease the amount of time spent waiting for an answer from name servers that cannot be contacted by 33% without measurably affecting the service's reliability. Just because three (or more) name servers *can* be listed in the `resolv.conf` file doesn't mean that this choice is a good idea. Also, remember that this performance tuning will be meaningful only if the local name server does not have the information in its cache.

Much like the `Timeout.iconnect` example given earlier, some mass-mailing servers may wish to cut the `Resolv.*.first` parameters to lower the latency imposed on the average injector, figuring that most of the DNS responses will come very quickly. For example, the following lines added to a `.mc` file might be quite reasonable under these circumstances:

```
define('confTO_RESOLVER_RETRY_FIRST','2')
define('confTO_RESOLVER_RETRANS_FIRST','2s')
```

Thus a message bound for a recipient whose MX record cannot be resolved quickly would remain in the queue. Queue runners, no longer attempting to make the first delivery, would use the default values during redelivery, in case the name servers are up but responding slowly. If the system uses a FallbackMX host, then the mass-mailing machine should never attempt a redelivery, so it might seem tempting to set these values for all situations, rather than just for the first attempt. Of course, the FallbackMX host might not respond all the time, so some reasonably polite behavior during redelivery attempts by the mass-mailing host is appropriate.

On a strategic note, while these tuning parameters may speed up email delivery, one technique may help even more, especially in the mass-mailing case: priming the DNS cache before sending the email. In fact, during less busy times, running a script on the email server that will do MX lookups on each domain for a site's large client or mailing list—say, once a day—can really improve performance. It will guarantee that for every site whose DNS service remains up and that uses TTLs of no less than 24 hours, the DNS information will always remain in cache, and no queries over the Internet during the mass-mailing phase need to be made. For those servers receiving email, this strategy will prove less productive.

Note that the `*.normal` and `*.first` parameters are consulted only when sending email. The `Resolv.retrans` and `Resolv.retry` parameters affect all DNS lookups.

6.1.2 Load Limits

Few things are more annoying for an email administrator than dealing with a mail bomb. With a mail bomb, some user or server sends an inordinate amount of email, often very large messages, to a single user to create a nuisance. If the amount or rate of email is large enough, and adequate safeguards are lacking, a mail bomb can progress from being merely obnoxious to becoming a denial-of-service attack against the entire server.

One can try to mitigate this possibility by setting `MaxMessageSize` so that `sendmail` will automatically reject messages over a certain size limit. Some (well-constructed) MTAs will specify the message size during the envelope exchange so that the rejection may occur before any resources have been consumed in transmission, which is a good thing. The following is an example of such an ESMTP exchange. Lines beginning with "S:" indicate the protocol provided by the server, and those beginning with "C:" indicate the client's portion of the exchange. Lines that begin with neither of these letters are continuations of the previous line.

```
S: 220 discovery.gangofone.com ESMTP Sendmail 8.12.2/8.12.2;
   Tue, 9 Feb 2002 17:59:55 -0800 (PST)
C: EHLO streaker.gangofone.com
S: 250-discovery.gangofone.com Hello streaker.gangofone.com,
   pleased to meet you
S: 250-ENHANCEDSTATUSCODES
S: 250-PIPELINING
S: 250-8BITMIME
S: 250-SIZE 1000000
S: 250-DSN
S: 250-ETRN
S: 250-STARTTLS
S: 250-DELIVERBY
S: 250 HELP
C: MAIL FROM:<npc@streaker.gangofone.com> SIZE=5000000
S: 552 5.2.3 Message size exceeds fixed maximum message
   size (1000000)
```

In the exchange, the client suggested it would send a 5 million byte message, and the server rejected the message as too large. Details of this SMTP extension appear in RFC 1870 [KFM95].

With a pest or an older MTA that doesn't support the SIZE message extension, a server will have to accept at least part of the message before discarding it, but resources may still be saved. The problem is that people have become used to sending the most inappropriate things via email, to the extent that 100MB messages are not out of the ordinary at many sites, so this tactic has limited effectiveness. Many ISPs limit messages they handle to 10MB or smaller. This decision can reduce some of the more egregious offenses, and every little bit helps.

It is also possible to set these parameters for different mailers using the SMTP_MAILER_MAX, LOCAL_MAILER_MAX, UUCP_MAILER_MAX, or other configuration parameters. In this way, one could allow the relay of relatively large messages through a machine without accepting them for local delivery:

```
define('SMTP_MAILER_MAX','10000000')
define('LOCAL_MAILER_MAX','1000000')
```

In the .cf file, this task is accomplished by specifying the message size using the M= parameter of the appropriate mailer definition.

Some sendmail configuration parameters are based on the nebulous concept of the system load average. Explaining exactly what this average entails would be complex and outside the scope of this book, but roughly it consists of an average count over some time period of the number of runable jobs. On some operating systems, "jobs" means processes; on others, it means threads of execution. If the value of the load average exceeds the number of processors in a system, then some jobs are unable to run because they are waiting for some resource to become available. These resources might include waiting for a CPU time slice or waiting for access to a special device file, such as a tape drive. Performance shortcomings on an email server are rarely well represented by this metric.

One thing that doesn't count toward load average on most systems is a process that's blocked waiting for file I/O, something that happens quite frequently on a busy email server. Under most operating systems, the load average generally skyrockets on a dedicated email server only if a system becomes so busy that process tables fill or it runs out of memory, or if something else runs into problems on the machine that either shouldn't be running or shouldn't be having problems. In the latter case, the solution is clear. In the former case, a high load average indicates that something is wrong long after the situation has reached a dire state. Because load average is so rarely useful for measuring the business of an email server, altering sendmail's behavior based on these parameters typically provides fewer benefits than we might hope. Nonetheless, sendmail configuration options such as QueueLA and RefuseLA deserve mention here.

With Linux, jobs that are blocked waiting for I/O do count in the load average. While load averages rarely reach very high numbers on operating systems such as Solaris or FreeBSD, busy email servers using Linux can have load averages that are quite high in fairly typical use, and exceptionally high when under heavy load. Therefore, when setting `sendmail` configuration parameters based on load average, don't assume that they can be cavalierly transferred between Linux and non-Linux systems—they cannot. Even between different Linux systems what constitutes a high load average will depend greatly on the specifics of the filesystem and the storage system in use. In general, I recommend setting these parameters very high, perhaps in the hundreds, and lowering them only if the system's total throughput demonstrably decreases as the load average increases.

The `RefuseLA` variable indicates the load average at which the MTA will stop accepting new connections via SMTP. Once the load average drops below this mark, new connections will be permitted. Because this event usually indicates an email server that simply cannot keep up with demand, having this machine stop responding for a period of time is not a long-term solution. It generally creates a greater pent-up demand by having email that has not yet been delivered back up across the Internet. Therefore, while traffic remains high, once the server's load average dips below the `RefuseLA` watermark, a flood of connections will come in, sending the load average skyrocketing. This, in turn, will cause the MTA to refuse connections again for some time. Unfortunately, changing the email server's configuration parameter will not diffuse the situation very much. The solution is to improve the throughput of the email server.

As the amount of email handled by a server increases, the total throughput (in bytes per second or messages per second) will increase in tandem. This situation continues until the server reaches its saturation point, where throughput is maximized. As demand increases beyond this threshold, total throughput will begin to decline. Depending on how large the load is and which operating system is running, the load average may then increase substantially. A good number for `RefuseLA` would be about half of the load average value at the point where total throughput begins to decline precipitously. Generally, one might be surprised at how high a number is appropriate here. Depending on the server's operating system and my direct experience with that particular load profile, I'll typically set this variable in a range between 12 and 20 on a dedicated non-Linux email server, and higher on a Linux server. Note, however, that the appropriate cutoff number will depend heavily on the resource being starved on the machine, so it's impossible to give hard and fast guidelines. One scenario where this variable does come in handy is if a busy email server near its capacity goes offline for whatever reason (network outage, hardware repair, power outage, and so on). It likely will get slammed with deferred connections when it first comes back up, but will eventually work its way out of the jam. An appropriately chosen `RefuseLA` parameter may help it do so in a minimum amount of time.

It is impossible to build a server that accepts connections from the Internet that cannot be pushed to saturation by external load. No matter how powerful an email service one builds, it can be brought to its knees by the cooperating horsepower of even a small fraction of "the rest of the Internet." Every significantly busy email service on the planet has been pushed beyond its saturation threshold at some point. Most of this book has discussed techniques that will raise the bar for this threshold, but if a high-capacity email server *never* reaches the saturation point, it probably has been overbuilt. As annoying as these situations can be, they're a fact of life on today's Internet.

Besides total capacity, another important characteristic of a well-designed, high-performance email server is its response to load saturation. If the demand for a service temporarily increases beyond the server's ability to respond to it, only minimal degradation in total throughput should occur. It's not sufficient to build an email gateway that handles 10 Mbps of email service gracefully, but crashes when the load reaches 15 Mbps. It should be expected that total throughput would be reduced by a few percentage points—even 10% or 20% is probably acceptable—when demand significantly exceeds capacity. If the server becomes so heavily loaded that it ceases to do work effectively, however, it may end up in a state from which it cannot recover. This outcome represents an unacceptably fragile situation.

The solutions adopted on an email server that risks occasionally running in a state where its throughput capability becomes saturated need to respond gracefully to overload. For example, even if the queue's filesystem doesn't need to support a hashed directory structure to handle the expected maximum load, having this capability is beneficial because it responds more gracefully to overload than a filesystem with a linear directory lookup. For the same reason, the system should have more RAM than one anticipates needing. Extra memory can act as a buffer against several types of resource shortages. It may be useful to perform a periodic queue rotation even if we don't expect this directory to grow very large under normal circumstances. Having more CPU horsepower than one expects to need can occasionally come in handy, as can having an additional unused disk or two on a server, which can be allocated toward swap space or used for an extra queue in case of emergency. Skilled email administrators don't just consider how their server will behave when demand is reasonable and within predicted values, but imagine what life might be like if demand exceeds available bandwidth. The best indicators of preparation are if a situation has the capacity to become a catastrophe yet turns out to be a mere disaster, or if a potential disaster ends up as a mere annoyance. Minimizing such damage rarely grabs headlines or results in awards, but these victories are very real when it comes to evaluating the bottom line.

The partner of `RefuseLA` is `QueueLA`, the load average at which an email server will simply queue incoming messages rather than trying to deliver them. On almost all busy email servers, it is an extremely dangerous parameter, and I strongly advise that it be set to a number not merely larger, but much larger, than `RefuseLA`. That is, a busy email server *never* wants to accept email and just queue it. When we consider that I/O to and from the queue constitutes one of the scarcest resources on a typical email server, and as the queue grows the server tends to run more slowly, it becomes clear why going into queue-only mode can have disastrous consequences. It will cause the queue to swell, reducing capacity in the one place most likely to cause the system to run slowly in the first place! The reader has been warned.

The last load average variable worth considering is `DelayLA`, which was introduced in `sendmail` 8.12. Exceeding this threshold introduces one-second delays into the SMTP session. Clearly, this variable should be set lower than `RefuseLA` to slow down the rate of incoming email without eliminating the flow entirely. In most situations, this tactic will not be very effective. If it's set, however, a value of about half of `RefuseLA` is probably a reasonable starting point. Setting this parameter tends to offer more benefits in situations where the email server receives messages from an SMTP injector or other fixed number of machines and bulk-mails them out to the Internet. This technique can help slow down a group of synchronously operating injectors if they're driving the senders faster than they can optimally operate.

On a machine receiving email from the Internet, this parameter proves less useful. Suppose an email server that receives email messages from the Internet has exceeded its `DelayLA` load average threshold and is now slowing down incoming connections. The rate at which the Internet will initiate new SMTP sessions won't be significantly affected by the fact that each individual SMTP session runs slowly. Instead of decreasing the rate at which a few machines send email to the overloaded server, connections will be started at the same rate, but each will take longer to complete. This result doesn't help the server to deliver email any faster.

If `DelayLA` is set, as long as the load average exceeds the parameter's threshold, a one-second delay will be introduced before any SMTP command is accepted and before a `sendmail` process performs an `accept()` call on an incoming connection. Therefore, when `DelayLA` is in effect, connections could potentially back up in the server's `listen()` queue. If `DelayLA` is set, it would probably be a very good idea to increase the depth of the `listen()` queue in the system's kernel. Generally, `DelayLA` should be viewed as a parameter that can help smooth out a transient surge in load over a short period of time, perhaps measured in minutes. It will not help an email server very much if it remains in a saturated state for hours.

`DelayLA` has an interesting side effect: If it is set, the system's load average is checked far more frequently than if just other `*LA` parameters are defined. Therefore, if the load average for `RefuseLA` is not checked as frequently as one might like, setting `DelayLA` to a large number might help mitigate this problem. On most contemporary operating systems, load average checking involves a very inexpensive lookup into a kernel data table. On an operating system where calculating the load average consumes a significant amount of system resources, it may not be advisable to use `DelayLA`.

SMTP Connection Cache

When looking through the copious list of features provided by `sendmail`, two leap out as possible sources for tuning: `ConnectionCacheSize` and `Connection CacheTimeout`. These parameters control the number of outgoing SMTP connections that a process can hold open at once. The dictum that "more is better" for performance is certainly true, but it's not nearly as big a help as one might think.

The reason for this small benefit is that these connections are considered on a per-process basis. They cannot be pooled among `sendmail` processes. Thus, if a process is spawned to relay email to a busy site such as `aol.com`, there's no sense in trying to hold this connection open. After all, the process will finish and exit after the SMTP session, and no other delivery will be able to take advantage of this open pipeline. This parameter rarely comes into play except when running the queue. Even then, however, the effect will be minimal if the queue is sorted by destination host. (The effect isn't zero because some messages may be bound to multiple recipients, so a later recipient on the list may take advantage of a cached connection. Nonetheless, as one would expect, this gain is a marginal win at best.) Generally, it would be rare to see a measurable performance enhancement from setting this parameter higher than "2" on most servers, unless a high percentage of the email traffic goes to each of several domains, and most messages handled by the server are destined for multiple recipients or the queue is not sorted by destination host. The *Sendmail Configuration and Operation Guide* gives fairly dire warnings about setting this value too high. These warnings are probably overwrought, but it's best to keep the value fairly low unless compelling reasons exist to think that a higher value would help significantly.

Some Other Parameters

Some other parameters are designed to help prevent an email server from failing under the weight of its own processes. `MaxDaemonChildren`, for example, limits the maximum number of `sendmail` processes that can be concurrently active that have been spawned by the master daemon process listening on TCP port 25. If `MaxDaemonChildren` is set and this threshold is reached, it does not prevent more `sendmail` processes from being spawned from the command line for the purposes of message submission or running the queue. The master `sendmail` process has no mechanism by which to detect these other processes. Instead, it simply imposes limitations on the number that it spawns itself.

The `MaxQueueRunSize` parameter is normally not set by default. Once a queue runner sorts the queue, it will attempt to deliver only as many messages as given by the value of this parameter. For busy and clogged queues, messages at the end of a queue that could be delivered may not be, because the first N messages cannot currently be delivered. Therefore, this parameter rarely proves useful in practice. When it is used, it is likely to be less detrimental when used in conjunction with the "`random`" queue sorting strategy. Queue sorting strategies are discussed in more depth in Section 6.1.3.

The `ConnectionRateThrottle` parameter controls the maximum number of new SMTP sessions that the master `sendmail` daemon will accept per second. Once a good threshold is known, setting this parameter may help smooth out the load on a mass-mailing server where the messages to be delivered are injected via SMTP. On other mass-mailing servers, this parameter will likely have no beneficial effect. It is also one of the few parameters that can help a server that receives email from the network smooth out some of the rough spots in message delivery without causing more trouble than it eliminates. Make certain before setting this parameter that it is set to a number that the server cannot handle on a medium-term basis. If it is set too low, `ConnectionRateThrottle` will restrict the server's ability to handle email.

In conclusion, `sendmail` supports numerous parameters intended to help it from getting overloaded. On busy, well-tuned email servers, setting many of these parameters is as likely to hurt performance as help, however. In general, I recommend setting very few of these parameters, or at least setting them to values that are known to be absurdly high, unless direct evidence from multiple incidents indicates otherwise.

6.1.3 Queue Operations

Much of this book has focused on tuning the queue, and for good reason. Besides speeding up I/O access by focusing on the filesystem and storage, some parameters within `sendmail` can speed up queue runs and vary the exertion required to process the queue.

When we start `sendmail` with a command line such as `sendmail -bd -q1h`, the first option tells the process to act as the master daemon and to run in the background. The second option tells the master daemon to spawn a process on start-up and again once every hour to run the queue. When a queue runner starts, it first sorts the messages in the queue, then sequentially tries to process and deliver them. Once it has processed all messages, it will exit, unless the system uses the `sendmail` 8.12 features allowing persistent queue runners. Many strategies are possible that may be employed in running the queue more efficiently.

The default `QueueSortOrder` strategy is by "`priority`," which means that the queue runner inspects the contents of every `qf` file for the `P` parameter, sorts all messages by this value, and attempts sequential delivery of each queue entry. The "`priority`" is partly based on a user-settable parameter specifying how important the user thinks the message is and partly based on how long the message has remained undeliverable. In practice, it means that the queue runner will try to deliver messages first that are not marked as "bulk" and those that haven't sat in the queue for a long time. This approach is generally desirable, but it does require that all `qf` files in the queue be read prior to the attempt to deliver the first message. If the queue is already a resource bottleneck, this effort can take a long time. In the real world, I have seen a `sendmail` queue runner take more than an hour to scan a queue directory before it opened its first SMTP connection, although these sorts of situations are rare. On email servers where the queue doesn't tend to get very large, "`priority`" is an excellent queue sorting algorithm.

If all messages in a queue will be processed anyway, one might adopt the strategy of trying to consume the least network overhead in attempting their delivery. In this case, a queue sort order of "`host`" represents the best strategy. This way, all messages (modulo those with multiple recipients) bound for the same host will be sent at the same time, minimizing the setup and teardown of TCP connections. If network bandwidth is precious, queue I/O bandwidth is relatively plentiful, and the goal is to send messages as quickly as possible, this tactic is an excellent strategy.

If queue I/O bandwidth is expensive compared to network bandwidth, then the queue sort order of "`file`" might be a good strategy. This method sorts the `qf` files based on their file name and starts a delivery attempt on the first one. Using this method, the `qf` files do not need to be opened and read before delivery is attempted;

instead, just a listing of the files in the directory is obtained. This method has a much lower I/O overhead, especially on start-up, than the methods previously described. If all messages are of roughly the same priority, and especially if the queued entries are already sorted by host, then a more sophisticated sorting algorithm offers no special advantages. This algorithm has the shortest start time before the first message delivery is attempted in general, and it works very well if the queue is characterized by heavy I/O contention.

Sometimes, perhaps due to network outage or other unfortunate circumstances, we might find ourselves with a deep queue of messages, most of which we expect to be deliverable on the first attempt. If we start several queue runners with any one of the above algorithms, each will proceed to process the queue in the same order. This operation won't be as efficient as we might like, because all queue runners will try to lock the same set of messages at the same time. For this reason, sites often start one queue runner with the sort order of "priority," one with "host," and one with "file," but that number might not be as many queue runners as one would like under some circumstances. Version 8.12 added the "modification" sort order, which sorts by modification time starting with older entries first, but the total number of alternative sorting methods remains rather small. Mitigating this limitation is the reason for the "random" queue sort order. It takes the file names of the qf files, shuffles them, and then processes them. Therefore, any number of queue runners will be statistically likely to be working on different parts of the queue at any one time while starting up almost as fast as the "file" strategy (the computational cost of shuffling file names is negligible on today's computers, even for queues with thousands of entries).

Generally, for single queue runners on small queues, either the "priority" or "host" strategy is probably the most effective. If queues become large or queue I/O bandwidth grows scarce, then "file" or "random" is probably the best strategy to adopt, with "random" being particularly effective if one wants to start several queue runners at the same time.

If a large number of queue runners are trying to process a single queue, and they're reading through each qf file to sort the deliveries, this approach can cause a great deal of I/O contention. Also, sorting the queue might take so much time that another queue runner will be spawned before the previous one starts its first delivery attempt. Under these circumstances, it might be appropriate to limit the number of processes that can run the queue at any time. MaxQueueChildren and the related MaxRunnersPerQueue are both designed to help control this situation. MaxQueueChildren controls the maximum number of queue runners that the master sendmail daemon will allow to exist at any time. Note that it does not track queue runners spawned by hand (`sendmail -q` or the equivalent), just those that would be periodically spawned by the master process—don't expect to see cooperation in this regard among several `sendmail` processes started from the command line at different times. In version 8.12, if queue groups and `MaxQueueChildren` are defined (by default, the latter is not), then the default value for `MaxRunners-PerQueue` is set to 1. If one has multiple queues, it's important to set this value appropriately. Typically, one would always want at least one queue runner per queue, and probably allowing for several is appropriate, especially if relatively few queues exist. Until the choice is demonstrated to be either insufficient or detrimental, I'd generally start with a value of 5 for `MaxRunnersPerQueue` if I had at least five queues, and a much larger value if I had fewer queues, or one primary queue that received more activity than the rest, if I felt the need to set this value at all. If `MaxQueueChildren` is smaller than the number of queues, then each will be processed in round-robin fashion.

Using the queue groups feature, one can create more complex sorting strategies. For example, to split off all email headed for the busy domain `hotmail.com`, add the following M4 lines:

```
FEATURE('queuegroup')
QUEUE_GROUP('hotmail', 'P=/var/spool/mqueue/hotmail, F=f')
```

The following line is then added to the `access` table:

```
QGRP:hotmail.com        hotmail
```

Now, messages whose first recipient on the recipient list is bound for this domain will be queued in a special area.

At first glance, even more complex strategies seem appealing. However, further consideration will reveal that moving too far down this path leads to madness. While notions such as one queue per domain or hierarchical queues might seem intriguing, how do they affect the number of queue runners per queue? How does one implement the `mailq` command? How can a person track what's going on in all parts of the "queue" without sophisticated tools? The use of multiple queues to increase parallelism and queue rotation are excellent strategies that busy sites should adopt. Sites with a disproportionate amount of traffic going to a single domain or sites with a large volume of mailing list and non–mailing list traffic may want to use queue groups to help minimize how performance problems in one area affect another area, but increasing complexity in one's queue structure to obtain a marginal gain in performance probably is not advisable. Keep a server's queue structure as simple as possible.

6.1.4 Ruleset Tuning

An unfortunate number of email administrators attempt to speed up `sendmail` operation by streamlining ruleset processing in the `sendmail.cf` file. Almost without exception, this tactic proves to be a serious mistake. Although many of the rules in the `sendmail.cf` file deal with very uncommon situations, some of them can prevent serious problems from happening if these rare events do occur. In any event, the amount of CPU time it takes to process a full-blown set of rules isn't significantly greater than the time needed to process those in a stripped-down `sendmail.cf` file. Also, as we've already seen, it's usually unlikely that CPU load will cause the system bottleneck in any case. Do not try to streamline the `sendmail` rulesets, and especially don't do so by hand-editing the `sendmail.cf` file.

Some configuration variations, however, can be tuned from M4, which may enhance performance, and they certainly would both be more effective and reduce the chance of serious negative side effects. Of course, each of these possibilities has its downsides, which should be carefully considered.

The "nocanonify" feature can be enabled by adding

```
FEATURE('nocanonify')
```

to the `.mc` file. If this feature is enabled, `sendmail` assumes that the email addresses it is passed are already canonical and, therefore, do not need to be expanded. This technique saves some effort, but it means that anyone sending email through that server to or from the address `npc@discovery`, for example, will not have that host name expanded to include the fully qualified domain name. As a consequence, that address won't be resolvable (at least not correctly) by other hosts on the Internet. For this reason, this feature is a good idea only on those hosts where all host names processed by a server will be canonical, such as on an email gateway where no one sends email from the command line or using on-server MUAs such as `elm` or `mutt`.

As has already been discussed, reducing internal computation, unless it's egregious, doesn't generally have a significant performance effect on email server operation. However, reducing unnecessary connections over the network, or even to other processes, can significantly boost performance. To limit spam, on each SMTP connection the envelope sender email address is checked to make sure it is plausible. That is, the addresses must represent valid domains, such that email returned to the sender might actually be delivered to a real mailbox. What would be the point of receiving email from a sender named `nobody@bite.me`? Performing these checks necessitates a DNS lookup, which requires a network connection to a root name server at least. Adding both `FEATURE(accept_unresolvable_domains)` and FEATURE(nocanonify) to the .mc file suppresses this check. As we've already seen, it is not appropriate to set FEATURE(nocanonify) on all email servers. If it cannot be set, then the only reason to set FEATURE(accept_unre-solvable_domains) is if it is necessary to accept email from domains that aren't in DNS. Frankly, this case means that a site's DNS is broken, and the problem should be fixed there. Of course, identifying spam early and refusing the connection could bring a performance savings. However, largely because of this sanity check that sendmail currently performs by default, it's rare for spammers to send email that lacks a sane return address, even if it's not theirs. I would generally recommend not enabling these two features in concert. On a server that handles email only from trusted hosts, such as a mass-mailing gateway, it probably would be appropriate to do so.

6.1.5 Table Lookups

The sendmail MTA provides an astounding number of options for relaying or rewriting both sender and recipient email addresses, through mechanisms such as the virtusertable, genericstable, and mailertable. The CPU-bound test server introduced in Chapter 1 must be set up in an extreme configuration for these map checks to produce a clearly measurable effect on throughput. If the machine is configured to use both interactive delivery mode and queueing to avoid queue writes, and it is set to deliver each message to /dev/null, then adding the checks associated with each new map will reduce the message discard rate by 1% to 2%. Therefore, we can conclude that most of these table lookups occur rapidly, and working hard to strip them is probably not necessary. If a table lookup isn't used, there's no reason to express that feature in a running configuration file.

An exception involves the access database. Adding

```
FEATURE('access_db')
```

to the sendmail.cf file and creating an access database causes throughput using the previously described configuration to drop by about 12% due to the number of access database lookups done in the rulesets. Of course, this example involves a CPU-bound server that never performs operations on any files. Something like this almost certainly won't be deployed in any real operation. The access database is invaluable as an anti-spam mechanism, but performance-sensitive systems should use it only if absolutely necessary.

Another configuration recommendation relates to .forward files. On many email servers, users do not have real accounts on the machine, in which case

`.forward` files will never be consulted. Thus the forward file search path, `ForwardPath`, should be null:

```
define('confFORWARD_PATH', '')
```

Further, by default, `sendmail` supports several `.forward` file naming conventions (and sometimes locations). The range of possibilities should be limited as much as is appropriate for that server.

The `hoststat` command can provide a lot of useful information about the state of the email system. It includes host-by-host information on volume, connection time, number of messages, and more transferred between those hosts and the local server. To enable the command, add the following line to an `.mc` file:

```
define('confHOST_STATUS_DIRECTORY', '/var/run/.hoststat')
```

This information needs to be stored on the server to be accessible to the `hoststat` program, which means more disk writes. The writes are asynchronous and small, but plentiful—at least one write for each delivery attempt. If this information is stored, putting it on a different disk than the queue or spool is probably a good idea, and putting it on a `tmpfs` or other memory-based filesystem is probably a better one. The downside to the latter approach is that these files aren't persistent across a machine crash, although that possibility may not be a concern. Of course, if this information isn't used at all, then support for this option should be disabled.

In contrast, the amount of data written to the `statistics` file for retrieval by the `mailstats` program is very small and shouldn't create a performance concern. The `statistics` file can be cleaned out by running `mailstats -p > /dev/null`. Future versions of `sendmail` will probably support an option to zero out the file without creating output. The output of `mailstats` is a good quick-and-dirty method for summarizing email throughput over a specified period without having to sort through the log files. Of course, the logs contain a lot of information that isn't available to `mailstat`. Both are valuable. A busy server might want to periodically (perhaps daily) run a script like the following to keep a running total of the statistics available to `mailstat`:

```
#!/bin/sh
# mailstat_archive.sh

ARCHIVE_DIR=/archive/email/
DATE=`date +%Y%m`
```

```
mkdir -p $ARCHIVE_DIR/$DATE
/usr/sbin/mailstats > $ARCHIVE_DIR/$DATE/mailstats.`date +%d`
/usr/sbin/mailstats -p > /dev/null
```

Many sites now use LDAP (Lightweight Directory Access Protocol) databases as a centralized site-wide information repository for aliases and authentication information, among other data. The appeal of such an approach is very compelling, and the last few releases of sendmail have included ever-increasing support for storing and retrieving LDAP data. However, each query of an LDAP database involves a network round trip. Despite largely living up to the billing of the first letter in the abbreviation, LDAP lookups simply aren't as fast as lookups in a local Berkeley DB hash table. Therefore, if an email system struggles while making these queries over the network, some benefits might be realized by moving the data closer to where it will be accessed.

Of course, centralizing user data has a considerable following for valid reasons: It's easy to maintain, it's convenient, and it minimizes cross-database "drift." These considerations can prove quite beneficial. Ideally, we could maintain this centralization without the expense of traversing the network every time a request needs to be made. One possibility is to install an LDAP replica, or a server replicating just the necessary subset of information, on a local network to speed up accesses and make them more reliable. Some replication is almost certainly necessary just from a reliability standpoint. If the LDAP directory is fairly small, one might even consider running the replica on the email server itself, much as this book recommends for DNS name servers.

If closeness isn't sufficient, then it may be appropriate to use something like the OpenLDAP [OPE] ldapsearch command to dump out the subset of interesting data and entries. This information may be formed into appropriate sendmail flat files using Perl or UNIX utilities such as sed and awk. We can then run makemap or newaliases to generate fast, locally accessible snapshots of the information in the LDAP database. Of course, this information wouldn't be as current, but if that consideration is not strictly necessary, performing this action in an automated fashion—say, once daily—might suffice for many organizations and could reduce the load on an email server significantly. Of course, dealing with these issues necessitates a balancing act, and the factors that go into designing a solution for a particular environment are so numerous that all cannot be listed here.

Some organizations have added similar hooks to sendmail to support their own home-grown databases. If these alterations take the form of code changes to sendmail itself, then maintaining these changes against continual releases of sendmail represents a serious endeavor, not to be undertaken lightly. In some situations, this is a requirement—doing periodic data dumps of the variety mentioned earlier will not suffice.

Some of these modifications include connections to SQL databases or connections to other data repositories. Regardless of how the data are stored, some general rules apply in designing these performance-enhancing interfaces. Let us assume that the equivalent of an organization's `virtusertable` resides in a SQL-based RDBMS somewhere, and the high-volume corporate email relay needs to access it. A site might want to provide a nearby replica of those data. If this strategy isn't possible, and the site's security architecture doesn't preclude it, perhaps giving the database server an extra network interface on a network shared by the gateway would be acceptable. It might even be worthwhile to create a network dedicated to this purpose on which only the data repository and email server reside.

SQL connections are not lightweight. If a `sendmail` process (and the database) must set up and tear down a session each time it wants to do a lookup, the email server will run slowly. A better design would have `sendmail` contact via IPC one or more dedicated proxy processes running on the email server, then have these processes maintain one or more persistent connections open to the database. This isn't a trivial programming task. Properly done, one has to communicate asynchronously with the database and several `sendmail` processes and keep track of and schedule all these sets of transactions. Fortunately, this problem has been solved many times before, and coding this sort of proxy should be straightforward. The question of whether to add a caching function to this daemon is left to the discretion of a programmer who has already gotten the proxy to work correctly.

6.2 Security and Performance

The topics of security and performance go hand in hand. In some cases, such as when preventing system abuse via spam or mail bombing, an improvement in security will result in an improvement in performance. In other cases, increasing security through additional database lookups, DNS requests, or use of strong encryption brings a cost in performance to some aspect of the system. This section will explore some of these trade-offs.

6.2.1 Don't Blame `sendmail`

A large number of configurable parameters appear under the heading of the `DontBlameSendmail` option in the configuration file. As the name suggests, it is risky to modify any of these options from their default (safe) settings. If the configuration of a given server seems to call for such a modification, rethink the configuration instead. None of the available options has a significant chance of measurably improving performance, so that excuse should not be used as a rationalization for potentially reducing the security of a server.

6.2.2 Privacy Options

The PrivacyOptions option is primarily designed to fine-tune how sendmail responds to SMTP queries. By default, sendmail is very permissive about what it will tolerate in terms of broken SMTP implementations on the Internet. As the name of this option implies, many sites may want to restrict the information they make available via remote SMTP queries. Some of these options may have modest performance implications. A complete list of the options available appears in the *Sendmail Installation and Operation Guide*. Some more relevant options are listed here. Note that not all of these options are available in every sendmail version.

novrfy If this option is set, sendmail will no longer respond to the SMTP VRFY command. The VRFY command is used to find out if a given email address is a valid one known to the server. Email administrators often disable this option to make it more difficult for spammers to find out what user names and, therefore, email addresses might be valid on a particular server. However, if this option is taken away, spammers may resort to sending email to all possible names on their list. Nonetheless, I generally recommend disabling this option on email servers connected to the Internet.

noexpn Similar to the situation with novrfy, if this option is set, sendmail will no longer allow the SMTP EXPN command. The EXPN command is a little more resource intensive. That is, it doesn't just return an indicator of whether an email address is valid, but also checks the aliases file, .forward files, and virtusertable to find out whether the email address in question is rewritten to some other email address, and returns that information. Certainly, if novrfy is set, noexpn should be as well.

noverb If either noexpn or novrfy is set, noverb is assumed. VERB is a nonstandard SMTP command that sendmail accepts to switch into a verbose mode. It is very useful for debugging email problems from a remote machine by using telnet to connect to the SMTP port. Unfortunately, it can also give outsiders a great deal of information. VERB should probably be disallowed on any email server connected to the wider Internet.

restrictmailq This option restricts running of the mailq command to the root user and the user who owns the mail queue(s). If a lot of email is queued, running mailq can be quite resource intensive. If general users have access to an email server that often has deep queues, and `mailq` is abused by being run too often, it may be prudent to restrict its use via this option.

`restrictqrun` If `sendmail` is set-user-ID `root`, then any user may start a queue run by typing `sendmail -q`. On lightly loaded servers, this ability shouldn't be a problem and might actually be a useful feature. On a heavily loaded server, the frequency with which queue runners are started may be closely managed. Again, if a potential for abuse exists, it may be necessary to disable this service.

`noreceipts` If this option is set, then successful delivery return receipt DSNs will not be sent back to people who request them. While this elimination will reduce the amount of email processed by a server, albeit not by very much at most sites, it's not very nice. I wouldn't recommend disabling this feature unless as a temporary measure, or if it is abused by antisocial folks at other sites.

`nobodyreturn` Usually when a DSN is sent, whether as a warning, a bounce message, a return receipt, or for any other reason, the entire message is returned to the sender. Sometimes this returned message body is useful for the context. If the `nobodyreturn` option is sent, just the headers are returned, not the body, saving some processing effort. If the email messages at a site tend to be large, or if the server is an outgoing mass mailer where the body contents are well known or don't contain any especially useful information, this option can prove useful. In any case, it is acceptable to set this option even if reducing load isn't the primary goal.

`authwarnings` This option will cause the addition of "`X-Authentication-Warning:`" headers to some email messages that originate from it. It indicates the user associated with the process that ran the `sendmail` command on that server if it's different from the individual who claims to have sent the message. This option adds an extra line to email headers if it's included, but the overall effect on server performance will likely be very minor. Nonetheless, no really good reason exists to enable it. On a relay host, because few, if any, email messages are sent from the command line, whether `authwarnings` was set is unlikely to make a difference. On a mass mailer, where email is generated and sent, it should probably not be enabled.

6.2.3 Blacklists

Spamming is an enormous problem on the Internet, so much so that some fairly desperate measures are widely used to help combat this scourge. One technique relies on blacklists, like the MAPS RBL [MAP]. This database contains a list of sites that the maintainers, in their estimation, consider to be spammers or havens for spammers, whether through ignorance or malice. Such a site typically works by having the email server query a site's database to see whether a connecting server is coming from a blacklisted network. If it is prohibited, a refusal is issued in response to the MAIL command during the SMTP connection, and the message is simply not transferred.

Of course, this approach requires yet another lookup over the network, and to a faraway server at that. It is possible to keep a copy of the MAPS database at a site, but one needs to jump through some hoops to do so. Information on how to obtain the necessary permission appears on the MAPS Web site. Given the staggering amount of spam traversing the Internet these days, reducing it by any significant extent may be worth the cost of the lookup, but this decision should not be made lightly. Moreover, enabling this service has much more profound consequences than mere performance issues. The folks who maintain these services tend to be more than a little draconian about which sites get blacklisted, and more than a few mistakes have been made. Subscribing to these services will reduce the amount of spam received by a site, but if general connectivity is important, it can carry a steep price.

In the relentless pursuit of cutting down on the amount of spam a site receives at nearly any cost, many choose to subscribe to services that aggregate lists of open relays, known spam sites, and other sites accused of antisocial behavior. In some cases, these aggregation lists require multihop queries to determine whether a given address is on the "bad guy" list. As an example, I might add the following lines in my .mc file:

```
FEATURE('dnsbl', 'spam-b-gone.example.org')
```

When I receive a message that might be spam, the email server will query the machine listed above. After consulting its own internal databases, spam-b-gone. example.org might turn around and query one, or perhaps many, other blackhole list servers to see whether the sender in question appears on anyone else's blacklist. This step can greatly increase the amount of time required to process each incoming email message. A small site might be able to afford this delay; a site concerned with email performance almost certainly will not.

6.2.4 Security

Beginning with sendmail 8.11, support for opportunistically encrypting email traffic between two SMTP servers became available to the Open Source community, via the Transport Layer Security (TLS) protocol [DA99]. This exciting feature allows two servers to exchange email without having the message contents become available to every prying eye on every intermediate network. The downside is that, like all cryptography, using this feature consumes CPU time.

Currently, very few sites support this option. A quick and unscientific count of my home machine's log file suggests that at the time of this writing, less than 10% of servers that send or receive email support STARTTLS, and I would suspect that I correspond with a crowd that's far more likely to use it than the average site. At the present time, probably less than 1% of all email sites support this option, although this number should rise over time. As long as the adoption rate stays low, supporting STARTTLS is unlikely to affect a server's loading, unless the computer is already CPU bound.

Even if adoption of STARTTLS does spread quickly, it remains unclear how much that change will affect email server load. Again, most email servers have CPU capacity to spare. Do they have enough to support encrypting the bulk of the email that they send or receive over the Internet? No one really knows. My advice would be to enable this option on servers that are not already CPU bound where it can do some good, and then keep an eye on these servers' CPU utilization rates. If CPU loading on the machine spikes up, this feature might be the cause, and evaluating the costs versus benefits of supporting this feature may become necessary.

6.2.5 Mail Filter Use

Beginning with sendmail 8.10, a quasi-official compile-time feature became available, and then became official with 8.12, called the Mail Filter API or "milter" for short. This general mail filter can operate on the envelope, message headers, and bodies to accept or reject messages based on the connection information or message contents. It also provides the ability to perform general header and message rewriting. Some potential applications include, but are by no means limited to, the following:

- Virus scanning
- Header rewriting/stripping
- Spam filtering
- Keyword search/spying on employees
- Removing excessively large attachments
- Removing especially risky attachments, such as Visual Basic programs

A milter application, which remains distinct from the sendmail program, runs as a single multithreaded daemon that can receive messages to examine from any number of `sendmail` processes. It receives the messages to be processed through either a UNIX domain or a TCP/IP socket, so the milter process doesn't even have to run on the same machine as the `sendmail` processes with which it communicates.

This technology is already incorporated into commercial products such as TrendMicro's Interscan VirusWall. Open Source projects such as the AMaViS email virus scanner [AMA] also take advantage of milter. While few applications are using milter as of this writing, its use is growing in both volume and sophistication. A milter advocacy Web site exists at `http://www.milter.org/`.

Of course, the text search-and-replace capability doesn't come cheap. If all email flowing through a busy server, or even a sizable percentage of it, passes through a global search-and-replace algorithm, it will consume significant resources and affect performance of the server as a whole.

Offloading the actual milter processing to another machine can help prevent an already busy server from becoming saturated, but memory will be consumed because `sendmail` processes will have longer durations due to the processing time of the milter application, the overhead involved in setting up the network connection, and the latency involved in a network round trip to the milter server.

To my knowledge no real-world performance studies using milter at high-volume email sites have yet taken place. I'd speculate that running servers in parallel that handle both email and their own filtering will be more efficient than running `sendmail` on one set of servers and milter applications on another. This strategy would eliminate network connections and their associated overhead, and most `sendmail`-only servers have CPU resources to spare that the milter application can use. However, we'll have to wait for real data to be collected to find out if this prediction is correct.

6.3 Other General Strategies

Other general architectural strategies can be undertaken to improve a site's email performance. While these strategies stray a bit from the "making single servers perform better" guideline set down in Chapter 1, some are compelling enough to warrant mention here.

6.3.1 FallbackMX Host

A FallbackMX host is a server set up by an organization to act as a temporary repository for queued email that is being sent from the organization to the rest

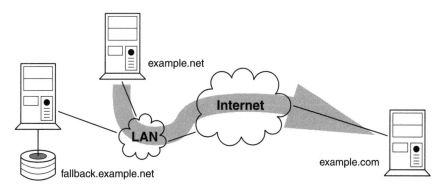

Figure 6.1. Normal email routing.

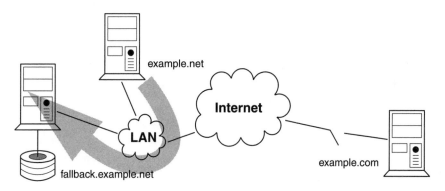

Figure 6.2. Email diverted to FallbackMX host.

of the Internet. Assuming the local domain is example.net, in M4, one can configure a FallbackMX host by adding the following line to a .mc file:

```
define('confFALLBACK_MX','fallback.example.net')
```

where fallback.example.net is the name of the host used as the FallbackMX host. When an email server looks up the host and domain portion of an email address for delivery, it generates a list of machines to try via querying DNS for MX, A, and CNAME records for that destination (and AAAA records if IPv6 support is enabled). If FallbackMXhost is defined, this host name (or set of host names if it is an MX record pointing to more than one actual server) is appended to the list. Thus, if the message cannot get through to its intended destination, it is funneled to the fallback machine for later delivery.

It may be easier to understand the function of a FallbackMX host by examining Figures 6.1, 6.2, and 6.3. Under normal circumstances, to move email from our

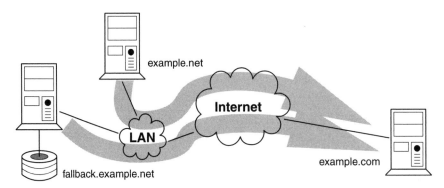

Figure 6.3. Connectivity reestablished.

site's outbound email server, `example.net`, to its destination, `example.com`, our server makes a direct connection to the destination machine (Figure 6.1). If our server cannot connect to `example.com` or any of the machines pointed to by `example.com`'s MX records, it will send email bound for that domain to its FallbackMX host, `fallback.example.net` (Figure 6.2). This host will attempt to send email on to its true destination—in this case, it cannot due to a network outage. Therefore, the messages are queued on this machine until delivery can take place. Once connectivity to `example.com` is restored, email can be sent there directly by `example.net`, and `fallback.example.net` can send the email bound for that destination that resides in its queues (Figure 6.3).

Using a FallbackMX host keeps the queues on the main server clear. In fact, as long as the fallback machine is accessible and handling SMTP connections, no messages should remain in the queue of the main server that are not currently being processed, and processed for the first time. On the other hand, the FallbackMX host might have relatively deep queues, but sending email from this machine need not occur extremely quickly, as every message in its queues has failed to be delivered to its intended destination at least once.

At a site with a FallbackMX host, the main servers responsible for sending email to the Internet need much smaller queues, which makes NVRAM and small solid state disks more practical, allowing for better throughput for the same amount of money. Further, because queues stay small, it may not be necessary to use a filesystem on these servers that performs efficient lookups in large directories, although performing fast metadata operations remains just as important as ever. At the same time, the FallbackMX host can have a small or moderate capability RAID system that doesn't need to be blazingly fast to store its queue. Multiple queue directories are appropriate here, as is a filesystem that handles large directories gracefully. Almost any site that traffics enough email volume such that it's appropriate to use multiple servers to handle the load will benefit from creating a FallbackMX host.

6.3.2 Spillover Host

At some sites, a single or small number of email servers may become overloaded on more than an occasional basis. In some cases, upgrading the service is not an immediate option. If so, then one might want to try the FallbackMX host concept in reverse. That is, set up a host that can handle deep queues to act as an email storage reservoir for an organization when the primary hosts are unavailable. Stated another way, a Spillover host is a machine set up by an organization to temporarily queue email sent from the Internet to the organization in question when the organization's main servers cannot accept the email that the Internet wants to send them.

To set up this host, configure DNS so that the main server has the highest precedence (lowest number) MX record for a given set of domains. The server may also have some resource limits set (such as MaxDaemonChildren) so that it doesn't become overloaded with incoming SMTP connections. At the same time, a second server would be configured in DNS with a lower-precedence (higher-number) MX record for those same domains. If the higher-precedence servers are not available, the Spillover host would accept email bound for those domains, but it would simply store that email in its queues. In other words, it wouldn't attempt to deliver email to local mailboxes. Once a higher-precedence MX server became available to receive email, it would forward the messages to that server.

It may be easier to understand how the Spillover host functions in practice by referring to Figures 6.4, 6.5, and 6.6. In this case, the highest-precedence MX record for the domain example.net points to the machine example.net. A lower-precedence MX record points to spillover.example.net, which is configured to relay email bound for example.net but not to deliver it locally. Under normal circumstances, other email servers on the Internet would send email directly to example.net (Figure 6.4). If this server cannot accept incoming email, email

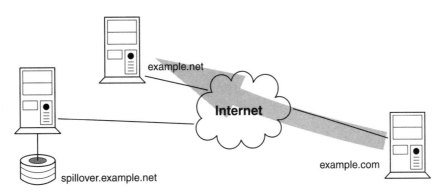

Figure 6.4. Connectivity reestablished.

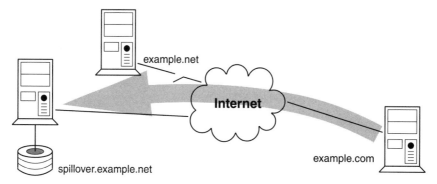

Figure 6.5. Connectivity reestablished.

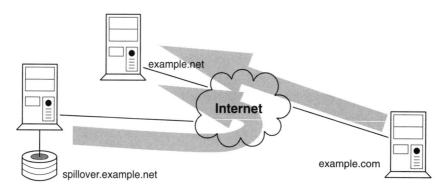

Figure 6.6. Connectivity reestablished.

for this domain would instead be sent to `spillover.example.net`, where it would accumulate in that machine's queues (Figure 6.5). Once connectivity is restored, new email from the outside world and messages that have accumulated in the Spillover host's queues would be delivered to `example.com` (Figure 6.6).

Even between two sites with good Internet connectivity and high-speed links, the effective bandwidth between them often remains surprisingly limited, and latency can be quite high. On the best of days it might be measured in the tens of milliseconds, and it may often be much worse. Therefore, if Server A sends a certain amount of email to Server B, performance implications will arise based on how the network between them behaves. Of course, generally speaking, the amount of disk I/O will be the same regardless of the quality of the network connection. In both cases, the data must be read and written to the disk, and it doesn't much matter how fast the data arrive. However, the slower the network between the two servers, the more time every `sendmail` process will take to conclude its task, and each process consumes system resources. The total number of messages and megabytes of email will be handled by a given server each day regardless of the quality of the network connection between a server and the rest of the Internet. Consequently, it stands to reason that the lower the latency between a server and its peers, the fewer simultaneous processes that need to run on a given server, and the less memory (and other system resources) that will be consumed at any one time. This consideration can cause a significant difference in overall system performance.

An email server getting email from its Spillover host over a low-latency connection can reduce some aspects of its load compared to a system that receives all of its email via a high-latency connection to the Internet at large. Additionally, a Spillover host provides the beneficial side effect that the email moves off the Internet and on to friendly hosts more swiftly. Further, it's being a good neighbor to not tie up email server capacity and disk space around the Internet when not necessary. A Spillover host typically doesn't provide nearly the performance boost that a FallbackMX host does, but in certain circumstances it can provide a significant benefit.

In many cases, the Spillover host will reside "nearby" the primary email server that it guards. Nevertheless, one can argue in favor of housing a Spillover host at an off-site location, especially if one's network connection isn't reliable or has limited capacity. Having a dedicated host that is up and able to receive email even if an organization's primary network connection becomes unavailable is good for the Internet, but it also can help keep the primary server from becoming overloaded when network connectivity returns. Instead of having the entire Internet waiting to deluge the primary server with the email volume that has been building up during the outage, this email will now reside on the off-site Spillover host. It cannot send email to the primary server faster than a single host can send out email, which should allow the primary server to absorb email at a tractable rate. At the same time, this transfer should occur quite efficiently, as the email backlog can be sent over a small number of SMTP connections, which will further reduce the amount of effort required to absorb those messages. This situation is in stark contrast to a FallbackMX host, which should always reside "near" the servers that send email to it. Preferably, these hosts will reside on the same network.

A Spillover host will be used more frequently when the primary server charged with receiving email for a particular organization is overloaded or down. As a consequence, it might not be a bad idea to raise the value for `Timeout.queuereturn` on the Spillover host. If the primary server stays off the air for an extended period of time, it would usually be beneficial to have as much email as possible eventually get through to its intended recipient.

6.3.3 Smart Host

One last type of additional dedicated server is the "smart host." It is set in the `sendmail.mc` file by adding the following line:

```
define('SMART_HOST', 'smarthost.example.org')
```

Originally, the smart host concept was created to allow a set of hosts within an organization that might not be able to route Internet-wide email (for example, if they didn't have access to Internet DNS information) to send all of their outbound email to a centralized server that could. The same strategy is also useful for reducing the load on an email server. Assume that a smart host is available for an email server that receives a great deal of email. With a smart host, outbound email will leave the sending host more quickly (going to a server that is always available and "nearby" in the networking sense). This approach will reduce the number of concurrent processes running on the sending machine as well as the number of entries in its queue at any one time. Both factors can reduce the load on the server.

6.3.4 Server Parallelism

When it comes to performing computer tasks, it's usually more cost-effective to run the task on two slower computers than on one computer that is twice as fast as either of the two. The trick is that the tasks to be performed must be parallelizable over the two computers, which is not always the case. The fact that not all tasks can be parallelized is primarily what allows vendors to sell very large computer systems. While the economies of parallelism often apply to CPU-bound problems, the cost-effectiveness of parallelizing I/O-bound applications is almost always considerable, and Internet applications such as email relaying are extremely parallelizable, although trying to parallelize a single image message store is not so easy to do.

Therefore, if an email relay is running at capacity, instead of implementing expensive upgrades, it's often a better strategy to buy a second server and split the load. In most cases, we point a domain's MX record at a host's single A record to indicate where email should go for that domain. Splitting the load is trivially accomplished by replacing the MX record pointing to the single host with two MX records that point to the two servers over which the load will be shared. The following example from a BIND zone file for the fictional `example.com` domain illustrates two equal-precedence MX records for the same zone split between two hosts:

```
$TTL 3600000
example.com          IN SOA ns1.example.com.postmaster.example.com. (
                        2002012001 ; Serial number
                        10800      ; Refresh
                        3600       ; Retry every hour
                        604800     ; Expire after 1 week
                        86400      ; Minimum TTL of 1 hour.
                        )

                     IN NS  ns1.example.com.
                     IN NS  ns2.example.com.

example.com.         IN MX  10 server1.example.com.
example.com.         IN MX  10 server2.example.com.

server1.example.com. IN A   10.5.4.11
server2.example.com. IN A   10.5.4.12
```

According to the RFC 2821, when presented with two equal-precedence MX records for the same domain, SMTP servers should select randomly between them to determine with which host it will connect. These days, almost all SMTP software behaves in this way; at the very least, a large enough percentage of it does so to effectively split the load between multiple servers.

One can also use layer 4 switches to provide a similar level of parallelism. These devices have their relative advantages and disadvantages compared to using multiple MX records to provide parallelism, but often become a good idea once the number of MX records for a single domain exceeds a very modest number. These devices are also quite useful compared to using MX records, as DNS records for a server one might like to remove from service may be cached around the Internet, which may make removing the server less transparent. Further discussions of the issues surrounding these devices is beyond the scope of this book. See Tony Bourke's book [BOU01] for more information.

If a host name is listed in the sendmail.cf file, it will be checked for MX records first. If the record points to multiple hosts, then a given sendmail process will contact a randomly selected host. If the host name is enclosed with square brackets, such as [server1.example.org], then MX record lookups are not performed. Instead, the host name or IP address within the square brackets is taken literally.

Of course, the fact that email services can be parallelized in this manner doesn't mean that one shouldn't tune a single server. In general, keep in mind that if the email operations (or any computing task) can be parallelized, one should assemble the most horsepower per dollar rather than build the fastest machine possible, remembering that support costs as well as equipment costs need to be factored into the financial equations.

6.4 Summary

- A few timeouts can improve email server performance, but most shouldn't be adjusted.

- On I/O-bound machines, throttling connections based on load limits usually isn't as effective as it might at first seem.

- Significant performance gains cannot generally be realized by making sendmail less security conscious than it is by default.

- Features such as STARTTLS and mail filters are wonderful from a utility standpoint, but they may have significant performance implications.

- A FallbackMX host can help relieve the load from email servers sending messages out to the Internet.

- A Spillover host can queue up messages coming from the Internet into an organization if the organization's primary machines cannot respond due to load problems or a network outage. Of the two types of hosts, deploying a FallbackMX host generally has the larger overall performance impact.

- When possible, it's generally more cost-effective and more scalable to distribute a given load over several smaller servers than to have one big server handle it.

## Chapter 7

Finding and Removing Bottlenecks

So far, this book has focused on up-front design and configuration of an email server. The goal of this chapter is to provide some methodology and explain the use of tools that will assist the email administrator in determining the cause of poor email server performance and rectifying the situation.

Over the years, operating systems have grown increasingly sophisticated. Today, several levels of data caches are typically internal to the operating system kernel. Most internal data structures are dynamically sized and hashed, so that they no longer have fixed extents and table lookups remain rapid as the amount of data they contain grows. This increased sophistication generally has been for the best, as these additional variables ensure that operating systems require less manual intervention to get them to work well in a high-performance capacity. Nevertheless, a system administrator needs to be aware of two facts. First, these benefits can have side effects. Second, this extra tuning often makes troubleshooting more difficult.

7.1 Kernel Parameters Run Amok

Let's consider a real-life example. The Solaris operating system from Sun Microsystems contains a kernel table called the Directory Name Lookup Cache (DNLC). The DNLC is a kernel cache that matches the name of a recently accessed file with its vnode (a virtual inode, an extra level of abstraction that makes writing interfaces to filesystems easier and more portable) if the file name isn't too long. Keeping this table in memory means that if a file is opened once by a process, and then opened again within a short period of time, the second open() won't require a directory lookup to retrieve the file's inode. If many of the open()s performed by the system operate on the same files over and over, this strategy could yield a significant performance win.

The DNLC table has a fixed size to make sure that it consumes a reasonable amount of memory. If the table is full and a new file is opened, this file's information is added to the DNLC and an older, less recently used entry in the table is removed to make space for the new data. The size of this table can be set manually using the `ncsize` variable in the `/etc/system` file; otherwise, it's derived from MAXUSERS, a general sizing parameter used for most tables on the system, and a variable called `max_nprocs`, which governs the total number of processes that can run simultaneously on the system. In Solaris version 2.5.1, the equation used to determine `ncsize` was

```
ncsize = (max_nprocs + 16 + MAXUSERS) + 64
```

In Solaris 2.6, this calculation changed to

```
ncsize = 4 * (max_nprocs + MAXUSERS) + 320
```

In Solaris 2.5.1, unless manually set, `max_nprocs = 10 + 16 * MAXUSERS`. I do not know if this calculation changed in Solaris 2.6.

If MAXUSERS is set to 2048, which is typical for large servers running very large numbers of processes, the DNLC on Solaris 2.5.1 would have 34,906 entries. On Solaris 2.6, using the same kernel tuning parameters, the DNLC could contain 139,624 entries. In Solaris 8, the calculation of this parameter had been changed to be more similar to the Solaris 2.5.1 method.

Performance on the new Solaris 2.6 system was horrible. File deletions on Network File Systems (NFS) took a very long time to complete, and it required a great deal of time to diagnose the problem. As it turns out, for some reason that I still don't fully understand, if one attempts to delete a file over NFS, and the DNLC is completely full, the operating system makes a linear traversal of the table to find the appropriate entry. The more entries the table holds, the longer this traversal takes. If it has nearly 140,000 entries, this operation can take considerable time. With the same `/etc/system` parameters on similar hardware running Solaris 2.5.1, these lookups did not cause a noticeable problem.

In my case, a colleague who had encountered this problem before suggested setting `ncsize` explicitly to a more moderate value (we chose 8192) in the `/etc/system` file. We then rebooted the system, and performance improved dramatically.

This is a pretty exotic example, but it indicates the following points:

1. Today's operating systems are complex. It's always possible that a server slowdown might occur under certain circumstances because of the misbehavior of some obscure part of the operating system.

2. It's always possible that very slight changes in an operating system—even changing minor version numbers or adding a single kernel patch—can have far-reaching consequences.

3. Larger cache sizes are not universally a good thing, especially if the system designers do not fully explore the consequences of having large caches.

4. There's no such thing as having too much knowledge about the hardware and software system that a site uses to operate a high-performance server.

This also leads to some obvious conclusions:

1. On a high-performance or mission-critical server, make even small changes with extreme caution.

2. One can never have too much expertise. Fancy tools rarely solve the problem, but a tool that can deliver one good insight during a crisis can prove exceedingly valuable.

3. Trust the data. When something is going wrong, the reasons may not be evident, but they will be consistent within their own logic. Although it may not seem obvious at times, once all the factors are understood, it will be apparent that computers are deterministic objects.

4. Test, test, and test again before deploying production system. Make the test as close to "real life" as possible. There's never enough time to be as thorough as one would like, but if there isn't enough time to test at least some extreme cases, there isn't enough time to do it right. In the preceding situation, we did test, but with data set sizes less than 140,000 files (the size of the DNLC). Because we never filled the DNLC, we never tripped over the bug. Obviously, our testing wasn't "close enough" to "real life." Chapter 8 will explore testing issues in more detail.

This example was not intended to criticize Solaris. Probably every operating system vendor makes comparable changes from release to release, and many similar stories could have been told that focus on other vendors.

There isn't enough space in this book to cover general troubleshooting methodology, but one aspect should be mentioned because it causes many people difficulty. In trying to focus on a problem, the troubleshooter often assembles a great deal of data. Some of it is relevant to the problem at hand, and some of it is tangential. Determining which data are relevant and which aren't often poses the most difficult aspect of solving a problem. There's no magic to categorizing data in this way;

rather, experience and instinct take over. However, when faced with a problem that isn't easily solved, it's often helpful to ask, "What would I think of this problem if any one of the facts involved was removed from the equation?" If one arrives at a conclusion that can be tested, it is often worthwhile to do so, or at least to reexamine the datum in question to make sure it is valid. This sort of analysis is difficult to do well, but in very difficult situations, it can prove a fruitful line of attack.

Another troubleshooting technique is preventive in nature—baselining the system. To understand what's going wrong when the system behaves poorly, it is crucial to understand how the server should behave when the system performs correctly. One cannot overemphasize this point. On a performance-critical server, an administrator should record data using each diagnostic tool that might be employed during a crisis when the server is in the following states:

- Idle, with services running but unused
- Moderately loaded
- Heavily loaded, but providing an adequate response

Then, when the server begins to perform badly, one can determine what has changed on the system. "What is different about the overloaded system from the state where it is heavily loaded, but providing quality service?" This is a much easier question to answer than the more abstract, "Why is this server performing poorly?"

The complexity of today's operating systems exacerbates this need. On most contemporary operating systems, it's much more difficult to tell the difference, for example, between normal memory paging activity and desperation swapping. It's difficult to know objectively what a reasonable percentage of output packet errors on a network interface would be. It's difficult to tell objectively how many `mail.local` processes should be sleeping, waiting for such esoterica as an `nc_rele_lock` event to wake them up. As with people, on computer systems many forms of unusual behavior can be measured only in relative terms. Without a baseline, this identification can't happen.

Previously, I mentioned how important it is to distinguish information related to a present problem from incidental information. Without a baseline, it can be difficult—if not impossible—to tell whether a given piece of information is even out of the ordinary. When something goes wrong, while looking for the source of the problem we've all encountered something unexpected and asked ourselves, "Was this always like that?" Baselining reduces the number of times this uncertainty will arise in a crisis, which should lead to faster problem resolution.

Run baseline tests periodically and compare their results against previous test runs. Going the extra mile and performing a more formal trend analysis can prove very valuable, too. It offers two benefits. First, it enables one to spot situations that slowly are evolving into problems before they become noticeable. Of course, not all changes represent problems waiting to happen, but trend analysis can also spot secular changes in the way a server operates, which may indicate new patterns in user behavior or changes in Internet operation.

Second, formal trend analysis allows administrators to become more familiar with the servers they are charged with maintaining, which is unequivocally a good thing. More familiarity means problems are spotted sooner and resolved more quickly. System administrators responsible for maintaining high-performance, critical servers who do not have time to perform these tasks are overburdened. In this case, when something fails not only will they be unprepared to deal with the crisis, but other important tasks will go unfulfilled elsewhere as a consequence.

In the "old days," many guru-level system administrators could tell how, or even what, the systems in their charge were running by looking at the lights blink or listening to the disks spin or heads move. They could *feel* what was happening in the box. Today's trend toward less obtrusive and quieter hardware has been part and parcel of the considerable improvements made in hardware reliability. This is a good thing. However, through these hardware changes, as well as the aforementioned increasing operating system complexity and the much larger quantity of boxes for which a system administrator is responsible, we've largely lost this valuable *feel* for the systems we maintain. Now the data on the system state are likely the only window we have into the operational characteristics of these servers. It should be considered an investment to periodically get acquainted with the machines we maintain so as to increase the chance of finding problems before they become readily apparent, and to give us the insight necessary to reduce the time to repair catastrophic problems when they do occur.

7.2 The Quick Fix

Despite our preventive measures, let us suppose a server does get itself into a jam and email backs up. Further suppose that we know the problem is that the disk on which the queue resides is not fast enough to handle the load. We may already have another disk ready and an outage window scheduled to perform the upgrade when the system will be less busy, perhaps after most people have gone home from work for the day. Once we can take the machine down, we plan to carefully back up the data on the queue disk, verify the backup, add the second disk, stripe the old and new disks together using software RAID, bring the system back up, test it, restore the backed-up data, verify that this restoration went well, restart services, monitor them for a while, and call it a success. All in all, this strategy sounds like a well-reasoned upgrade plan.

The question is, What should we do *now*? The upgrade window may be hours (or perhaps days) away, the system is running slowly at this moment, and users or management may be asking if something can be done in the short term. Sometimes a quick fix is possible. If the server normally serves other functions, perhaps they can be suspended temporarily. With a POP server, perhaps incoming email could be turned off or at least dialed back long enough so that users can read the email they already have. Temporarily turning off lower-priority services is a reasonable reaction to a short-term performance crunch.

In some circumstances, one might be tempted to try to make short-term alterations to the server to get through the crisis. One could attempt to move older messages out of the queue and into another queue to expedite processing of the main queue. One could lower the `RefuseLA` parameter in the `sendmail.cf` file to try to lower the load on the system. Many other things could be attempted as well. In reality, these attempts at short-term fixes rarely help. Usually, it's best to just let the server work its way out of a jam.

Some assistance, such as rotating the queue or perhaps changing the queue sort order to be less resource intensive, can prove beneficial, but most of the other problems won't be mitigated by just stirring the pot. For example, if one wants to move messages from one queue to another queue on a different disk, what operations must happen on the busy disk? The files will be located, read, and then unlinked. This is exactly the same load that will be put on the disk if the message is delivered. If the message will be delivered on the next attempt, we gain *nothing* by trying to move it. If the message will not be delivered for a while, we can lower the total number of operations on the disk by rotating the queues, and then suspending or reducing the processing of the old queue temporarily. Performing a queue rotation requires far fewer disk operations while deferring or reducing the number of attempts that will be made to deliver queued messages.

Similarly, attempting to reduce the number of processes, the maximum load average on the system, or otherwise trying to choke off one resource in order to reduce the load on another typically arises from a spurious assumption. One may be able to reduce the load on the queue disks, for example, by reducing the number of `sendmail` processes that run on a server. However, reducing the load on the disk doesn't solve the problem, because the load on the disk is a *symptom* of the problem. The real problem is that more email is coming in than the server can handle. In this case, having a saturated disk is a *good* thing. It means that the disk is processing data as fast as it can. If we lower the amount of data it processes, the server will process less email. The external demand on the busy server will not decline because of our actions, but rather increase because we have voluntarily decreased the server's ability to process data, which is the last thing that we want to do.

Some administrators might voice concerns that a system under saturation load will run less efficiently and, therefore, process fewer messages per unit time than a less busy server does. With some types of systems, this concern is well founded, but two points make this possibility less of an issue for the sorts of email systems discussed in this book than for other types of systems.

The first point is that while there exist a large number of fixed resource pools on an email server (CPU, memory, disk I/O, and so on), each process on that server remains largely independent. Thus one process running slowly generally does not cause another process to run slowly, other than through the side effect that both may compete for a slice of the same fixed resource pie. For example, if a system is running so slowly that the process table fills and the master `sendmail` daemon can't fork off a new process to handle a new incoming connection, this issue doesn't cause a currently running `sendmail` process to stop working. These events are largely independent of one another. It doesn't matter to a remote email server whether an SMTP session with the busy server couldn't be established because the master daemon cannot fork a child process or whether the connection is rejected by policy to avoid loading the server.

On the other hand, if, for example, `sendmail` were a multithreaded process running on the server with one thread handling each connection, and it didn't have internal protection against running out of memory, then the process running out of available memory could affect any or all other `sendmail` threads of execution, which could have catastrophic consequences. Fortunately, today's UNIX versions do a remarkably good job of isolating the effects of one process on another. If yet another process is competing for a fixed resource, that conflict may cause the other processes using that resource to run more slowly, but the resource will almost always be allocated fairly and *the total throughput of the system will stay roughly constant*, which is what we really want to happen.

The second point is that even if the system is processing less total data in saturation than it would under a more carefully controlled load, maneuvering the system to achieve higher throughput is very tricky. If some threshold, such as `MaxDaemonChildren`, is lowered too little, it will have no effect on the system's total throughput. If it is lowered too much, resources will go unused, which will lower aggregate throughput—a disaster. The sweet spot between these two extremes is often very narrow, hard to find, and, worst of all, time dependent. That is, the right value for `MaxDaemonChildren` might differ depending on whether a queue runner has just started, how large the messages currently being processed are, or how user behavior contributes to the total server load.

In summary:

1. When a server gets busy, the most important thing is to find the real cause of the problem and schedule a permanent fix for it at the earliest convenient moment.

2. In the meantime, one might be able to do some things to help out in the short term, such as temporarily diverting resources away from lower-priority tasks.

3. Making configuration changes to overcome short-term problems is difficult at best, and will often cause the total amount of data processed by the server to go down, not up, which is not desirable.

4. Because an email server generally allocates limited resources fairly, even when saturated with requests, the best course of action is often to let the server regulate its own resources, as it will likely do so more efficiently than it would with human intervention.

When a real fix for a saturated email server can't be implemented immediately, it's usually better to let the server stay saturated and, hopefully, work its way out of a jam rather than to try to interfere.

7.3 Tools

In this section, we examine just a few of the tools that are likely to be useful to the email administrator. Many possibilities are available—many more than are listed here. Some are very specific, whereas others have broad applications. The tools discussed here are both generally useful and widely available. Email administrators interested in tuning, or just understanding, an email system should not restrict their studies to just the utilities mentioned here. Magazine articles, books, Web sites, and other system administrators can all provide insight into very helpful tools.

Each tool discussed has different options and displays slightly different information on each operating system version. While this inconsistency is annoying, some of the differences are tied to the internal workings of the operating system and are unavoidable. Also, some of the less common options are the most useful. It's just not practical to limit the use of these utilities to their common flag and output subsets, so that won't be done here. Instead, this section will generally provide examples using the FreeBSD (version 4.5) operating system utilities, throwing in some examples specific to other operating systems.

A final note: As we know from science, it is impossible to measure a system without affecting it. Just by running a tool we necessarily change the behavior of the very computer we're monitoring. These utilities consume memory and CPU time, they open sockets and files, and they read data off disks. Therefore, we can never be entirely sure that a problem that we observe on a system isn't at least partially influenced by the fact that we're monitoring it. Although this is rarely the case, it's a good idea to not go overboard by continually running top or by having scripts run ps every five seconds to capture the state of the machine. A much more modest approach to capturing data (running ps every five minutes, for example) will provide equally useful information without adding substantially to the server's load.

7.3.1 ps

The venerable ps utility comes in two flavors: the Berkeley flavor (found on BSD-based systems and Linux) and the System V flavor (found on AIX, HP-UX, and other systems). Solaris provides the System V flavor in /usr/bin, and the Berkeley flavor appears in /usr/ucb. My preference is for the Berkeley-style output of ps; I like the information it provides and the way that the Berkeley ps -u sorts the data. Essentially the same information is available from either version, however, so other than remembering which option does what, one shouldn't be handicapped by any particular flavor.

A lot of information is available from ps, and it's especially useful for such tasks as tracking the number of certain types of processes running on a machine or seeing which processes are the largest resource consumers. A great deal of information is available from this program, which varies depending on the option flags selected. Everyone performing system troubleshooting would be well advised to become very familiar with the ps man page for the operating system that runs on their email server.

For both varieties of ps, some command-line flags require more processing to resolve than others. On Berkeley-type systems, it is more computationally intensive to resolve commands with the -u flag than without it. For System V versions, adding the -l flag requires more computational resources than if the command is run without it. Therefore, these flags, which produce extra output, should be used only when they relate important information. One thing that ps provides is rough process counts, for example:

```
ps -acx | grep -c "sendmail"
```

These sorts of data are useful, and periodic counts are often scripted. Especially in automated systems, it's worthwhile to make sure that they produce minimal strain on the server. Determining which options are more resource intensive than others isn't always straightforward, but the `time` command or shell built-in can aid in this calculation. On quiet servers, the response time for this command might be too fast to measure, so the aggregation of several commands may provide a more precise measurement. For example:

```
/usr/bin/time sh -c 'for i in 1 2 3 4 5 6 7 8 9 10; \
    do ps -aux > /dev/null; done'
```

Some `ps` output from the CPU-bound test server during one of the tests cited earlier in this book appears in Table 7.1. At the moment that this snapshot was taken, `syslogd` was the most active process. While it is a busy process on an email server, it rarely does the most work at any given time. However, unlike the MTA and LDA processes that move data, this persistent process reads data from the IP stack and writes it to disk on every delivery attempt.

Adding all numbers in the RSS column, they roughly equal the system's total main memory (only 32MB), which doesn't count RAM consumed by the kernel or the buffer cache. Because much of the memory consumed by the processes is shared, it provides enough space to keep the parts of the programs that run while resident in memory and still allow extra space for the kernel and the buffer cache.

On this machine, the `script` command is used to capture output from the `iostat` and `vmstat` commands, which will be discussed shortly. The `stat` entry is a home-built script that adds date and time information to the output of these two utilities. As we'd expect, most of the CPU time is consumed by `sendmail` and `mail.local` processes. Also as we'd expect, concurrent MTA processes outnumber LDA processes, even though the email is sent to this server over a low-latency local area network.

Most of the rest of the processes running on this server are either standard parts of the operating system or processes related to remote connections to the server.

7.3.2 **top**

Many UNIX operating systems include the venerable `top` utility, which is also one of the first Open Source programs installed on many other operating systems. The `top` utility lists the largest CPU resource consumers on a system and updates this list periodically, typically every few seconds. For understanding the general state of the system, some of the most valuable information appears in the first few lines of the program's display. A system consistently showing a CPU idle state at or near 0% is

Table 7.1. Sample `/usr/ucb/ps -uaxc` Output from the CPU-Bound Test Server

```
% /usr/ucb/ps -uaxc
USER        PID %CPU %MEM    SZ  RSS TT        S   START   TIME COMMAND
root      11302  1.3  3.3  3480 1004 ?         S 15:03:18  0:23 syslogd
root      23420  1.1  4.3  2296 1304 ?         R 16:05:56  0:02 sendmail
root      24881  0.9  5.6  2392 1700 ?         S 16:13:11  0:00 sendmail
root      24884  0.8  5.3  2352 1592 ?         R 16:13:11  0:00 sendmail
root      24861  0.7  5.6  2392 1700 ?         S 16:13:07  0:00 sendmail
root      11009  0.6  3.9  2012 1172 ?         S 14:47:30  0:08 nscd
root      24871  0.6  3.4  1552 1016 ?         S 16:13:08  0:00 mail.local
root      24886  0.5  5.0  2312 1516 ?         R 16:13:12  0:00 sendmail
root      24892  0.5  2.9  1140  860 pts/4     O 16:13:13  0:00 ps
test1     24890  0.5  3.4  1552 1012 ?         R 16:13:12  0:00 mail.local
root      24889  0.4  5.0  2312 1516 ?         R 16:13:12  0:00 sendmail
root      18650  0.3  3.8  1712 1160 ?         S 15:45:14  0:01 sshd
npc       18716  0.2  2.5  1016  756 pts/4     S 15:45:24  0:00 csh
root      24891  0.2  1.7  2296  492 ?         S 16:13:12  0:00 sendmail
npc       23454  0.2  1.9   856  580 pts/3     S 16:08:02  0:00 stat
root      23449  0.1  1.9   856  580 pts/2     S 16:08:00  0:00 stat
npc       23434  0.1  1.9   788  560 pts/0     S 16:06:48  0:00 script
root          3  0.0  0.0     0    0 ?         S  Feb 04 19:27 fsflush
root          0  0.0  0.0     0    0 ?         T  Feb 04  0:00 sched
root          1  0.0  0.5   652  132 ?         S  Feb 04  0:26 init
root          2  0.0  0.0     0    0 ?         S  Feb 04  0:02 pageout
root        156  0.0  1.8  1464  548 ?         S  Feb 04  0:01 cron
root        159  0.0  2.4  1644  724 ?         S  Feb 04  1:46 sshd
root        174  0.0  1.6   852  480 ?         S  Feb 04  0:00 utmpd
root        203  0.0  2.1  1404  632 ?         S  Feb 04  0:00 sac
root        204  0.0  2.1  1496  624 console   S  Feb 04  0:00 ttymon
root        206  0.0  2.3  1496  688 ?         S  Feb 04  0:00 ttymon
root      10540  0.0  3.1  1800  936 ?         S 14:19:23  0:10 sshd
npc       10543  0.0  1.5  1012  448 pts/1     S 14:19:33  0:00 csh
root      10554  0.0  0.0   276    4 pts/1     S 14:20:03  0:00 sh
root      11262  0.0  3.0  1712  904 ?         S 15:01:22  0:02 sshd
npc       11265  0.0  2.5  1028  756 pts/0     S 15:01:25  0:00 csh
root      11456  0.0  2.7  1052  800 pts/1     S 15:05:33  0:00 csh
root      23429  0.0  1.8   764  536 pts/1     S 16:06:46  0:00 script
root      23430  0.0  1.9   788  560 pts/1     S 16:06:46  0:00 script
root      23431  0.0  2.4   996  732 pts/2     S 16:06:46  0:00 csh
npc       23433  0.0  1.8   764  536 pts/0     S 16:06:48  0:00 script
npc       23435  0.0  2.7  1024  804 pts/3     S 16:06:48  0:00 csh
root      23448  0.0  2.2   840  660 pts/2     S 16:08:00  0:00 vmstat
npc       23453  0.0  2.3   848  684 pts/3     S 16:08:02  0:00 iostat
```

almost certainly CPU bound. The caveat is that some systems list an `iowait` state indicating what percentage of processes are waiting for I/O. This number doesn't represent CPU time being consumed, but rather consists of the system's best guess as to the amount of CPU time that would be consumed if no processes were blocked waiting for I/O. If a significant percentage of processes are in the `iowait` state, then the system may show 0% idle while the CPU is barely being used.

In the upper-left corner is the last process identifier (PID) used by the system. From its rate of change, one can deduce how many new processes are spawned per second, giving some idea of how fast sessions are coming and going on the server. This method isn't useful on those few operating systems, such as OpenBSD, that assign new PIDs randomly rather than sequentially.

The memory information displayed isn't as useful as one would first expect. On nearly any system that has been running for a few minutes, or even a few seconds if it's busy, we should expect the amount of free memory listed to stay very near zero. On contemporary operating systems, any RAM that goes unused by processes will be allocated to caching some data. Thus, just because there is very little memory free, it doesn't mean that the system is memory starved. On some operating systems, `top` will show more memory information, such as how much RAM is allocated to filesystem caches; if this number drops near zero, it would likely indicate that the server would use additional RAM effectively.

Even more so than with `ps`, the information displayed via `top` varies from operating system to operating system. A thorough reading of the utility's man page should be performed before its results are interpreted.

7.3.3 `vmstat`

The `vmstat` utility explores the activity of the virtual memory system, which includes real memory used by processes, memory used for caching, and swap space. The first line of data produced summarizes the activity since the system was booted. Generally, this information should be ignored.

While it's much less impressive than the output that one will find on a true high-performance email server, some example output from the CPU-bound server during one of the test cases discussed in this book can be instructive. This output appears in Table 7.2.

Excessive memory activity will cause heavy paging, which translates into relatively large numbers in the `pi` and `po` columns. Of course, what constitutes a large number depends heavily on the particular system. Interpreting these numbers without a baseline will be next to impossible. In the example case, these numbers are so small that we can safely conclude that the system is not memory bound.

Table 7.2. Sample `vmstat` 15 Output from the CPU-Bound Test Server

```
% vmstat 15
 r  b  w  swap   free   re    mf pi  po    fr de sr   in    sy   cs us sy  id
 0  0  0  4692   1804   0      0  0   0     0  0  0    3    39   22  0  0 100
 7  1  0 64440   1956   5    925  6  38    38  0  0  256  2150  328 31 68   2
 8  0  0 64008   1800   8    923  0  40    44  0  1  249  2030  285 24 67   9
 8  0  0 64612   2276  10    950  1  46    48  0  0  249  2079  283 27 66   7
 7  1  0 64712   2956   4    954  6  23    94  0 22  262  2101  294 28 67   5
 7  1  0 64320   2852   0   1024  2   0     0  0  0  271  2260  317 27 73   0
 9  0  0 61684   1960   8    995  6  62   170  0 37  281  2186  329 29 71   0
 7  0  0 62968   3836   0   1061  4   0     0  0  0  255  2209  315 29 71   0
15  1  0 58508   1800  12    956  7  71   138  0 27  288  2302  342 30 70   0
 6  0  0 62936   4860   2   1035  1  10    10  0  0  252  2072  299 26 71   2
```

On those systems whose `vmstat` provides this information, another column worth tracking is `de`. It gives a system's expected short-term memory deficiency, for which memory space will have to be actively reclaimed. A nonzero entry will show up occasionally in this column on a healthy but busy system. The more often this result appears, though, the more likely the system could use more memory. Our sample data show no deficiencies, another indication that this system is not memory bound.

The first column, labeled `r`, indicates the number of runnable processes, which provides a snapshot of the system load average. In this example, a number of processes want to run but can't because they have no CPU time slice available to them. The second column, labeled `b`, gives the number of processes that are blocked from proceeding because they are waiting for I/O. If a significant number of processes are listed in this column, the system is likely I/O bound. In our example, we occasionally see a blocked process, but this event is rare, giving us an indication that this system isn't I/O bound. Yet one more variable worth tracking is the third column, labeled `w`. It represents the number of processes that are either runnable or have been idle for a short period of time and have now been swapped out. Frequent nonzero numbers in this column also indicate that the server may be desperately short of RAM. The example looks like it's in good shape on that point.

In the past, one could tell whether a system was memory starved just by looking for swapping activity, as opposed to the more healthy activity of paging. Paging is the process of writing parts of process data to swap space to make room for pages of other data in active memory. An operating system may "page out" part of a process if that page hasn't been accessed in a while, even if the process is running. This efficient behavior allows new processes to start up more quickly because memory reclamations don't need to occur first, and it leaves more room for caching data, leading to better performance. Some amount of paging will occur on all operating systems and is considered normal and healthy.

Swapping usually refers to taking a process and moving its entire memory image to disk. It might happen if the process has remained idle for a very long time (tens of seconds, which is a very long time in computer terms) or if the system desperately needs to make room for new processes. "Desperation swapping" and "thrashing" are terms used to describe a system that is so memory starved that nearly every time a process receives a CPU slice, it must be read in from swap to active memory before it can proceed. This horrible circumstance effectively slows memory access (typically measured in tens of nanoseconds) to disk speeds (measured in ones to tens to hundreds of milliseconds, a difference of two to four orders of magnitude). Once a system starts thrashing, it will not operate efficiently. One should aggressively avoid this situation.

Somewhat unfortunately, as virtual memory algorithms have become more complex and sophisticated over the years, it's become more difficult to tell in a vacuum whether a system is thrashing. In fact, many operating systems don't distinguish between paging and swapping, eliminating the latter behavior altogether. Here is where a baseline becomes crucial. One must understand what sort of paging statistics occur on a heavily loaded but properly operating server before one can determine whether a system is beginning to thrash. However, once the disks with swap on them begin to get loaded, it will be painfully obvious that the system has simply run out of memory. Of course, this behavior will occur beyond the point where a server starts to slow down noticeably.

Solaris 8 introduced a new system for managing the buffer cache. Now the page daemon is no longer needed to free up memory used to cache filesystem information. Consequently, the page daemon does not have to do any work to reclaim memory space for new processes. The upshot is that on Solaris 8, if the `sr` field of `vmstat` output is nonzero, running processes are being paged to disk to make room for new processes. On this operating system, it has now become more straightforward to identify significant memory deficiencies. Significant activity in the `sr` field on other operating systems can indicate that the machine is memory starved, but the demarkation point is not as obvious as it is on Solaris 8.

7.3.4 `iostat`

The `iostat` tool is similar to `vmstat`, except that it measures system I/O rather than virtual memory statistics. On many systems, it can measure not only disk-by-disk data transfers, but also I/O information to and from a wide variety of sources,

Table 7.3. Sample `iostat -cx 15` Output from the CPU-Bound Test Server

```
% iostat -cx 15
                        extended device statistics              cpu
device  r/s   w/s   kr/s   kw/s  wait  actv  svc_t  %w  %b  us  sy  wt   id
sd0     0.0   0.6   0.1    3.0   0.0   0.0    9.2   0   1    0   0   0   100
sd3     0.0   0.0   0.0    0.2   0.0   0.0   22.8   0   0

                        extended device statistics              cpu
device  r/s   w/s   kr/s   kw/s  wait  actv  svc_t  %w  %b  us  sy  wt   id
sd0     0.5  12.0   1.7   62.0   0.0   0.1   10.9   0  12   27  68   1    4
sd3     0.0  47.9   0.0  225.8   0.0   0.4    7.4   0  30

                        extended device statistics              cpu
device  r/s   w/s   kr/s   kw/s  wait  actv  svc_t  %w  %b  us  sy  wt   id
sd0     0.7  10.7   1.9   54.3   0.0   0.1   11.0   0  11   29  71   0    0
sd3     0.2  51.2   0.4  251.9   0.0   0.5   10.0   0  34

                        extended device statistics              cpu
device  r/s   w/s   kr/s   kw/s  wait  actv  svc_t  %w  %b  us  sy  wt   id
sd0     0.7  13.9   2.4   71.1   0.0   0.2   11.1   0  14   29  71   0    0
sd3     0.9  47.6   1.3  235.7   0.0   0.4    9.2   0  33

                        extended device statistics              cpu
device  r/s   w/s   kr/s   kw/s  wait  actv  svc_t  %w  %b  us  sy  wt   id
sd0     0.7   9.8   2.3   51.3   0.0   0.1   10.2   0  10   30  70   0    0
sd3     1.0  54.0   1.8  268.9   0.0   0.5    8.3   0  36
```

including tape drives, printers, scanners, ttys, and so on. Like vmstat, this command displays CPU information in the last set of columns. On many systems, if one specifies no I/O devices, it can be a good mechanism to track CPU usage in scripts, such as running `iostat -c 60` to get basic output of CPU information every minute on a Linux or Solaris system. As with vmstat, the first line of output by the iostat program is a summary since boot time and is effectively useless. Table 7.3 gives some data gathered with iostat while testing earlier examples in this book.

Typically, iostat reports its data as kilobytes per second or transfers per second. In this example, reads and writes per second for each device are listed in the second and third columns, while the amount of data being moved appears in the fourth and fifth columns. Some versions also show how long the average transfer takes, svc_t in this example, which can be very useful metric for determining loading. If this number starts going up, it indicates that the device is heavily loaded.

On Solaris and some recent versions of Linux, the -x flag gives even more valuable information, as in this example, including the average amount of time each request spends in the wait queue and the percentage of time I/O requests are waiting to be serviced by the disk device. These numbers represent some of the best indicators of disk contention in the absence of a baseline, but they're no substitute for one. A disk can be 100% busy and yet the system can still provide adequate service. In our example, we can clearly see that the two disk devices (sd0 contains the message store and sd3 contains the logs and the email queue) are not saturated and, therefore, this system is not I/O bound.

Knowing that a disk always has requests sitting in the wait queue doesn't explain why a change in server behavior has occurred. If kilobytes per second increases while tps remains constant, it would indicate that we're dealing with larger requests, which may alert us to a temporary or permanent change in the type of email flowing through the system.

On some operating systems, iostat has problems reporting useful information about disks managed by software RAID or from a hardware RAID system. This is especially true for those numbers indicated on a percentage basis. Absolute throughput numbers such as numbers of reads and writes per second or bytes per second compared against a baseline are likely to be more reliable. Because email servers so often become I/O bound, iostat may be the single most important utility in the email administrator's toolkit. Anyone who expects to maintain such a system would be well advised to become very familiar with it.

In the operating system used in the examples here (Solaris 2.6), note that the CPU loading information given by the iostat command lists an I/O wait stat (the wt column), whereas the vmstat command lumps it in with the idle CPU state (the id column). Someone who looked at just the vmstat output might conclude that the system is not quite CPU bound, whereas this result would become more obvious if the CPU loading information was examined via top or iostat.

7.3.5 netstat

The third tool in the "*stat" trio is netstat. As one would expect, netstat provides information about system networking. It can display either a snapshot of very detailed information about nearly every conceivable network parameter (netstat -s) or periodic data like that found with vmstat or iostat (e.g., netstat -w 5 on BSD systems, netstat -i 5 on Solaris, or netstat -c on Linux).

Obviously, in its periodic mode, some of the parameters provided by netstat that we want to carefully observe include the number of packets per second and the number of bytes per second. Both statistics, and especially trends in them, can provide the most direct information on the objective external load on a system, so they should be tracked. How the ratio of input to output statistics might change can also be highly informative.

On some types of shared networks, such as Ethernet, when computers are connected to the network via a hub rather than a switch, two machines could potentially try to send a network packet at the same time. This attempt can result in a collision. Both senders will then wait for a small, random amount of time and try to send their packets again. On a shared network, the number of collisions is a good indicator of general network load. Again, hard and fast numbers are difficult to identify, as they depend on the speed of the network, packet sizes, and the number of other machines on the network, but as a rule of thumb a busy email server should not reside on a network that consistently shows hundreds of collisions per second. On a switched network, no collisions should occur. If they do arise, it might mean that the switch, or the connection between the server and the switch, dropped into a nonswitched mode for some period of time. To avoid this possibility, one can lock network interfaces on switched networks into full-duplex, rather than letting them autonegotiate speed and mode.

The other piece of data of special value from `netstat` in periodic mode involves the error rates. An error usually indicates that a packet has failed its checksum—that is, its contents don't match what the packet header indicates. An output error indicates that this problem occurred somewhere between the formation of the packet by the operating system and its transmission over the wire. This result is never good. Even a handful of entries in this field can indicate a serious problem with the server's NIC and should be investigated. Input errors are less severe, as a packet might legitimately have become corrupted traveling over a network to the server, but input error rates of even 0.1% may indicate a network problem, such as bad cabling, electrical interference, or a bad NIC. An error rate of 1% means something is seriously wrong with the network somewhere, and this problem should be tracked down and eliminated before it worsens and interferes with operations.

7.3.6 sar

On System V-derived UNIX versions, you can run the System Activity Reporter (`sar`) program in the background to gather statistics and accounting information, including much of the data reported by the tools that have already been mentioned in this section. It is an excellent baselining tool, and collecting data every 1 to 15 minutes on a system via `sar` and archiving those data is something that every server administrator should seriously consider. This effort will be worthwhile on any system where performance monitoring is important.

Just about every piece of data one could want to examine is available via `sar`. In fact, it's more likely that one will miss key information due to the presence of too much data than that information on the nature of a given problem isn't available. This tool provides a superset of the information available from vmstat, iostat, netstat, and other utilities. Any performance-critical server administrator should become very familiar with sar and its affiliated utilities.

7.3.7 Other Utilities

Many other utilities could have been mentioned here, such as pstat, lsof, ifconfig, systat, pstack, ad nauseum. They have been omitted not because they're not valuable, but because a line must be drawn somewhere. Playing around with these other possibilities is worthwhile with the proviso that before one makes a new utility part of the "canon," it should be demonstrated that programs that are more familiar and already on the system cannot easily generate the same information.

Finally, if for no other reason than to satisfy the reader's curiosity, I'll explain the stat shell script that appeared on the example ps output. This trivial script receives output from commands such as vmstat and iostat that do not indicate the date and time the data were gathered, and adds this information. Thus, instead of

```
% vmstat 15
 procs          memory ...
 r b w swap  free  re ...
 0 0 0  4692  1804   0 ...
 7 1 0 64440  1956   5 ...
 8 0 0 64008  1800   8 ...
 8 0 0 64612  2276  10 ...
```

we could run

```
% vmstat 15 | /usr/local/etc/stat
020315 15:14:03  procs          memory ...
020315 15:14:03  r b w swap free  re ...
020315 15:14:03  0 0 0  4692 1804   0 ...
020315 15:14:18  7 1 0 64440 1956   5 ...
020315 15:14:33  8 0 0 64008 1800   8 ...
020315 15:14:48  8 0 0 64612 2276  10 ...
```

Now data from one source can be matched up in time against data from another source.

The stat script is trivial:

```
#!/bin/sh

OLDIFS=$IFS
IFS=
while read LINE
do
        echo -n `date "+%y%m%d %H:%M:%S"'
        echo " " $LINE
done
IFS=$OLDIFS
```

IFS is redefined to be null so that the whitespace isn't adjusted when each line of input is collected by the read command.

7.4 syslog

The syslog facility isn't a program used to evaluate system performance, but rather a set of library calls and a daemon, syslogd, that records information that the system and its programs think is worth logging. All email server applications mentioned in this book, but especially sendmail, use syslog to log data about their behavior, and it would be unwise for an email administrator to ignore this fact. The syslog package was originally developed as a part of the sendmail distribution to help maintain the information it would log. It was later adopted by the rest of Berkeley UNIX around the BSD 4.1 timeframe, and from there spread to other UNIX versions. Now it has become so ubiquitous that the fact that its origin is tied to sendmail has been largely forgotten.

7.4.1 syslog and sendmail

During an SMTP message reception, sendmail logs the sender information at the end of the message transaction, whether the message is actually sent or not. If the message is accepted, then the log entry occurs after the end of the DATA phase. If the message is rejected, then the log entry is made immediately after the rejection. During a successful SMTP message reception, sendmail logs the recipient information at the end of the session, although the precise timing can vary depending on sendmail's delivery mode. At the conclusion of each failed delivery attempt, that attempt is also logged. At least two log entries for each successful delivery and one log entry for each unsuccessful attempt, plus various other entries for start-up, encountering errors, STARTTLS information, and so on, will be made. The two types of log entries mentioned initially make up the bulk of the log messages generated, however, and are the two that occur as a result of a successful delivery. All of these log messages can result in a lot of data, and this information can provide significant insight into what is happening on the server.

Here is an example sendmail log entry for a successful message delivery:

```
Mar 12 14:39:49 discovery sendmail[44639]: g2CMdnkq044639:
 from=<npc@acm.org>, size=1047, class=0, nrcpts=1,
 msgid=<200203122239.g2CMdcQL044635@mail.acm.org>,
 proto=ESMTP, daemon=MTA, relay=mail.acm.org [199.222.69.4]
Mar 12 14:39:49 discovery sendmail[44641]: g2CMdnkq044639:
 to=<npc@gangofone.com>, delay=00:00:00, xdelay=00:00:00,
 mailer=local, pri=30052, dsn=2.0.0, stat=Sent
```

The first question asked might be, "How do we count the total number of messages that flow through the system?" This question isn't as simple to answer as it might seem. The answer depends on whether one wants to count the number of SMTP connections, the number of unique messages as sent by a sender, or the number of messages (often sent to multiple recipients) that end up in someone's mailbox somewhere. Each of these metrics is a valid choice, but in my judgment the bulk of the work is done for each successful message recipient, so I generally choose to count the number of syslog entries with both the to= pattern and stat=Sent in them. I call that measure the number of messages that the system has successfully processed, mindful that it is merely one statistic that is much more nebulous than it appears at first glance.

If we consider the format of these log entries to contain a set of fields delimited by whitespace, the first three fields contain information about the date and time when the log entry was made. This information can be parsed to track the busiest time of day for the server. In the from entry, the eighth field contains the size of the message in bytes, which we can use to find out the average message size handled by the system. On the same entry, the tenth field lists the number of recipients per message, another interesting statistic to track. In the to entry, the information in the delay and xdelay fields are of particular interest. The delay field measures the total amount of elapsed time between the receipt of the message and this particular delivery attempt. The xdelay field, which stands for transaction delay, measures the amount of time consumed on this particular delivery attempt, which should reveal something about the current connectivity to a particular site.

A great deal more information available in the logs can be extracted for various purposes, but at this point the next step will be left to the imagination of the reader. Section 2.1.1 of the *Sendmail Installation and Operation Guide* provides additional information on the sendmail log entries.

A similar set of information can be extracted from the logs left by any of the POP or IMAP daemons discussed in this book. Combined with other statistical information gathered with the tools described here, one can plot number of processes versus load average, connection rates versus disk activity, and so on to obtain a thorough understanding of any email server's performance. These checks can be easily automated, and at least the most basic ones should be part of an email administrator's baselining effort.

7.4.2 `syslog` and Performance

If a server handles a large volume of email, the resources consumed by syslog in writing out the many log entries can be significant. On very large servers, mounting /var/log or its equivalent on its own disk might be appropriate. Beyond this point, an additional syslog issue directly affects performance that should be mentioned. On Linux systems, by default the syslog daemon will fsync() its log files after each entry is written to them. On a busy email server, this operation can cause a measurable slowdown. In most organizations, email server logs aren't so critical. This behavior can be switched off by preceding the appropriate entry in the /etc/syslog.conf file with "-":

```
mail.* -/var/adm/mail
```

If logging continues to pose a performance problem for a host, it may be appropriate to log the information to a dedicated remote logging host. If this step is taken, replacing the mail. entries in /etc/syslog.conf with one like the following may be appropriate:

```
mail.* @loghost.example.com
```

The loghost.example.com machine may end up aggregating log information for a large number of hosts. Because the host name is included in each log entry, it should be straightforward to split the entries out again on the log host if desired. On the log host, a RAID system with a high-performance filesystem may be mounted on /var/log to handle this load.

One downside to remote logging is that syslog sends its messages to the log host using UDP. Thus, if a log message becomes lost en route, it will not be retransmitted. This behavior makes this method less useful if saving each log message is critical. One way to work around it is to replace the default `syslog` daemon with `syslog-ng` [SYS] or one of several packages with similar feature sets that support logging over TCP.

7.5 Removing Bottlenecks

Let's assume that the system bottleneck has been revealed using the techniques described earlier in this chapter. The next logical question to ask is, "What should be done about it?" Some of the methods for effecting an improvement in system performance will be obvious, and many have been discussed already. In this section we will explore some of the ways in which bottlenecks may be alleviated and some of the pitfalls that may be encountered.

It may seem that identifying the bottleneck and planning the fix should be the most difficult part of improving system performance, and they usually are. Additional frustration may arise, however. We never really completely eliminate bottlenecks—we just improve the throughput of one aspect of a system. A truism of information technology seems to be that the load placed on servers increases over time. As the load on an email server grows, it is inevitable that we will eventually encounter another bottleneck that must be removed. Perhaps this next bottleneck lurks just around the corner, raising its ugly head after our capacity increases just a few percentage points from the level at which the last obstacle was removed. If we have a set of disks on a SCSI-2 interface that is saturated at peak times while delivering 8 Mbps of data to our applications, we won't have long to wait after upgrading the disks before the SCSI controller becomes a bottleneck. Sometimes, as in this example, the next hurdle that will need to be overcome is easy to see. At other times, it's almost invisible. With experience comes better instincts about where the next problem lurks, and with some support from the folks who control budgets, perhaps some of these roadblocks can be eliminated before they slow down the system again. No matter how much experience a person has, no one can anticipate everything. This uncertainty is just one of the things that makes the job so challenging.

7.5.1 CPU-Bound Systems

With a CPU-bound system, the first step is to see if anything currently running on the server can be stopped or moved to another server. If that's possible, it would be a fortunate fix. Of course, one cannot eliminate unnecessary tasks indefinitely.

Sometimes a shortage of CPU power really masks another problem—for example, the system may be working very hard to move processes in and out of swap space. The danger in interpreting utilities that seem to report CPU utilization but also report I/O utilization, such as some versions of `top` or `vmstat`, has already been discussed.

By some measures, having a CPU-bound system is a good thing. It usually indicates that the rest of the system is well tuned and operating efficiently. Besides, CPU is often the easiest component to upgrade. Even in the worst-case scenario, we can expect the new chip released in the next quarter to offer a larger percentage improvement over the current product line than for any other computer component of the next-generation system.

Finally, the email applications discussed in this book have all run many processes simultaneously to handle multiple requests. Thus they operate in parallel very nicely to work on multiprocessor computers. If an email server with two processors becomes CPU bound, it's almost certain that the same vendor has an upgrade plan to a four-CPU box, and upgrading to a system with more CPUs is almost always easier to plan and execute than upgrading I/O controllers, software, or storage systems. Not only is there typically less to configure, but also it's straightforward to estimate the actual improvement in CPU capability between the old and new systems. This factor is generally much easier to predict than the effects of upgrading a storage system or increased RAM.

7.5.2 Memory-Bound Systems

As we've already learned, some amount of paging on a system is normal. Excessive paging, or "thrashing," causes problems, however. This condition is not always easy to detect when it is mild, but it is patently obvious when severe. If the system is truly memory bound, the only solution is to add more RAM. Fortunately, memory is relatively cheap when it comes to system costs. For most applications, having extra memory will help reduce I/O by providing more filesystem cache space. Email is helped less than many other applications by surplus RAM, but extra memory does help, sometimes a great deal. Rarely will a recently constructed email system require more memory storage than can fit in that machine. That is, CPU, networking, and I/O all tend to make an entire computer chassis obsolete before it needs to be completely filled with RAM.

Another pitfall may become evident: It's very easy to be fooled into thinking a system problem is a memory problem when that's not the case. In point of fact, *every* time a server runs out of a finite resource, if the load keeps coming, the system will *always* run out of memory. Consider the following scenario:

- A computer is relaying email from the Internet to an internal email server. The internal server can handle anything the gateway can throw at it.

- The gateway's queue resides on a single disk, and just today, the load has reached the point where metadata operation contention exhausts the I/O capability of the disk.

- The server is now processing as much email as it possibly can, but the rest of the Internet won't be sympathetic and back off. Instead, email keeps getting sent, and at a faster rate than data can be moved into and out of the queue. Putting some numbers to this scenario, let us suppose that email comes into the server at a rate of 5 Mbps, but the queue is processed at 4 Mbps.

- Consequently, more `sendmail` processes are spawned on the server than exit in a given time period, causing the number of processes to start to increase.

- While they share a single text image in memory, each process has its own data image that starts eating away at available RAM.

- This shortfall in memory causes the system to reduce the size of the buffer cache, placing more I/O demands on the queue disk that cannot be satisfied. The total number of processes increases further as each process takes longer to complete its work and exit.

- Eventually, real memory pages become exhausted by all of these surplus processes, and the system starts to thrash.

When email administrators come to this machine and start running diagnostics, they will see that the server is out of memory and thrashing. Stopping there, they will erroneously conclude that the system needs more memory. They can obtain more and install it, but next time this situation occurs the server will merely flail around for a longer period before it begins to thrash. Adding memory will not correct the real problem.

In fact, this example leads to a general maxim about Internet servers. *Surplus RAM acts as a buffer against temporary resource shortages. More RAM does not eliminate the problem, but it does buy the server more time in which the shortage might become resolved, or at least be abated.* In our example, the resource shortage was disk I/O, but the same sort of scenario plays out for an email server that communicates directly with other servers around the Internet when the organization's Internet link is severed. Email backs up on the server filling the queue. As the queue grows deeper, the amount of time any one process spends in the queue increases, leading to resource contention that may become apparent to POP or IMAP users. Having more RAM on the server means that a longer outage may be tolerated before intervention becomes necessary.

Similar sorts of outages occur frequently and can be mitigated by good planning and architecture, but cannot be completely eliminated no matter how much effort is expended. DNS server outages, routers being given bad information or rebooting, "backhoe fade," or even unusual transient spikes in load can all cause these sorts of problems. A good server will be resilient against these sorts of situations, but it can never be made impervious to them. For this reason, it's more difficult to provide reliable Internet services than it is to provide many other utility services such as reliable dial-tone phone service. When a phone switch runs out of circuits, it can say "no" to the next entity wanting to use its resources; the process of saying "no" does not significantly drain the switch's resources. This result is much harder to achieve in the Internet case. Even saying "no" takes more resources, and the load will keep coming despite the refusal.

If a server is running normally at full capacity without any problems, but occasionally runs out of resources without having to process either more email messages (transactions) or larger messages (overall volume), then running out of memory is not the cause of the problem, but rather a symptom. The server is running out of "something else," where that something could be network bandwidth, I/O, CPU, or any number of other possibilities. If a server running out of memory is correlated with a higher demand being placed on that machine, that condition may indeed be a memory shortage.

7.5.3 I/O Controller-Bound Systems

On most disk systems, the data may be accessed by only a single I/O controller. If this controller becomes saturated, few remedies exist. Splitting up the load onto multiple storage systems using different controllers is the first thing to try, but that can't happen beyond the limit of one disk/SSD/RAID system per controller. If a controller with one device becomes saturated, the only option is to upgrade to a faster controller. However, this upgrade is a solution only if the storage device on the other end of the bus can support the faster speed. If a SCSI-2 controller is saturated talking to a single SCSI-2 disk, upgrading the controller isn't enough, because the disk will still speak SCSI-2 and the faster controller won't make a difference. In this case, the disk must be upgraded as well.

The use of system NVRAM can help mask controller saturation, but disks and controllers aren't that expensive, so upgrading shouldn't impose any special burden. It's generally a good idea to buy a high-end SSD or RAID system that comes with the highest-speed interface supported by the device, even if one has to buy a new controller to match. Even if the bandwidth isn't needed now, it would be a tragedy to purchase an ultra-fast storage system that must be completely replaced at a later date solely because its controller runs out of bandwidth before the storage system does. Only the very highest-end storage devices (SSDs and the most powerful RAID systems) can saturate the fastest controllers on the market by themselves in typical email environments. If this event comes to pass, the only solution is to divide the load over multiple disk systems on separate controllers, either with multiple mount points or by using software RAID to create a single storage image out of multiple devices by striping them together.

Because email data access patterns tend to be small and random, one can usually place several, or even many, disks on a single controller with confidence. In an environment where only a single large file will be read at a time, two or three disks per controller might be the maximum supportable. For email servers, it's usually safe to put several disk drives on the same SCSI bus—perhaps as many as six on a SCSI-2 chain, or even a dozen on high-speed controllers. It's still a good idea, though, to dedicate controllers to email tasks. Controllers can become saturated on email servers, especially if solid state disks or high-performance storage systems are employed.

7.5.4 Disk-Bound Systems

Conceptually, upgrading disk systems is fairly easy. Get faster disks, get faster controllers, and get more disks. The problem is predicting how much of an improvement one might expect from a given upgrade.

If the system is truly spindle bound, and the load is parallelizable such that adding more disks is practical, this route is almost always the best way to go. When a straightforward upgrade path exists, there's no more likely or predictable way to improve a system's I/O than by increasing the number of disks. The problem is that a straightforward path for this sort of upgrade isn't always obvious. As an example, assume we have one state-of-the-art disk on its own controller storing sendmail's message queue, and the system has recently started to slow down. There are two ways to effectively add a second disk to a sendmail system. First, we could add the disk as its own filesystem and use multiple queues to divide the load between the disks. This upgrade will work, but will become more difficult to maintain and potentially unreliable if it is repeated too many times. Second, we could perform a more hardware-centric solution, upgrading to either create a hardware RAID system, install a software RAID system to stripe the two disks together, or add NVRAM to accelerate the disk's performance. With any of these solutions, upgrading the filesystem might also become necessary. None of these steps is a trivial task, and there's no way to be nearly as certain about the ultimate effect on performance with the addition of so many variables.

Obviously, we can't add disks without considering the potential effect on the I/O controller, and sometimes limits restrict the number of controllers that can be made available in a system. While we rarely push the limits of controller throughput with a small number of disks because email operations are so small and random, it's possible to add enough disks on a system such that we run out of chassis space in which to install controller cards.

Any time a system has I/O problems, it would be a mistake to quickly dismiss the potential benefits of running a high-performance filesystem. This solution is usually cheap and effective, and where available can offer the best bang for the buck in terms of speed improvement. If I am asked to specify the hardware for an email server, in situations where I have complete latitude in terms of the hardware vendors, I know I can get fast disks, controllers, RAID systems, and processors for any operating system. The deciding factor for the platform then usually amounts to which high-performance filesystems are supported. This consideration is that important.

If a RAID system is already in use, performance might potentially be improved by rethinking its setup. If the storage system is running out of steam using RAID 5, but has plenty of disk space, perhaps going to RAID 0+1 will give the box some more life. If it is having problems with write bandwidth, lowering the number of disks per RAID group, and thus having a larger percentage of the disk space devoted to parity may help. Losing unused space is certainly preferable to buying a new storage system. Changing the configuration of the storage system is especially worth consideration if it wasn't set up by someone who really understood performance tuning. The vendor could very easily have given some advice that wasn't optimal for email applications.

If a RAID system has been set up suboptimally, it may also be possible to improve its performance via upgrading. Vendors often provide upgrade solutions to their RAID systems that can improve their throughput, both in terms of hardware components and the software that manages the system. Also, to save money, the system might have originally included insufficient NVRAM or read cache; performance might improve dramatically if more, or any, is installed.

7.5.5 Network-Bound Systems

Two networks are considered: the network(s) under one's control, typically one or more LANs, and the network connection(s) to the Internet, which are usually much more difficult and expensive to upgrade. If the problem lies with the latter, one can do little except to upgrade the server or add an off-site Spillover MX host to ride out the times when network contention causes email to back up. Unfortunately, this tactic doesn't really solve the problem, but merely mitigates it. Further, it's fairly costly in terms of server hardware, maintenance, and potential rack space at a better-connected site. When the problem lies with an internal network, the solution is usually much more tractable.

Reducing the number of other servers contending for time on a cramped network and going to a switched topology are the first things to try if the email server resides on a shared network. If the network is already switched, upgrading speeds and NICs will be necessary, and one will want to make sure the switch itself isn't overloaded.

7.6 Summary

- If an email server sometimes runs out of memory, it may not be memory bound. Swapping can be a symptom that the system has run out of "something else," which has caused processes to back up on the server. This problem eventually leads to memory exhaustion.

- I/O-bound email servers are a common occurrence. Generally, fixing this problem requires adding disks, upgrading storage systems, or upgrading filesystems.

- Often, if a system is network bound, it will be impractical to upgrade the network in the short term. Instead, the email server may need to be upgraded to support deep queues and many concurrent processes.

- When a server becomes saturated, very often the best option is to just let it "work its way out of a jam," rather than trying to find some way to reduce its load. If a server can't handle the load being thrown at it, the demand for its services won't decrease in the short term. The email will keep coming.

- Many tools are useful for determining why a server might run slowly.

- Email applications tend to log a lot of information. This logged information is valuable for assisting in performance tuning, but the logging process itself consumes resources.

Chapter 8

Load Generation
and Testing

T here are a great many variables to account for in building and tuning a high-performance email server. Because of the many variables and because much of the information available from hardware and software vendors cannot be easily incorporated into a model that will accurately predict the real-world capacity for any configuration, the only way to gain any confidence in how much email a server can process is to set it up and see how it performs in practice.

Obviously, several problems arise with this strategy. First and most important, no matter how much preparation and planning one does, very real risks will always arise in replacing one operating server that holds critical data with another server. Moving the data from one repository to another is always perilous. If the new server configuration doesn't perform adequately, then the data may need to be moved back to the original machine and then again to another new server configuration, with no guarantee that another configuration will perform any better.

Every equipment substitution in the upgrade process creates a window of downtime. In some roles in some environments, this process can be relatively pain-free. For example, if an organization plans to replace the email gateway responsible for relaying email through their firewall, and that organization can tolerate a few hours of deferred incoming and outgoing email during nonwork hours, then the cost of having to perform any particular upgrade is likely to be rather small.

In other situations, any outage window, no matter how small or well coordinated, can be expensive. For example, if one needs to replace a server that holds an email message store for a large ISP, doing so will be expensive by some measure. The customers will expect the server to operate on a 24/7 basis, and no matter how diligently an organization works to inform the customer base about the impending outage, some people will inevitably not get the message, ignore it, or forget they received it. When they go to retrieve or send email and find that they cannot, it will cost the ISP real money. Every outage will generate calls to customer support, which consumes personnel time, telephone resources, and customer goodwill. Therefore, in this sort of environment every effort should be made to ensure that any particular upgrade takes the minimum amount of time and has the maximum chance of achieving its goals.

The best way to obtain confidence in a new solution is to test and tune that configuration prior to going live with it in as realistic an environment as one can manage. This chapter discusses the issues involved in designing a test system as well as the difficulties in making a test system approximate real-world use as closely as possible.

8.1 Test System Setup

Before an email server or server configuration change can be tested, one must have a system to test. If new equipment has been purchased, then it can be assembled and tested. If, however, one wants to determine whether a given configuration change on an operating server is more or less likely to improve the performance of that server, then the change has to be made either on the real server or on another machine. The choice of whether an organization elects to purchase a test server, and how closely the test server will resemble the production server, comes down to economics. How does the cost of downtime for testing and iteration compare to the cost of purchasing extra hardware and potentially extra software licenses? Each site must evaluate this issue, but the final decision is best made explicitly by people who have both the authority to decide on the best course of action and the information necessary to properly evaluate the risks and rewards of all possibilities. This decision is often, if not usually, out of the hands of the people responsible for performing the upgrades. Nevertheless, the system administration staff have the responsibility to make sure that the decision makers are armed with all knowledge necessary to make an informed choice.

The decision on whether to set up a test environment is rarely as black and white as having nothing or replicating every piece of gear. Invariably, some compromise becomes necessary. For example, although an organization may choose not to purchase a complete test system that duplicates an expensive centralized IMAP server, that doesn't mean that the only alternative is to have nothing on hand. A less expensive, lower-powered machine can provide valuable information when used as a test platform. For example, if the production IMAP server is a Sun Enterprise 4500 server that is in danger of becoming memory bound, testing a recompilation of the IMAP daemon on a Sun Ultra 5 to see whether its memory footprint is smaller will yield results that could be expected to apply to the larger server. However, extrapolated test results are not always guaranteed to be valid.

In fact, results from *any* test environment are never guaranteed to be applicable in actual practice. Every test environment is merely an approximation of the real environment. The more effort expended to make sure the test environment resembles the real environment, the more likely the test results will resemble the behavior of the real system. Of course, no amount of effort expended on a test system can translate into absolute certainty about real-world behavior. Each organization needs to decide how much money it should spend on equipment and how much effort it should expend on configuring the system to mimic the production environment. The organization's resources, tolerance for risk, and applicability of the results of any particular test will all determine the appropriate amount of effort. This book cannot provide enough information to thoroughly evaluate the first two conditions. Some rough guidelines for determining how much confidence should be placed in certain test scenarios appear later in this chapter.

In an email test environment, we distinguish between three categories of servers involved in testing: source, sink, and target machines. The target is the server—sometimes a set of servers—to be tested. As stated earlier, the more closely this machine's configuration matches the production system, the more reliable the results of the test will be. Source machines, also known as load generators, provide data—in this case, usually email messages—to be processed by the target. We might want to test many situations, such as email relaying or POP3 server performance testing where the target machine will generate traffic that it will send to some other system. Machines that accept data from the target are called sink machines. Some tests will not require sources and some will not require sinks, but some tests will require both types of servers. All tests will, of course, require a target.

Each of the machines involved in a particular type of test must be able to communicate with the others, which means they're linked together via a network. This network should typically have the same properties as the network of the production server that the target is emulating. For example, if the production server is a well-tuned Intel-based server running FreeBSD on a 100 Mbps network, and if the target is an identically configured machine, then the test network should also be 100 Mbps. If the production network is switched, the test network should be switched, preferably using the identical networking equipment, including cabling.

If, however, the production server is a Sun E4500 connected to the outside world using Gigabit Ethernet and the test server is a Sun Ultra 5, it's probably not productive to run Gigabit Ethernet in the test environment. We do not expect the Ultra 5 to be able to handle the same throughput as the E4500, so going to the extra expense of matching networking technologies when such a great disparity in the performance capabilities between the production and test servers exists is usually not productive.

Remember, though, that production email servers with performance problems are usually I/O bound rather than CPU bound. An E4500 acting as an email gateway with a single SCSI disk connected to it as its queue may have a very similar throughput to an Ultra 10 with the same disk attached. If a bottleneck exists on a production server, it's usually safe to provide a test network sufficient to handle the same ratio of networking traffic, if the test network cannot support the same absolute throughput. For example, if I/O controller throughput acts as the bottleneck, and if the test target has a slower controller than the production server, then it's usually safe to provide a test network sufficient to handle the same ratio of networking traffic.

For example, a production server connected to the Internet via Gigabit Ethernet might be I/O controller bound on an 80 Mbps SCSI controller. At peak times, the production server may exchange 160 Mbps of traffic with the outside world. If a test server has only a 20 Mbps I/O controller, then a switched 100 Mbps test network might suffice to handle the projected 40 Mbps of network load during a scaled-down test. Of course, if the test server isn't I/O controller bound, then all bets are off. If this is the case, our test is unlikely to produce valid results no matter how the network is configured.

If the test network is connected without restriction to the general Internet, a simple configuration error could cause test email to interact with the rest of the world, which could prove disastrous. While it undoubtedly would be too restrictive to suggest that the test network be "air gapped" (that is, cut off completely) from the rest of the Internet, some precautions should be taken to ensure that any tests that run amok won't spew bogus email to the general Internet. One solution is to configure a packet-filtering router to block all commonly used email ports: SMTP (25/TCP), POP3 (110/TCP), IMAP (143/TCP), and message submission (587/TCP). This router could then provide connectivity to the test network. Alternatively, a dual-homed bastion host that doesn't route packets could be set up to screen the rest of the world from the test network. Any host with two network interfaces could serve this purpose as long as no routing daemon runs on the host (such as `routed` or `gated`), and the kernel is configured to not forward IP packets between interfaces.

To add another layer of protection against flooding the Internet with test email, one can use a block of private IP addresses, as discussed in RFC 1918 [RMK+96]. In this way, if a host on the test network tries to make a connection with external hosts, it will be prohibited from doing so because its IP address won't be routable across the Internet (or at least it shouldn't be). Some organizations use private IP addresses for many machines within their organization and network address translation (NAT) servers to proxy connections from these hosts to Internet servers. In such a case, the test network should use a different block of private IP addresses than the computers that are allowed to make these connections, and the NAT gateway should be explicitly set up not to translate the test network addresses. In many cases, using RFC 1918 private addresses is not a good idea; this instance is a case where using them most definitely *is* a good idea.

Another service that needs to be set up within the test network is DNS. As discussed earlier in this book, very good reasons support running a high-volume email server with a caching-only domain name service daemon. To replicate the production system as closely as possible, one can run a similarly configured name server on the test network target machine. If the test network uses private IP addresses, then the test machine will not be able to contact the root name servers. As a consequence, it won't be able to identify any of the machines attempting to connect to it, because a caching-only name server contains no information about any DNS zones. Further, an externally accessible DNS server may not be configured with accurate information about the machines on the test network.

There are two good ways to solve this problem, either of which may be the best option depending on the circumstances. First, instead of setting up the name server on the target machine to be a caching-only server, set it up to be a caching-forwarder pointing to a name server that knows about all domains used in the test network. If a bastion host is used to screen the test network from the rest of the Internet, it represents a good candidate to run this name server if it isn't practical to set up a machine in the test network for these purposes. The test network name server may or may not be able to query the root name servers. If it cannot, then the second solution to this problem is to create a fake root name server on the test network that contains the domains to be used. Again, it could consist of a machine on the test network dedicated to this task, or it might be combined with the bastion host if one is available. Whichever solution is chosen, I'd recommend not running either the forwarder or fake root name server on a machine used as a source, sink, or target host. Having one of these hosts perform this function might adversely affect the repeatability of certain tests.

Before running any test, make sure that DNS is working properly. Situations in which the target machine (or source or sink machines) delay connections waiting for DNS timeouts to occur will seriously skew test results. If the bastion host separating the test network from the outside world runs a name service daemon, this host does not have to have its resolver (typically via the /etc/resolv.conf file) point to itself. It can query another name server for its DNS information, which is important if it is running as a fake root name server.

Finally, having an inexpensive computer sitting on the test network that isn't directly involved in the testing can prove very valuable. This machine can be used for network monitoring, storing log files, processing data, and as a long-term repository for information in general. On test networks, the targets, sources, and sinks tend to get wiped out and rebuilt from scratch fairly frequently, so it's nice to have a nearby repository where one can put files and expect to find them again next month.

8.2 Testing Tools

Besides the hardware required for a test system, software is necessary. In this regard, the tester can pursue a course anywhere along a continuum between two extreme strategies. One extreme is to merely take existing email programs and adapt them to the test environment. The other extreme is to write all test software from scratch. An organization must always do at least some work, no matter how much it would like to use only existing code. Even so, anyone writing a complete system can typically benefit by leveraging portions of existing tools or at least libraries to reduce the amount of effort necessary to produce a test system. This section will discuss some popular Open Source software packages available on the Internet that can be adapted for load testing, consider which pieces must be developed by the tester, and discuss places where home-built tools might provide considerable benefits compared to existing software.

8.2.1 `sendmail` as Source

Not surprisingly, the first software tool we'll consider is `sendmail` itself. The `sendmail` MTA can be used effectively as both a source and a sink for SMTP messages. A source server that generates email messages to send to the target must have software on it that can speak SMTP, or at least fake it well. The SMTP protocol, especially if one includes the ESMTP extensions, can require some fairly complex implementations. In most environments, it's not worthwhile to duplicate this effort. However, we don't want or need to run a normal `sendmail` implementation on these servers. As this effort isn't "real" email, we can safely cut some corners to improve performance. Following is a sample `.mc` file for use on a Linux-based source machine using `sendmail` version 8.12:

```
OSTYPE(linux)
FEATURE('nocanonify')
FEATURE('use_cw_file')
define('QUEUE_DIR','/ramdisk/mqueue')
```

```
define('confDELIVERY_MODE','interactive')
define('confSAFE_QUEUE','False')
define('confDF_BUFFER_SIZE','110000')
define('confXF_BUFFER_SIZE','16384')
define('confCHECKPOINT_INTERVAL','0')
define('confQUEUE_SORT_ORDER','Filename')
define('confDEAD_LETTER_DROP','/var/mail/dead.letter')
define('confREFUSE_LA', '25')
define('confQUEUE_LA', '100')
define('confTO_IDENT','0')
MAILER(local)
MAILER(smtp)
```

Before we go through this file, let's discuss some prerequisite machine configuration issues. In this example, we'll use a Linux server, although any operating system would suffice. We'll run a name daemon on this machine to speed DNS resolver lookups. When we send email messages from this machine, we will do so with a script that assembles a message and pipes the data to sendmail invoked from the command line. We want the queue to be as fast as possible, so we create a memory-based file system, which the Linux folks call a "RAM disk," and mount it on /ramdisk. We also create a directory called mqueue under /ramdisk that sendmail will use as our queue directory. We set appropriate permissions on these two directories. That is, we make /ramdisk readable, writable, and executable by root and readable and executable by everyone else. We make the mqueue subdirectory owned by the user root and the group mail, and make it readable, writable, and executable by the owner and inaccessible by everyone else.

In some cases, the source machines will mimic several users from several domains. In this circumstance, each domain should be set up on the name server, and each user name should be set up in the passwd or aliases files so that bounce messages can be recovered and inspected later. Each host or domain name that a source or sink is pretending to be should be recorded in /etc/mail/local-host-names. A regular sendmail daemon should be ready to receive mail on each source host specifically to receive DSNs from the target. After each test run, we inspect the mailboxes for the sending users to identify bounced messages. If any are found, the reasons for them should be well understood and be acceptable if they were generated in the production environment. Before running a new test, these mailboxes and the message queue should be cleaned out and the log file rotated to prevent statistical contamination from occurring between tests. In a Linux environment, email-related file names listed in the `syslog.conf` file should be preceded with a "`-`" sign so that the system won't become bogged down waiting for them to be `fsync()`ed.

Now that the server configuration is well defined, we can look through the source machine `.mc` file. The familiar `OSTYPE` macro appears at the top of the file. Next, we add the `nocanonify` feature. If this feature is turned on, then `sendmail` does not attempt to fully qualify domain names, but rather assumes they are already fully qualified. Therefore, sending email to `npc@host.example.com` will be handled properly but `npc@host` won't, even if the domain of the server is `example.com` or `host.example.com` is the local server's name. Because all the sending and receiving addresses are explicitly listed for the test software on the source machine, it's a simple matter to make sure they're always fully qualified, and so the extra resources canonification consumes on the server won't be needed. This gain will generally be very small, but a gain nonetheless. We also add the `use-cw-file` feature so that `sendmail` will consult the `/etc/mail/local-host-names` file.

Next, we see that the queue is defined so as to reside in our memory-based filesystem. This choice is made for speed reasons: We don't want disks moving for mail to be queued as we're sending email messages. If the operating system used on our source machines doesn't support a memory-based filesystem, or if it doesn't have enough memory to use one as a queue without swapping, then the queue should go on a separate disk, if possible. If a physical disk holds the queue, it would be appropriate to mount it using the `async` and `noatime` options because the data it will contain does not require protection.

To further reduce the amount of queue writing needed, we set the delivery mode to be `interactive` and turn the `SuperSafe` option off. We're writing messages to a memory-based filesystem, so not running `fsync()` doesn't reduce data integrity in the face of a system crash, and we want as much throughput as we can get. Note that this case is one of the very few occasions where it might be considered acceptable to set `SuperSafe` to `False`. As neither the queue nor the logs are being saved synchronously, accurate information about a test run may not be recoverable if a server reboots during the test. If this event happens, the test must simply be rerun, which shouldn't create a significant burden.

The `DataFileBufferSize` generally should be configured to be just a little bit larger than the largest message that will be sent from the source. If buffering the data causes the source machine to start to swap, the best solution is not to lower this value, but rather to add more memory to the source. Many people have an ill-advised tendency to acquire load generation machines as inexpensively as possible.

A better strategy is to provide as much load on the target server for as little money as possible, which is an entirely different thing. Underpowering these machines tends to waste money. Even though these servers will never be put in production, they do need to be fast. There's no reason to buy gold-plated components, but one shouldn't skimp either. While an `xf` file is unlikely to grow as large as the 16,384 bytes buffered in this configuration file, setting the configuration parameter to this value won't hurt us. Again, if there might be a large number of recipients per message because one is simulating mailing list behavior, then it might be beneficial to raise this number. Because `CheckpointInterval` controls how often the `qf` file in the queue is updated, we set this value to zero to prevent updates from occurring.

We set the queue sorting algorithm to be `Filename` to require the least resources in processing the queue. In most tests, all messages in the queue will head to the same server anyway, so a more sophisticated sorting algorithm would consume resources to no useful purpose. We fully expect that queue runners won't be necessary to deliver messages unless the target server becomes saturated. In fact, we may not start a `sendmail` process using the `-q` flag at all.

The Dead Letter Drop serves as the repository for email that a server can't deliver and can't bounce. Such email messages shouldn't occur, but sometimes they do. They are more likely to be generated in a test environment, which explains why we list the repository's location explicitly. For example, we might forget to create an account or alias for the user name `test38`, which will send email from a source machine. We might also forget to configure the target machine's `/etc/mail/local-host-names` file to include `target.example.com`. If the source sends email from `test38@source.example.com` to `user1@target.example.com`, the message will bounce from the target. The sending host will try to deliver it to the sender. If that attempt fails, it will try to deliver the message to the `postmaster` alias on the local host. If it still can't deliver the message, the email will go in the Dead Letter Drop. This file should also be inspected and cleaned out after every test run.

We don't care if the load generator becomes saturated, so we set `QueueLA` to an absurdly high value. We want to do so explicitly because this environment involves a Linux system. As has already been mentioned, Linux is one of the few operating systems where threads of execution blocked waiting for I/O count toward the system's load average. We also set `RefuseLA` to a high value, although we don't expect our source machine to receive a large number of messages at all. Finally, our source machine does not need to verify the real user name associated with any email it receives, so we turn IDENT checking off.

After setting up the server, we want to be able to send messages. The simplest tests involve a single sending address and domain and a single test message. The most naive attempt might look something like the following:

```
#!/bin/sh
# sendmessage.sh

while [ 1 ]
do
        /usr/sbin/sendmail -t -f srcuser@source.example.org \
            < /tmp/messagefile
done
```

where the file `messagefile` contains

```
To: destuser@example.org
Subject: Testing

This is a test message.
```

This test script uses the `-f` flag to communicate the sending user to `sendmail`. The `-t` flag suggests that the recipient should be determined from the `To:` line in the header of the message itself. Usually, we'll want to send messages that are more representative of real traffic, but it's easy enough to invent and generate a larger message.

This method has several problems. First, it will send only one message at a time. Under no circumstances will this technique be able to maximize the source machine's throughput, because most of the time it takes for both ends to process this message will be dominated by the latency of the SMTP request/response conversation, even over a fast local network. Second, it doesn't exercise multiple users or multiple sender or recipient domains. Third, a single small message doesn't accurately represent the distribution of traffic flowing through the system. All of these problems can be remedied.

The easiest way to fix the "one message at a time" problem is to run several copies of the test script in parallel. How many should be run? The answer depends, but one can readily fire off, for example, two of them, and then keep launching more scripts in groups of two until some part of the load generator or target becomes saturated. Once the system has reached a "steady state," where the number of relevant processes such as `sendmail`, `mail.local`, test scripts, and so forth on all machines involved in the test stop varying significantly over time, then measurements can be taken.

One can simulate multiple users by using a randomizing function with a predefined list of names. For example, it is trivial to create a program in C, which we'll creatively call `random`, that will print out a random number between 1 and an integer argument (inclusive) given on its command line. Its usage might look like the following:

```
% random 8
4
```

This code could be used to select a random entry from a file containing a list of N entries:

```
line=`random N`
sender=`head -n $line sender_list.txt | tail -n 1`
```

After some minor extra work, the same process can be applied without needing to know the number of lines in the file list:

```
maxlines=`wc -l rcpt_list.txt`
line=`random $maxlines`
recipient=`head -n $line rcpt_list.txt | tail -n 1`
```

Faster and more efficient ways to do this exist, but this example is about as simple as matters get. Often, the time taken by the person in writing the test scripts is at least as valuable as the amount of time saved by using fewer load generation resources. The simple method should be demonstrated to be inadequate before more complex mechanisms are pursued.

The same method used to select recipients can be used to select from a variety of message bodies. Suppose we want to test a new email gateway and to reproduce in our test environment both the aggregate amount of traffic per message and the distribution of various message sizes. After creating a histogram from analyzing all the `size=` fields from our `sendmail` message logs, we find that we can reasonably approximate the distribution of our messages as follows:

Size Range	Average	Frequency
<4KB	2.5KB	0.6
4–32KB	8.5KB	0.3
>32KB	128KB	0.1

First, we create a directory, called `messages`, in which to store our standard messages. Because 60% of our messages are less than 4KB, and the messages in this range average 2.5KB, we create six files in this directory with that size. This can be simply the first 2.5KB of the `/usr/share/games/fortune`, `/usr/dict/words`, or similar file on any available system. To make matters even simpler, we can call these files "1" through "6". The files "7", "8", and "9" would each be 8.5KB of data, and the file "10" would be 128KB in size. More or fewer files of different sizes or types could be substituted depending on what a histogram of the actual sizes suggests.

Putting this information together, we can alter our email submission script to look like the following:

```sh
#!/bin/sh
# sendmessage.sh
# Determine number of recipients, senders, and messages.
# We have to do this only once, so it goes outside the loop.
maxrcpts=`wc -l rcpt_list.txt`
maxsenders=`wc -l send_list.txt`
maxmessages=`ls messages | wc -l`

while [ 1 ]
do
    # Generate parameters for email message to be sent.
    messagefile=`random $maxmessages`
    rcpt_number=`random $maxrcpts`
    sender_number=`random $maxsenders`
    recipient=`head -n $rcpt_number rcpt_list.txt | tail -n 1`
    sender=`head -n $sender_number send_list.txt | tail -n 1`

    # Send the message
        /usr/sbin/sendmail -f $sender $recipient < \
            messages/$messagefile
done
```

It should be straightforward to modify the script to add the possibility (and probability distribution) of multiple recipients per message. It is trivial to write a script that would fire off some number of these load generators in parallel. Extending this script even further to more closely approximate the production load is left to the reader's imagination. (As an aside, the specific testing done earlier in this book was accomplished with scripts that are almost identical to the ones presented here.)

8.2.2 `sendmail` as Sink

Next, we examine the use of `sendmail` as an SMTP sink. In this case, we want to absorb messages as quickly as possible, but we really don't care about the integrity of those messages, nor would we even need to store them in most cases.

As far as basic machine setup, much as in the source example, we will run a name daemon on this server to speed DNS queries. We will also set up the queue, if possible, on a memory-based filesystem. All hosts and domains for which this server is supposed to receive email will be added to `/etc/mail/local-host-names`. We also want to add each recipient user name to whom email will be sent to the `/etc/mail/aliases` file as follows:

```
user1:        /dev/null
user2:        /dev/null
user3:        /dev/null
...
```

Now the sink won't have to write all email messages it receives to disk, but rather will just eliminate them upon reception. Obviously, this method eliminates disk writes. Someone might want to verify that the messages are actually received intact, which would require writing the messages out to a message store. Generally, however, we would need to be this careful only if we were testing a new LDA or had modified some part of the code that processed the email messages along the way. For testing configurations, it usually suffices to compare the size of the email message on the sending machine with that on the recipient machine. Note that the size recorded by `syslog` in the mail logs considers the size of the body and the headers together. We want `syslog` to log its entries without `fsync()`ing them; in fact, we may want to not run it at all.

This same behavior could also be accomplished without the need to explicitly list each recipient by combining the `aliases` file with the `virtusertable`:

```
FEATURE('virtusertable')
```

We enable the `virtusertable` by including the previous line in the `.mc` file, and an entry like the following is added to `/etc/mail/virtusertable` for each domain in the `local-host-names` file:

```
@example.com          devnull
@other.domain         devnull
```

Now all messages for any user in the listed domains will be readdressed to the user `devnull`. Add the following line to the `aliases` file:

```
devnull: /dev/null
```

We no longer need to list every possible user name to which email might be sent. In fact, the source machines could even generate user names randomly.

In most cases, when `sendmail` writes email to a file it will obtain a lock on the file first, thereby avoiding the possibility of message corruption. However, if `sendmail` detects that the destination file is specifically `/dev/null`, not only will it not lock the file, but it won't write the message to the file. Instead, it will just acknowledge that the message was delivered successfully.

The configuration listed in the previous section is already set up to process email as efficiently as possible without regard to data integrity, which is what we want. If we can use neither `sendmail` 8.12 with its fast queueing nor a memory-based filesystem as a queue, it would be possible to use the DISCARD feature of the `access` database to reject the message even before it is queued.

The `access` database can be supported by adding the following line to the `.mc` file:

```
FEATURE(`access_db')
```

Then, in the `/etc/mail/access` file, we can add an entry like the following:

```
Connect:target.example.com               DISCARD
```

To have it take effect, we create database files by running `makemap hash /etc/mail/access</etc/mail/access`.

Any message coming from `target.example.com` will now be silently discarded.

Note that the DISCARD function of the `access` database is not as efficient as one might expect. Consider the CPU-bound test server that has been used in examples throughout this book; it runs `sendmail` 8.12.2 using `interactive` delivery mode and `interactive` queueing. It is capable of receiving and discarding around 600 messages/minute using the method combining the `virtusertable` with an alias pointing to `/dev/null`. When the system is reconfigured to use the DISCARD function of the `access` database, throughput drops to around

270 messages/minute. Of course, if we weren't using version 8.12 we would expect a less pronounced difference between these two methods, as using the `virtusertable` would require queue writes. Even so, on this test server the number of messages that can be discarded per minute using `access` is on the order of the number of messages per minute that can be delivered to mailboxes, which points out some significant inefficiencies in the discard mailer. At the present time, it would generally be better to use version 8.12, `interactive` mode, and `/dev/null` to receive and discard messages.

8.2.3 `postfix` Tools

Other tools besides `sendmail` can be used for SMTP sources and sinks. One set consists of the tools that come with the `postfix` distribution in the `src/smtpstone` directory. These tools, which are called `smtp-sink` and `smtp-source`, are used just how their names would imply. Each program contains rough documentation, but these utilities aren't that difficult to figure out how to use. They make good substitutes for `sendmail` in the configurations listed previously. The shell scripts documented earlier could readily be modified to use these tools instead of `sendmail`.

8.2.4 `popclient`

Besides SMTP testing, an organization may want to do performance testing of POP access. To do so efficiently, one needs a tool that will perform a POP session in a scripted environment. One package that can accomplish this goal is `popclient`.

The `popclient` utility was written by Carl Harris, Jr., of Virginia Tech University, and has been floating around the Internet unmodified, as far as I can tell, since August 1995. The operating system OpenBSD makes `popclient` available as an installable package, but no central authoritative FTP or Web site for this software exists at the current time. Nonetheless, it's available via HTTP or anonymous FTP access at several software repositories. Most of the people who once used it to download their email have switched to Eric Raymond's improved `fetchmail` package; unfortunately, however, `fetchmail` is not well suited for use in email performance testing.

The command syntax for use in a test environment is simple. Retrieving and discarding all email for a given account on a target server can be accomplished as follows:

```
#!/bin/sh
popclient -s -u username -p SeCrEt -o /dev/null \
    popserver.example.org
```

```
logger -p "local3.debug"-t "popclient" \
        "Exited with status: $?"
```

In this example, we begin with the `-s` flag to suppress the status information ususally printed to STDERR. We then issue the user name and password on the command line using the `-u` and `-p` flags, respectively. Of course, we wouldn't issue a password on the command line in a real-world situation, but in a test environment with fake accounts and fake email this choice is a perfectly acceptable optimization. We list the server name as `popserver.example.org`; `-o` indicates that the messages `popclient` downloads should be written to `/dev/null` so we don't perform local disk I/O. Information on the number of messages and quantity of email transferred in bytes can be recovered from the POP daemon's log files on the target machine. A great deal of information is available via `popclient`'s exit codes, which prove especially valuable when using the application in an automated mode. The codes and their meaning are well documented in the `popclient` manual page. We use the `logger` program to log this useful information to `syslog` along with the tag (`-t`) "popclient" using the facility `local3` and the priority `debug`. If `logger` isn't already available on the operating system used for load testing, it can be written readily or the exit status of the `popclient` can just be appended to a file.

Other command-line flags that may prove useful in scripting include the `-k` flag, which causes `popclient` not to issue instructions to delete the read messages on the POP server, and the `--protocol APOP` flag, which allows connection using the APOP authentication mechanism. Many other options are available as well. Consult the manual page for more information.

As with the `sendmail` source and sink examples, we can populate mailboxes on the target machine for a wide number of users, keep a list of these users on the sink (client) machine, and make random selections from this list to exercise the server. The most common POP client behavior is to connect to the server, download all email, delete the messages from the server, and then disconnect. As `popclient` shares this default behavior, it makes the program useful for this testing. Again, a script should be written to invoke this process. To simulate a real-world load, the sink would run several of these scripts in parallel.

8.2.5 c-client

The variety of modes in which POP clients connect and download messages is really very restricted. IMAP, on the other hand, offers a great deal more freedom. Determining what a typical IMAP session looks like for a server is by no means an easy feat. Some IMAP daemons can be switched into a debugging mode, which will log the commands used by each session. Similarly, a utility such as `tcpdump` may be used to perform a packet capture of IMAP sessions. Either of these techniques may violate users' privacy, and neither should be undertaken without express permission.

Even armed with many sample sessions, there are probably as many IMAP profiles as there are IMAP clients multiplied by the number of IMAP users. This fact makes it extremely difficult to have any real confidence in performance numbers generated in an IMAP test environment. Nonetheless, some rough numbers are better than none, as long as their limitations are well understood.

Once one or more "typical" IMAP session profiles have been defined, the next step is to create an automated client that can simulate these usage patterns. No IMAP equivalent of `popclient` that can be used for scripting IMAP sessions exists. Instead, the best that can be hoped for is a toolkit that allows someone to write an application that mimics an IMAP client without having to write the entire client side of the IMAP protocol.

Fortunately, such a toolkit exists. Called `c-client`, it comes with the University of Washington IMAP server distribution. Its primary Internet repository is at `ftp://ftp.cac.washington.edu/mail/imap.tar.Z`. A C library, `c-client.a`, is created in the `src/c-client` directory when this distribution is unpacked and compiled. As the name suggests, it contains a set of library calls to perform IMAP functions that can be called from a C program that links with it. The documentation is sparse, but the file `internal.txt` in the `docs` directory and the source code itself provide enough information to allow a programmer to build something that will work. The often-used `pine` UNIX IMAP client links with the `c-client` library, so one can use its source code as an example. Even better examples are probably the utilities included in the associated `imap-utils.tar.Z` package found in the same directory of the previously mentioned FTP site. Despite the documentation and examples, creating an automated IMAP client will almost certainly represent a serious undertaking for even the most experienced email programmers.

8.2.6 Perl Modules

All of the tasks we sought to accomplish using the programs and scripts discussed earlier in this section can also be accomplished in other languages, including Perl, which is commonly used for writing test harnesses by system administrators. Certainly, a reader who is very familiar with Perl programming may already have thought about how to carry out some of the test tasks described earlier in this language, in some cases perhaps much more efficiently and thoroughly than the examples presented here.

The Perl language is supported by an online library of preexisting Perl soft-ware modules and documentation called CPAN (Comprehensive Perl Archive Net-work) [CPA]. The CPAN archive contains a number of modules that can assist those writing email test utilities in Perl, some of which will be discussed here. The contents of CPAN change often, so the information presented in this book inevitably gives an out-of-date snapshot of what is currently available. Anyone interested should browse the online repository to see whether updates or new modules are available.

Mail::Bulkmail

The Bulkmail module contains routines for sending email messages, including a Perl version of a stripped-down SMTP client. Its purpose is to efficiently send out large amounts of email, such as announcements. The module sends those messages to an SMTP server, which will relay them. For testing, the destination could easily be the target server. In essence, this code is an example of a simple SMTP-based injector, like those mentioned in Chapter 5.

The code in the module is less careful about timeouts than a complete SMTP client should be. For instance, it assumes that the server used to relay the messages is "well behaved" and will respond to queries reasonably quickly. This assumption shouldn't be a problem in most test environments. The module also doesn't handle all possible SMTP error codes that can be returned, but it does include cases for handling some of the most common ones. Again, this simplification will usually be acceptable in a test environment.

With all of these modules, the entire module itself may not be directly useful. Nevertheless, even if it's not, the module may contain subroutines that can be copied to save a programmer some extra effort.

Mail::POP3Client

As its name suggests, the POP3Client module contains code for accessing email servers via the POP3 protocol. Rather than being a complete POP client, it com-prises a set of routines that can be used to build a POP session. Most MUAs that support the POP protocol tend to access email in the same sort of ways, but often some small differences crop up. If one type of POP client is commonly used in a given organization, then once the sequence and timing of commands for that client has been determined, they can be duplicated using the routines in this module without the need to write RFC 1939–compliant code.

As an example, suppose that the most widely used POP client in an organization performs the following default behavior: It authenticates with the server, asks for the UIDL of all messages, and retrieves the headers using the TOP command asking for the first 20 lines. Then, if new email has arrived, it prompts the user whether it should be retrieved. In taking a profile, we find that 85% of the time users answer "yes," and they wait an average of 45 seconds before making that response. The email is downloaded, the client sleeps for five minutes, and then it repeats the process. While this scenario may not be a very realistic or very well-designed POP process, it is easy to model, and an accurate simulation of such a client can be written using this module with little effort. It would take more work to try to get `popclient` to behave in this manner.

Mail::IMAPClient

The IMAPClient module contains a set of routines and data structures that may be helpful in creating an IMAP client. It will come as no surprise that this module is larger and has more features than the POPClient module. Nonetheless, once a profile has been created of an IMAP session that one wishes to automate, it will almost certainly take much less work to code it using this module than to write all of the client-side code from scratch.

At the time of this writing, this module seems to be fairly well documented within the code itself, and its implementation of the IMAP protocol is very thorough. Of course, turning even a well-considered IMAP profile into an automated client will not be easy. A lot of coding will be required, but using the IMAPClient module should simplify the process.

8.2.7 Mstone

While developing their Messaging Server product, Netscape programmers also developed a set of testing tools called Mailstone. They kindly provided these tools to their customers for the purpose of testing the installation of their new email systems before it was placed in production. When Netscape chose to release its browser technology under an Open Source license, the company also elected to release its Mailstone test suite under the same license, albeit under a slightly different name: Mstone. This test suite can be of great assistance to anyone who wants to load-test an email server.

Obtaining the Mstone package can be a bit tricky, as a `tar` bundle isn't available via FTP or HTTP on the Internet. Instead, one must use anonymous Concurrent Versions System (CVS) to download the package. Instructions on how to contact the Mozilla anonymous CVS server are available at the following URL: `http://mozilla.org/cvs.html`. Information on which modules to download is available at `http://mozilla.org/projects/mstone/`. Anyone with an Internet connection and a working CVS client should be able to download the package from the information provided in these two Web pages.

Building Mstone should be straightforward on any supported platform for Netscape Messaging Server version 4.15, including Solaris, Linux, and several others. Before building, the installer must have the GNU version of the `make` utility and a version of Perl at least as recent as version 5.005. The `gnuplot` and `gd` graphics utilities may also prove beneficial, although they are not strictly required. The system is well documented, although some of the URL links mentioned in the documentation are no longer valid, and some information hasn't been rewritten since the package underwent its name change and became widely distributed. A careful reading, especially of the `doc/MailStone.html` file, will still provide the information needed to create profiles and run SMTP, POP, and IMAP tests against a target machine.

8.2.8 Testing Tool Summary

None of the tools mentioned here represents the only, or even best, method for generating a load so as to measure the capability of an email server in a test environment. However, this section does cover a reasonable set of tools that can provide a useful starting point for further exploration. While one can easily write more sophisticated and efficient tools than those that can be obtained by cobbling together the components mentioned in this section, the items discussed here should at least provide some reasonable examples from which to draw, even if they do not give a complete load-testing solution.

One final note: Before venturing too far down the road of modifying or rewriting test tools to more specifically meet an organization's needs, remember the adage that "time is money." Time spent programming costs money just as surely as buying hardware does, and it's important that the money be spent most efficiently. It's often cheaper to buy more hardware to run an inefficient test suite than to spend a great deal of valuable time writing complex software.

8.3 Load Testing Pitfalls

Several tricky issues arise in setting up a test environment for an email system. Some of these issues may seem obvious, but others probably won't be. In any case, it's always best to be aware of these potential problems before getting started so the necessary choices are made explicitly.

Suppose we have an email test environment in which we have set up a single target machine with a dedicated disk for the queue and a reasonable RAID system for the message store. Further suppose that we plan to test how many messages per second the system can receive and store. Besides its overall capacity in absorbing email messages, we'd like to know the location of the next bottleneck so that we can evaluate whether we might need multiple disks for the queue, a high-performance filesystem for the message store, or some other improvement to provide adequate headroom for future growth. To test this target server, we also have set up two computers to be the load generation (source) machines and connected them with the same type of network and switch we plan to use in production.

Generally, we expect that when the target machine reaches its saturation point, it will become I/O bound somewhere in the system. Because the actual messages used in testing don't matter, a source machine can generate meaningless messages rather than read data from its own disks. It could just send the same message over and over again to the target, or it could select randomly from some pool of messages that are representative of the distribution of message sizes that are typical of that organization's expected load. In this case, we'd expect that if the source and target machines had the same configuration, a single source should be able to overwhelm the target with load, because the source isn't moving its disks and the target is. Oddly, in many cases this result doesn't happen. In fact, it sometimes takes several times the target server's horsepower in source machines to saturate the target. The reasons for this behavior are often difficult to determine, but a partial list of some of the more likely culprits follows:

1. The tools used are not always efficient load generators. Software such as `sendmail` and `popclient` is not designed with load generation in mind. When these tools were written, the programming priorities were data integrity and correctness rather than blinding speed. Even if one modifies their behavior to improve performance, such as by having `popclient` write its output to `/dev/null`, the utility continues to perform at least one extra data copy that wouldn't need to be done in a tool designed purely for load testing. These little inefficiencies add up, especially when running large numbers of load generators. When hundreds or more of these processes run on a single machine, the shell scripts that drive them will fork a very large number of processes, and the original `popclient` author almost certainly didn't expect that 1,000 concurrent copies of his program would run on a single server at the same time. Conversely, the programmers working on `sendmail` and the Cyrus IMAP daemon, for example, spend a significant amount of time considering how their code will run in high-stress environments, like those on the target server.

2. A program that is active but not running still consumes resources. When a test program starts it consumes memory, at least one network socket, one or more file descriptors, and a slot in the process table. Due to the latencies involved in the synchronous request/response conversation of the email protocols covered in this book, most of these processes will spend most of their time waiting. This is even more true once the target server starts slowing down, as it will when it becomes more heavily loaded. This feedback causes the testing machine to slow down even more. Soon memory consumption and context switching become enough of an issue that the load generator starts slowing down itself.

3. Once a target configuration goes beyond the most basic setup—that is, its I/O system becomes fairly well tuned—handling large amounts of I/O becomes easier for the server. Even without other inefficiencies, the source and sink machines don't have sophisticated I/O systems on which to offload part of the work done by the server. As a consequence, the load generation and target machines can be closer to parity in the effort they actually expend than might seem likely at first.

4. Aside from its I/O capabilities, the target server is likely to be a more powerful system than each of the load generators. Certainly, it wouldn't be completely fair to criticize load generation software running on two Linux PCs for not being able to saturate a well-configured, four-processor Sun E420R. Of course, dollar-for-dollar and processor-for-processor comparisons aren't strictly fair either. Nevertheless, with a significant disparity in the class of machines used for load generation and the target server, we shouldn't be surprised if this difference manifests itself during testing.

5. Sometimes the source and sink machines actually perform more work than the target server. For example, if the target server acts as an email gateway, relaying email between an SMTP source and sink, then the nontarget machines might be expending more effort. While it's true that the target receives email and sends it, the sink receives email, and the source sends it, a well-configured target has the option of using the same data buffers to write out the incoming email, and then read the outgoing email. The source and sink can't employ the same optimization, nor could they even if both functions resided on the same machine. The two load generation machines have to manage some work items that the target doesn't have to perform in some cases.

Many other reasons exist as to why it might take several load generators to saturate a single target server; the ones mentioned here are just some of the most common. Nonetheless, if the load testing machine and the target machine consist of otherwise identical hardware, even if the fastest, most efficient I/O system is attached to the target, a well-tuned source should be able to saturate an equally well-tuned target. I haven't tested this theory in all cases, but one of the reasons for the lack of rigorous testing goes back to the issue of overall efficiency. There are a few environments in which it makes sense to tune anything except the target server in a test environment. Hardware is usually plentiful and almost always cheaper than expertise.

8.3.1 Difficulties in Approximating the Real World

At the beginning of this chapter, it was stated that no matter how much effort is put into creating a test environment, it can never be more than an approximation of what the server will face in a real-world environment. As specific tools were discussed, some of the ways in which it will be nearly impossible to simulate every detail of what an email server will actually experience probably became evident. It is worth explicitly exploring where some of these difficulties will occur so that the limitations of a given test environment will be well understood.

One of the more obvious differences between a production environment and a test environment relates to the number of hosts, domains, and IP addresses that the target machine encounters. When testing a gateway server, it might be possible to simulate the number of internal servers that will actually be encountered in a production environment if the number is small and virtual hosting is used. If the number of internal hosts is very small, then the number of internal IP addresses may even equal the number of servers set up as SMTP sinks. However, one cannot count on these cases. Even when they do apply, no practical way exists to simulate the variety of hosts, domains, and IP addresses that the production machine will find on the Internet side. In the test lab, DNS caches will be always be smaller, SMTP connection caches will always be more effective, information such as `sendmail`'s persistent host status will always be stored more efficiently, and items such as route tables will always be smaller.

In a test environment, the number of different user accounts used, for example, on a target POP server, will often be smaller than in the production environment. If possible, a similar number of accounts should be tested as are expected in the production system. For all except the largest corporations, this type of testing is probably feasible. Tools can be written so that a test environment simulating the use of tens of thousands of accounts isn't out of the question. Simulating the entire user base of a large ISP or email portal is a different matter, however—testing millions of accounts is a much more difficult problem than testing thousands. Just the extra effort required to select an item from a list with 1 million entries will place different demands on these two test systems. As the anecdote in Chapter 7 shows, testing with an improper number of accounts can generate misleading results.

Another set of circumstances that is challenging to account for in a test environment focuses on the collection of unusual events, misconfigured hosts, and antisocial denizens of the Internet with which an email server must cope on a daily basis. Most test suites won't include miscreants probing whether the target server is an open relay by trying to bounce 100 email messages off of it. Most test suites won't include POP clients that disconnect without informing the server through the POP protocol. Most test suites don't simulate rebooting backbone routers, misconfigured DNS servers, or email servers that don't strictly adhere to SMTP. Generally, this approach is appropriate. This sort of detail usually lies far beyond the threshold of what is worthwhile to explicitly account for in a test environment. However, while an email server may be subjected to more load in the lab, it will encounter far more unusual events in the field than any test writer can imagine.

When designing a test scenario, the primary interest is typically simulating the load that an email server will encounter during the period of its peak usage. To make things easier, we often use average loads and average message sizes. Sometimes, an email server's load is dominated by a single unusual event. A gateway might be called upon to relay or bounce an enormous message, a POP client might download an especially large message, or some client might issue an IMAP SEARCH command on an enormous volume of email. Averaging out some of these extreme cases might mean that the server is not tested under its most stressful circumstances.

A critical difference between production and test environments that is extraordinarily tough to simulate is the fact that in a test environment the network link between two hosts typically has much lower latency than in the real world. On the same subnet, the network latencies between client and server will be less than 1 ms. Across the Internet, they can easily reach 100 ms. Indeed, over a modem link, a latency of 300 ms is not uncommon. The addition of these latencies in interactive protocols fundamentally changes the nature of the connections. Let's look at this point in some detail.

Let us perform a fairly naive calculation on how long it will take to transfer a 10KB message from one host to another using SMTP. First, let us consider how long it will take with the two hosts on adjacent 10 Mbps Ethernet networks connected by a router that introduces a 1 ms latency. Let us also assume, for the sake of simplicity, that each of the two servers in question is an authoritative name server for its respective domain. We also assume that the CPU time for processing the message is

Table 8.1. Latency During Various Phases of an SMTP Conversation

Duration	Event
3 ms	Send initial SMTP connection request using TCP
1 ms	Server looks up PTR record of connecting host
1 ms	Server looks up A record of connecting host
1 ms	Receive the initial SMTP banner
1 ms	Send the ESMTP EHLO
1 ms	Respond with 250 EHLO
1 ms	Send the MAIL FROM:
1 ms	Verify that the domain of the sender exists
1 ms	Canonify sender host name
1 ms	Respond to the sender information
1 ms	Send the RCPT TO:
1 ms	Canonify the recipient host name and perform MX lookups
20 ms	Create a `sendmail` queue entry
1 ms	Respond to the recipient information
1 ms	Send the DATA start
1 ms	Respond with the 354 "go ahead" message
8 ms	Send the message
40 ms	Queue the message data body
1 ms	Respond to the message terminator
1 ms	Send the SMTP session QUIT
1 ms	Give the 221 "closing connection" response
	Total elapsed time: 88 ms

arbitrarily fast, a reasonable assumption; even if it were not true, however, it would add only a few milliseconds to the transaction in each case. Table 8.1 presents a list of the durations of most of the events that occur during the message transfer, assuming `sendmail` will receive the message and runs in `background` mode, using a typical configuration. Obviously, the duration of the session is dominated by waiting for disk writes to occur.

Now, let's replace each 1 ms of latency for each part of the conversation with 200 ms of modem latency, which is quite generous, and replace the 8 ms of message transmission with 1400 ms, assuming a 56 Kbps modem. In this case, the same set of transactions will now require more than 5 *seconds* to complete, almost a 60-fold increase in the duration of a single process. Of course, this calculation is crude and the receiving server would rarely need to make DNS requests across a modem line, but this example is not completely outlandish. Note that both sessions required the same amount of CPU calculation, I/O capacity, and total network consumption—the first session simply required far less wall-clock time than the second session did.

As a result, system utilization usually looks quite different in the lab than it does in the field. Processes that interact with the outside world stick around a lot longer than the same tasks when run on a low-latency test network, even though they move the same amount of data. Under a test suite, a heavily loaded, saturated email server receiving and storing messages from the outside world, transferring some number of megabytes per second of data in and out of its network interfaces in the lab might, at any one time, have 30 `sendmail` and 12 `mail.local` processes running concurrently on that server. The same system deployed at a dial-up ISP handling the same throughput might easily run the same 12 `mail.local` processes but in excess of 300 `sendmail` daemons, due to the additional duration of each session caused by high-latency connections to the outside world.

This point leads to an important maxim in network profiling. Assume we have a set of synchronous network transactions, such as email protocols, that are running and consuming a constant amount of network bandwidth. Then, if the latency of the connections increases significantly, the primary effect on the servers involved in these transactions will be a substantial increase in memory consumption. A hint of this result can be seen in the CPU-bound test examples cited earlier in this book. The target server could quite capably handle the load thrown at it in a test environment without swapping, despite having a mere 32MB of RAM. When put in production, however, this system would begin thrashing under even a small fraction of its tested capacity. This problem would arise because the latencies between the target server and its peers in production would be much larger than they were in the lab.

Besides the obvious risks of swapping, this additional memory requirement for a production email server creates ripple effects that influence the performance of the entire system. The extra memory in use means less memory is available for things such as the filesystem buffer cache, DNS cache, and write-behind buffer space for asynchronous data (e.g., log files). These alterations in system behavior will probably reduce total I/O capability. Occasional bursts of higher traffic may be far more noticeable on the production server than they would be during testing. Larger process tables will make `fork()`ing, context switching, and memory reclamation more CPU intensive. Because more sessions operate concurrently in a production environment, the system will be characterized by more concurrent queue entries, more open files, and, therefore, longer waits for synchronous data operations. In general, one cannot expect to achieve the total throughput of an email server in a production environment that has been measured in a test lab. It's important to take this point into account.

Other than setting up a farm of load generators on the other end of a modem bank, there exists at least one good way to simulate high-latency networks. Work has been done on modifying network drivers to allow a computer to operate as if it resided on the other end of a low-bandwidth and/or high-latency network connection. One of these development efforts has been included in the FreeBSD operating system beginning with version 2.2.8 called `dummynet` [RIZ97]. The `dummynet` facility is built on top of the `ipfw` (IP firewall) facility in the FreeBSD kernel. One must configure `ipfw` to use `dummynet`. A very good tutorial on configuring `ipfw` and `dummynet` is available online [RIZ]. The availability of `dummynet`, along with the robustness and performance of FreeBSD, makes it my operating system of choice for load-testing servers, even though getting Mstone to work there requires some minor programming.

A similar facility is available for Linux called NIST Net [NIS]. Its implementors claim that it should be considered beta code, but many sites are already running it, and it has the advantage of being configurable from a GUI. Additional information on NIST Net can be found at [DAW00].

8.4 Summary

- While it is impossible to completely simulate the demands of a production system in a test environment, testing remains the best way to achieve confidence in a solution before its deployment.

- Setting up a test environment should be done with careful consideration. Simulating the Internet in a lab environment poses many challenges.

- Efficient configuration of servers that are used for load testing is likely to be very different than the configuration of production email servers.

- It is almost certain that a combination of publicly available and homegrown solutions will need to be amalgamated into a comprehensive package of testing tools.

- Examine all testing results with a critical eye. Many pitfalls may be encountered in attempting to accurately test the capabilities of an email server.

Chapter 9
Conclusion

By this time, I would expect readers to have had their fill of information on email performance tuning. If information seemed a bit repetitive toward the end, it shows that the reader has been paying attention and ideally is well on the way to understanding how to improve the performance of email servers.

As comprehensive as this book has attempted to be, there remains much more to learn that hasn't been covered. The reader would be well advised to continue researching and learning everything possible about the topic. An almost unlimited amount of good information is available today, and the industrious student shouldn't lack for ideas about where to look.

Specifically, some additional sources that may be useful to the reader include the following:

Books on General System Administration That Cover Email Issues

- *UNIX System Administration Handbook*, 3rd edition, by Evi Nemeth, et al.
  If I were teaching a "how to" course on system administration, I would use this handbook as a textbook. It contains a great deal of good information on how to maintain a wide variety of UNIX servers under many circumstances. Necessarily, its coverage of configuring and running `sendmail` is abbreviated compared to specialized books, but what it provides is quite good.

- *The Practice of System and Network Administration*, by Thomas Limoncelli and Christine Hogan
  This book isn't about the "nuts and bolts" of everyday system administration, but rather discusses the "big picture" issues. If someone wants to learn how to install new disk drive, read the book by Nemeth and colleagues. If someone wants to learn how to set up a file server to minimize the amount of effort it will take to maintain going forward, read this text. It's an excellent book with which all professional system administrators should become familiar.

Books Specifically About `sendmail`

- *Linux Sendmail Administration*, by Craig Hunt
  Because it covers `sendmail` through version 8.11, and because it emphasizes
  building configurations using M4, it is my opinion that this book is the best
  tutorial on learning `sendmail` available today. Its apparent focus on Linux
  should not dissuade administrators who favor other operating systems from
  looking through this book, as it's quite easy to separate out the Linux specifics
  from the more general `sendmail` advice.

- *sendmail*, 2nd edition, by Bryan Costales and Eric Allman
  Despite the fact that it covers `sendmail` only through version 8.8, the
  "Bat Book" remains the definitive reference on `sendmail`. While a third
  edition is in progress, at the time of this writing it's uncertain when it will be
  released. In the meantime, any `sendmail` email administrator who doesn't
  have a copy should acquire one. My main argument with this book is it
  spends too little time discussing configuration using M4.

Other Books About Email

- *Managing IMAP*, by Dianna and Kevin Mullet
  Anyone running either a UW or Cyrus IMAP server will almost certainly want
  a copy of this book, although it's unfortunate that it says very little about
  Cyrus version 2. A lot of other information in this book may be useful to email
  administrators who are not running IMAP.

- *Programming Internet Email*, by David Wood
  This very good book describes both Internet standards and issues involved in
  developing email applications.

Books on General Performance Tuning

- *Sun Performance and Tuning: Java and the Internet*, by Adrian Cockroft and
  Richard Pettit
  Even though this book covers only Solaris, and only up to version 2.6, it
  contains a lot of very good information. It's especially strong in explaining
  how to diagnose problems and use system performance monitoring tools. If I
  could own only one book on performance tuning, I'd choose Musumeci and
  Loukides's book because it is more current. However, *Sun Performance and
  Tuning* is still well worth reading.

- *System Performance Tuning*, 2nd edition, by Gian-Paolo Musumeci and Mike
  Loukides
  This excellent book focuses on how what goes on "under the hood" in a
  computer system affects performance. The book emphasizes Solaris and
  Linux, but its coverage of many tools is very good, and more thorough than
  that presented here.

Bibliography

[AMA] *AMaViS Mail Virus Scanner.* http://www.amavis.org/.

[ASA] Eric Allman, Gregory Shapiro, and Claus Assmann. *Sendmail Installation and Operation Guide.* Distributed with the sendmail source distribution.

[BAD+92] Mary Baker, Satoshi Asami, Etienne Deprit, John Ousterhout, and Margo Seltzer. Nonvolatile Memory for Fast, Reliable File Systems. In *Proceedings of the 5th ASPLOS Conference*, Boston, MA, October 1992.

[BCF+94] Nanette Boden, Danny Cohen, Robert Felderman, Alan Kulawik, Charles Seitz, Jakov Seizovic, and Wen-King Su. Myrinet—A Gigabit-per-Second Local-Area Network. *IEEE-Micro*, 3(1):1–30, 1994.

[BES00] Steve Best. *JFS Overview: How the Journaled File System Cuts System Restart Times to the Quick*, January 2000. http://www-106.ibm.com/developerworks/library/jfs.html.

[BLU00] Richard Blum. *Running qmail.* SAMS Press, 2000.

[BOU01] Tony Bourke. *Server Load Balancing.* O'Reilly and Associates, 2001.

[CA97] Bryan Costales and Eric Allman. *sendmail*, 2nd edition. O'Reilly and Associates, 1997.

[CBB97] Nick Christenson, Tim Bosserman, and David Beckemeyer. A Highly Scalable Electronic Mail Service Using Open Systems. In *Proceedings of the First USENIX Symposium on Internet Technologies*, Monterey, CA, December 1997.

[CER99] CERT. *CERT Advisory CA-1994-04 Melissa Macro Virus.* Technical report, Computer Emergency Response Team, March 1999.

[CHK+98] Strata Rose Chalup, Christine Hogan, Greg Kulosa, Bryan McDonald, and Bryan Stansell. Drinking from the Fire(walls) Hose: Another Approach to Very Large Mailing Lists. In *Proceedings of the 12th Systems Administration Conference (LISA)*, Boston, MA, December 1998.

[COU] *Courier Mail Server.* http://www.courier-mta.org/.

[CPA] *Comprehensive Perl Archive Network.* http://www.cpan.org/.

[CRI96] Mark Crispin. *Internet Message Access Protocol—Version 4rev1.* RFC 2060, Internet Engineering Task Force, December 1996.

[CTT94] Remy Card, Theodore Ts'o, and Stephen Tweedie. Design and Implementation of the Second Extended Filesystem. In *Proceedings of the First Dutch International Symposium on Linux*, Amsterdam, Netherlands, December 1994.

[CUC] *Cubic Circle.* ftp://ftp.cuci.nl/pub/.

[CYR] *Project Cyrus.* `http://asg2.web.cmu.edu/cyrus/`.

[DA99] Tim Dierks and Christopher Allen. *The TLS Protocol Version 1.0.* RFC 2246, Internet Engineering Task Force, January 1999.

[DAW00] Terry Dawson. NISTNet: Emulating Networks on Your Own LAN. *O'Reilly Network*, June 2000.

[EXI] *Exim Home Page.* `http://www.exim.org/`.

[FON00] John Fontana. E-mail Growth Hogs Enterprise Resources. *NetworkWorldFusion News*, January 2000.

[FRE00] Ned Freed. *SMTP Service Extension for Command Pipelining.* RFC 2920, Internet Engineering Task Force, September 2000.

[GP94] Gregory Ganger and Yale Patt. Metadata Update Performance in File Systems. In *Proceedings of the USENIX Operating Systems Design and Implementation (OSDI) Conference*, Monterey, CA, November 1994.

[HUN01] Craig Hunt. *Linux Sendmail Administration.* SYBEX, 2001.

[JOH93] Michael St. Johns. *Identification Protocol.* RFC 1413, Internet Engineering Task Force, February 1993.

[KAT00] Jeffrey Katcher. *PostMark: A New File System Benchmark.* Technical Report TR3022, Network Appliance, October 1997. `http://www.netapp.com/tech_library/3022.html`.

[KFM95] John Klensin, Ned Freed, and Keith Moore. *SMTP Service Extension for Message Size Declaration.* RFC 1870, Internet Engineering Task Force, November 1995.

[KLE01] John Klensin. *Simple Mail Transfer Protocol.* RFC 2821, Internet Engineering Task Force, April 2001.

[KOL97] Rob Kolstad. Tuning Sendmail for Large Mailing Lists. In *Proceedings of the 11th Systems Administration Conference (LISA)*, San Diego, CA, October 1997.

[KR94] Brian Kernighan and Dennis Ritchie. *The M4 Macro Processor, 4.4 BSD Programmer's Supplementary Documents*, Chapter 17. O'Reilly and Associates, 1994.

[M-O00] AOL Per-User Email Figures Climb 60 Percent in 1999. *Messaging Online*, February 2000.

[MAP] *MAPS RBL.* `http://www.mail-abuse.org/`.

[MAS97] Paul Massiglia. *The RAID Book*, 6th edition. Peer-to-Peer Communications, 1997.

[MBKQ96] Marshall McKusick, Keith Bostic, Michael Karels, and John Quarterman. *The Design and Implementation of the 4.4 BSD Operating System.* Addison-Wesley Publishing, 1996.

[MD90] Jeffrey Mogul and Steve Deering. *Path MTU Discovery.* RFC 1191, Internet Engineering Task Force, November 1990.

[MET97] Rodney Van Meter. Observing the Effects of Multi-Zone Disks. In *Proceedings of the USENIX Annual Technical Conference*, Anaheim, CA, January 1997.

[MG99] Marshall McKusick and Gregory Ganger. Soft Updates: A Technique for Eliminating Most Synchronous Writes in the Fast Filesystem. In *Proceedings of the USENIX Annual Technical Conference*, Monterey, CA, June 1999.

[MJLF84] Marshall McKusick, William Joy, Samuel Leffler, and Robert Fabry. A Fast File System for UNIX. *ACM Transactions on Computer Systems*, 2(3):181–197, August 1984.

[ML02] Gian-Paolo D. Musumeci and Mike Loukides. *System Performance Tuning*. O'Reilly and Associates, 2002.

[MM00] Dianna Mullet and Kevin Mullet. *Managing IMAP*. O'Reilly and Associates, 2000.

[MR96] John Myers and Marshall Rose. *Post Office Protocol—Version 3*. RFC 1939, Internet Engineering Task Force, May 1996.

[MYE96] John Myers. *Local Mail Transfer Protocol*. RFC 2033, Internet Engineering Task Force, October 1996.

[NEW99] Chris Newman. *Using TLS with IMAP, POP3 and ACAP*. RFC 2595, Internet Engineering Task Force, June 1999.

[NIS] *NIST Net Home Page*. http://is2.antd.nist.gov/itg/nistnet/.

[NSSH01] Evi Nemeth, Garth Snyder, Scott Seebass, and Trent Hein. *UNIX System Administration Handbook*, 3rd edition. Prentice Hall, 2001.

[OBS99] Michael Olson, Keith Bostic, and Margo Seltzer. Berkeley DB. In *Proceedings of the 1999 USENIX Annual Technical Conference, FREENIX Track*, Monterey, CA, June 1999.

[OPE] *OpenLDAP Project*. http://www.openldap.org.

[PAM] *Pluggable Authentication Modules (PAM) for Linux*. http://www.kernel.org/pub/linux/libs/pam/modules.html.

[POS] *Postfix Home Page*. http://www.porcupine.org/postfix-mirror/start.html.

[PRO] *procmail*. http://www.procmail.org/.

[QMA] *qmail Home Page*. http://www.qmail.org/.

[QPO] *qpopper*. http://www.eudora.com/qpopper/.

[RAC97] Steven Rodrigues, Thomas Anderson, and David Culler. High-Performance Local Area Communication with Fast Sockets. In *Proceedings of the USENIX Annual Technical Conference*, Anaheim, CA, January 1997.

[REI] *ReiserFS*. http://www.reiser.org/content_table.html.

[RIV92] Ronald Rivest. *The MD5 Message-Digest Algorithms*. RFC 1321, Internet Engineering Task Force, April 1992.

[RIZ] Luigi Rizzo. *dummynet Tutorial*. http://info.iet.unipi.it/~luigi/ip_dummynet/.

[RIZ97] Luigi Rizzo. dummynet: A Simple Approach to the Evaluation of Network Protocols. *ACM Computer Communication Review*, 27(1):31–41, January 1997.

[RMK+96] Yakov Rekhter, Robert Moskowitz, Daniel Karrenberg, Geert Jan de Groot, and Eliot Lear. *Address Allocation for Private Internets*. RFC 1918, Internet Engineering Task Force, February 1996.

[RO92] Mendel Rosemblum and John Ousterhout. The Design and Implementation of a Log-Structured File System. *ACM Transactions on Computer Systems*, 10(1):26–52, February 1992.

[SA99] Gregory Shapiro and Eric Allman. Sendmail Evolution: 8.10 and Beyond. In *Proceedings of the 1999 USENIX Annual Technical Conference, FREENIX Track*, Monterey, CA, June 1999.

[SDH⁺96] Adam Sweeney, Doug Doucette, Wei Hu, Curtis Anderson, Mike Nishimoto, and Geoff Peck. Scalability in the XFS File System. In *Proceedings of the USENIX Annual Technical Conference*, San Diego, CA, January 1996.

[SEN] *Sendmail Consortium*. http://www.sendmail.org/.

[SG98] Alan Schwartz and Simson Garfinkel. *Stopping Spam*. O'Reilly and Associates, 1998.

[SGM⁺00] Margo Seltzer, Gregory Ganger, M. Kirk McKusick, Keith Smith, Craig Soules, and Christopher Stein. Journaling versus Soft Updates: Asynchronous Meta-data Protection in File Systems. In *Proceedings of the USENIX Annual Technical Conference*, San Diego, CA, June 2000.

[SHB⁺98] Yasushi Saito, Eric Hoffman, Brian Bershad, Henry Levy, David Becker, and Bertil Folliot. The Porcupine Scalable Mail Server. In *Proceedings of the SIGOPS European Workshop*, Sintra, Portugal, September 1998.

[SHO94] Kurt Shoens. *Mail Reference Manual*, 5.5 edition, *4.4 BSD User's Supplementary Documents*, Chapter 7. O'Reilly and Associates, 1994. http://docs.FreeBSD.org/44doc/usd/07.mail/paper.html.

[SIL01] Dave Sill. *The qmail Handbook*. APress, 2001.

[SLE] *Sleepycat DB Online Documentation*. http://www.sleepycat.com/docs/index.html.

[SYS] syslog-ng Home Page. http://www.balabit.hu/en/downloads/syslog-ng/docs/.

[TWE98] Stephen C. Tweedie. Journaling the Linux ext2fs Filesystem. In *Proceedings of the 4th Annual LinuxExpo*, Durham, NC, May 1998. ftp://ftp.kernel.org/pub/linux/kernel/people/sct/ext3/journal-design.ps.gz.

[UM] *United Messaging Year-End 2000 Mailbox Report*. http://unitedmessaging.com/assets/pdf/mailboxreport_full.pdf.

[UWI] *UW IMAP*. http://www.washington.edu/imap/.

[VEN92] Wietse Venema. TCP WRAPPER: Network Monitoring, Access Control, and Booby Traps. In *UNIX Security Symposium III Proceedings*, Baltimore, MD, September 1992.

[VER] VERITAS File System, Part 1. http://eval.veritas.com/downloads/pro/fswht1.pdf.

[VH01] William von Hagen. *Linux Filesystems*. SAMS Press, 2001.

[VI97] *Virtual Interface Architecture Specification*, December 1997. http://www.viarch.org/html/collateral/san_10.pdf.

[WOO99] David Wood. *Programming Internet Email*. O'Reilly and Associates, 1999.

Index